DEVOTIONS®

*I*f any man serve me, let him follow me; and where I am, there shall also my servant be. —John 12:26

JANUARY

Photo © Digital Stock

Gary Allen, editor

God Is . . . Smiling?

I was shown mercy so that in me, the worst of sinners, Christ Jesus might display his unlimited patience as an example for those who would believe on him and receive eternal life (1 Timothy 1:16, *New International Version*).

Scripture: **1 Timothy 1:12-20**
Song: **"Grace, Greater than Our Sins"**

While in college I was shocked when a fellow student said, "I have come to realize that God is always smiling on me!" I argued that she was surely mistaken. Of course, what I was really saying was that God couldn't possibly be smiling on *me.* I was just too much of a mess.

I am a mess. You are a mess. Paul was a mess. He says he was "a blasphemer and a persecutor and a violent man" and "the worst of sinners" (see 1 Timothy 1:13, 16). Yet this whole passage reminds us that God pours out His grace on us abundantly. We're so tempted to dwell on our mistakes and shortcomings that we may downplay the passionate love God has for us.

Yes, you and I are a mess, but every moment is a second chance with God. (Okay, today maybe the millionth chance!) He has unlimited patience for those of us who come to Him. He is smiling on us, His children.

Dear Father, as I begin this New Year, remind me that I can begin anew with You each day. Thank You for not holding my sins against me, for being a God of second chances and new beginnings. In Jesus' name I pray. Amen.

January 1. **Glen Elliott**, now a minister in Tucson, has served as a missionary to the Ukraine, starting several churches and a Christian college there.

Being a Blessing

I thank my God upon every remembrance of you (Philippians 1:3).

Scripture: **Philippians 1:3-11**
Song: **"Precious Memories"**

Can you imagine being such a blessing to someone that every time they thought of you they thanked God? The church at Philippi was such an encouragement to the apostle Paul that he gave thanks to God for them every time they crossed his mind.

In my life I have several friends that, when I think of them, I thank God for bringing our paths together. One particular friend is someone who is encouraging to me and supports me, although she does not always agree with me. She speaks the truth to me honestly and lovingly. She prays for me and loves me in the Lord. Who is my special friend? My wife!

Maybe you know someone like that—someone who loves you enough to be honest with you and pray with and for you. Perhaps it's your own spouse, or another family member, or a dear friend. If so, what a blessing that is! And with the blessing comes a reminder: I can be a blessing to others in just the same way!

Heavenly Father, as I start the New Year, open my eyes to the condition of people around me, and help me to be a blessing to them. In the name of Your Son, my Savior, I pray. Amen.

January 2-8. **Pete Anderson** is a senior minister in Ocala, Florida, where he lives with his wife, Barbara, and two boys. His hobbies include taking mission trips.

No Matter What

Give thanks in all circumstances, for this is God's will for you in Christ Jesus (1 Thessalonians 5:18, *New International Version*).

Scripture: **1 Thessalonians 5:16-22**
Song: **"Give Thanks"**

Christian comedian Mark Lowery asked, "Did you have a bad year last year? Don't worry, it will pass. Did you have all sorts of trouble last year? It will pass. Did you have a good year last year? Don't worry, it too will pass!"

No matter what type of year you had last year, it is now history. It's the beginning of a new year, and all that matters now is the present and the future. You cannot change the past, but you can learn from the past.

Notice that our Scripture today does not say, "In *some* circumstances give thanks." No, the passage is clear; in the midst of *all* circumstances—the joyful ones and the painful ones—we are to keep giving thanks to God.

We can give thanks, no matter our circumstances, because we know that God will be with us, no matter what trial we're facing, even when we feel that God is far away. I like the way writer Madeleine L'Engle put it in *Two Part Invention*: "It is when things go wrong, when the good things do not happen, when our prayers seem to have been lost, that God is most present. We do not need the sheltering wings when things go smoothly. We are closest to God in the darkness, stumbling along blindly."

Lord, although I cannot always understand why I am going through trials, I know that You are with me. I bless Your holy name. Amen.

Living in Harmony

All of you should be of one mind, full of sympathy toward each other, loving one another with tender hearts and humble minds (1 Peter 3:8, *New Living Translation*).

Scripture: **1 Peter 3:8-12**
Song: **"We Are One in the Bond of Love"**

Being a Christian would be easy if you didn't have to live with anyone else! Imagine that the only requirement for being a Christian was to go some place private and just study the Scriptures. That way, you would have no contact with anyone else, no interference, no conflict. It could be much easier to live the Christian life.

But Christianity is so much more than just studying God's Word. It is a relationship with Almighty God. It is sharing that relationship with others. It is living in harmony with others who are all made in the image of God. In other words, we could live without the conflict; could we live without the love?

God knows that it can be difficult to love others who are different. Yet we are not to allow our differences to separate us. We are to live in harmony with one another as brothers and sisters.

I have several brothers. Sometimes I argue with them, but I know that while we might argue, we are still brothers. We still love each other. That is what God has in mind for all Christians.

Dear Lord, *help me to live in harmony with other Christians that I might demonstrate the kind of love You have for me. In Christ's name, amen.*

No Off-the-Cuff Requests

I'm going to see that she gets justice, because she is wearing me out with her constant requests! (Luke 18:5, *New Living Translation*).

Scripture: **Luke 18:1-8**
Song: **"Footprints of Jesus"**

When I was younger, I remember reading a story about a boy who wanted a watch for Christmas. He would remind his parents constantly about getting a new watch. He was so annoying that his parents finally told him that he couldn't say another word about the watch. At family devotion time that evening, the boy shared this verse with everyone sitting around the kitchen table: "And what I say unto you I say unto all, Watch" (Mark 13:37, KJV). You do have to admire that boy's persistence!

Why do we think that while circumstances are good, we are in the middle of God's will, but when things start to become difficult, we think God has left us? The widow in our Scripture passage was persistent about going to the judge. The boy was persistent about getting a watch. Christ is persistent about loving us.

We should also be persistent in our prayers. When we cry out, God will hear us! But He wants us to come to Him with an open, needy heart. Perhaps to bring us into that blessed place, God lets us continue to repeat our petitions.

Lead me, Lord, to pray for the things that most deeply move me, for the things I must have and cannot provide for myself. Let me offer no trivial or off-the-cuff request, lest I treat You with disrespect. In Jesus' name, amen.

Loving Enemies

Love your enemies, bless them that curse you, do good to them that hate you, and pray for them which despitefully use you, and persecute you (Matthew 5:44).

Scripture: **Matthew 5:43-48**
Song: **"I Am His, and He Is Mine"**

I find it rather easy to love those who love me. I love my parents, my wife and children, and my friends—no problem. I also find it fairly easy to love myself. Problem is, as Benjamin Franklin once pointed out: "He that falls in love with himself will have no rivals."

So we are called by the Lord to love another class of humanity: our enemies. Yet how to do it? Do we convince ourselves that our enemies actually *deserve* such a blessing? Impossible!

Here's the key: God loved us "while we were yet sinners." We didn't deserve salvation, but God saved us anyway. We can do likewise with those who persecute us.

I think the great writer and defender of the faith G.K. Chesterton put it perfectly: "The way to love anything is to realize that it might be lost." If we see our enemies only in terms of the hurt they've caused, we may just want to hurt back. If we see their true humanity, their likeness to ourselves, their belovedness in the eyes of God, and their essential lostness—as we too were lost—well, then how can we help but reach out in love?

Help me to love my enemies, Lord, *and help me not only to love them and see them as You see them, but to be a blessing to them. In Christ, amen.*

Living Peaceful Lives

That we may live peaceful and quiet lives in all godliness and holiness (1 Timothy 2:2, *New International Version*).

Scripture: **1 Timothy 2:1-7**
Song: **"Peace Like a River"**

I am not a fan of afternoon television. What comes on in my area of the country are "talk shows" that focus on a variety of problems. One of the shows is famous for its guests' abilities to throw chairs—and fists. Much of what the guests say is censored because the television stations don't want to air such language. If the television talk shows are to be believed, people do not live in peace these days!

One of the hallmarks of the Christian life is living in peace and quiet. Because the Holy Spirit lives inside of us, we can exhibit a special kind of calm. Although the circumstances of life swirl around us, we can trust that God is in control and will provide the way for us.

When my brother was murdered, my family was understandably shocked by the news. But we knew that God would be honored somehow. We could live in peace because we knew that God was still in control. Nothing has happened in the past—nor is anything going to happen today—that God cannot handle.

Father, help me to live at peace with my neighbors. Help me to live as Jesus would live if He were physically present in our world today. And help me to trust You, even when I am deeply grieved by what has happened. In the name of Jesus, my Savior, I pray. Amen.

Powerful Prayers

The effectual fervent prayer of a righteous man availeth much (James 5:16).

Scripture: **James 5:13-18**
Song: **"Kneel at the Cross"**

Maybe you've heard the complaint that "my prayers don't seem to go higher than the ceiling." As a minister, I have heard that statement more times than I care to remember. But isn't it true that sometimes it *feels* as if God just isn't listening?

Yet I certainly *believe* that God listens to the prayers of His children. And it seems quite important to have our minds settled on the issue when we, or someone we care about, is suffering. Our passage today asks: "Is any among you afflicted?" Then Scripture tells us to pray. Why do we see prayer as our last resort rather than the first thing we should do?

I believe our heavenly Father considers each prayer and responds according to His will, with our best in mind. We cannot manipulate God, of course. He will do those things that honor and glorify His name while, if we allow it, bringing us to a new level of spiritual maturity.

Even when we fail to get the warm feeling we're seeking in our prayers, let's faithfully continue to bring all our concerns before the throne of the Lord almighty.

Dear Lord, I have so much on my heart today. Help me lay these needs and concerns before You in all openness and faith. And help me to trust You completely for the answers. In Christ's name, amen.

Celestial Reminders

The Lord your God hath multiplied you, and, behold, ye are this day as the stars of heaven for multitude (Deuteronomy 1:10).

Scripture: **Deuteronomy 1:9-18**
Song: **"Standing on the Promises"**

Trudging through the snow on a clear night, I looked up at the sky. So many stars, everywhere, sparkling like diamonds! Then I discovered the pale haze of the Milky Way stretching across part of the sky, encompassing a trillion stars or more, incomprehensible to my mind. Whenever I observe the heavens in this way, I automatically turn to the promises of God. Such awesome celestial lights make all His assurances seem overwhelmingly real.

So, too, God's people must have felt loved. After all, God had promised they would become a large nation, as vast as the number of stars that could be seen on a clear night. When we consider that "Father Abraham" first received this promise from God at a time when he had no children, God's faithfulness shines even brighter.

What does the Lord do for you? While taking in the dazzling display He's placed above you, take a moment to ponder His unconditional love, His tender care, His inner peace, and His ability to keep His promises.

Forgive us, Father, for the times we concentrate more on our immediate tasks than on the many wonders that testify to Your care. In Christ, amen.

January 9-15. **Jane Stanford** lives with her family in Maine and, when not hiking in the hills near her home, enjoys writing nonfiction.

No Barriers

They might bring us into bondage: to whom we gave place by subjection, no, not for an hour; that the truth of the gospel might continue with you (Galatians 2:4, 5).

Scripture: **Galatians 2:1-10**
Song: **"The Song of the Soul Set Free"**

I walked through a wide archway into a spacious religious building far from my homeland. It was Sunday, and my tour group decided to attend a Christian service unlike any I had experienced. Gilded ornaments and jewel-like windows seemed to shout for attention. Yet my mind was focused on the focal point of the service, the partaking of the Lord's Supper.

As we all stood up to sing a hymn in a language unknown to me, I glanced around at the smiling faces and listened with joy to the loud, happy voices. These people, I thought, were strangers to me and practiced many traditions unique to their culture. And yet they were also my brothers and sisters in the Lord.

This was the attitude of Paul with the Galatians. He stood against anyone who wanted to divide believers based on traditions such as dietary regulations or, in this case, rules about circumcision. He wrote that the saving work of Christ flowed out to all believers by grace—not according to what customs or traditions we may follow.

Dear Lord, help us to treat our Christian brothers and sisters as You would have us do—unhindered in our love for each other and for You. In the name of Jesus Christ we pray. Amen.

Looking Out

See that none render evil for evil unto any man; but ever follow that which is good, both among yourselves, and to all men (1 Thessalonians 5:15).

Scripture: **1 Thessalonians 5:6-15**
Song: **"On and On We Walk Together"**

Two lines of cars and trucks wait for the traffic light to turn green. Beyond the light, the right lane merges into the left. A yield sign reminds all right-lane drivers to give preference to those already in the left lane.

I was in that left lane, stopped at the light. Several cars stopped next to me on the right. Occasionally some drivers revved their engines, ready to pull out in front me. In the past when drivers on the right edged close to my front bumper and passenger door, I would back off, slow down, and let them charge ahead. But yesterday I didn't feel like giving in at all, especially since I needed to reach my destination on time.

After reading the apostle Paul's instructions to do what is best for everyone, I feel a little guilty about the times I didn't give in but fought hard to maintain my place in traffic. Now I wonder, who was the loser? Was I really helping anyone by stubbornly forging ahead as if the other cars didn't exist?

Dear Heavenly Father, please forgive me for those times I have looked out more for our my interests than for the interests of others. Help me to find ways to show others consideration and politeness, even if I don't receive any in return. In Jesus Christ's name I pray. Amen.

Forming a Good Habit

Holding fast the faithful word as he hath been taught, that he may be able by sound doctrine both to exhort and to convince the gainsayers (Titus 1:9).

Scripture: **Titus 1:5-9**
Song: **"Tell Me the Old, Old Story"**

It's six o'clock in the morning, and neither of our children has gone downstairs to eat breakfast. The school bus arrives at 7:15 A.M. Both bedroom doors, still closed, emit a faint yellow glow around the edges. All is quiet.

What are they doing? Our kids are practicing a habit that began several years ago during elementary school. Back then, they read juvenile fiction books by the dozen, but they hardly touched their Bibles. Then we began seeing certain changes in their behavior. For example, they'd come home from school and argue when we asked them to wash the dishes or set the table for dinner.

Out of desperation, we set down a crazy house rule: no Bible, no breakfast. Both kids liked to eat almost as much as they liked to read. The rule somehow stuck, by God's grace. Soon the habit became so ingrained that nowadays we know which book they're reading first. We also hear less arguing. As the apostle Paul instructed Titus, we're hoping that our children will continue to absorb God's Word so their actions and speech can be an encouragement to others.

Dear Lord, *help me to retain Your words in my mind and heart so I can speak wisely to others. In the name of Jesus Christ I pray. Amen.*

Being Watched

Whosoever shall receive one of such children in my name, receiveth me; and whosoever shall receive me, receiveth not me, but him that sent me (Mark 9:37).

Scripture: **Mark 9:33-37**
Song: **"Jesus Loves the Little Children"**

A few years ago our family befriended a young couple with three children. They lived in another town but came every Sunday to our church fellowship. Because services often ended late, we frequently invited them to our house, at the last minute, for a meal.

Sometimes our three youngest guests, freed from the confinement of church, loved to run from room to room, laughing and trying to get into mischief. When one would sneak into the kitchen, my daughter or I would stop whatever preparations we were doing, take a deep breath, and ask if he or she wanted a glass of water or a piece of fruit.

Later on, the mother surprised me by confiding that she always watched closely how other adults treated her children. "If they ignore my kids or only talk to them when they're angry or annoyed," she said, "I know they aren't the kind of people we want to be around."

We never know who may be watching how we interact with the little ones or what influence, for the Lord's sake, our actions may have.

Help us, heavenly Father, to treat children with the respect and care that You desire. Thank you for the children in our lives, and help us to be godly examples to them as well as to their parents. In the name of Jesus, amen.

Reputation at Risk

Moreover he must have a good report of them which are without; lest he fall into reproach and the snare of the devil (1 Timothy 3:7).

Scripture: **1 Timothy 3:1-7**
Song: **"Anywhere with Jesus"**

Years ago I watched my father agonize over a decision. A young friend had asked Dad to write a letter of recommendation to a loan agency. Dad wanted to help, but he also felt the man needed a few more years of experience before starting a business on his own, just as Dad had needed when he was that age. He feared that if his advice went unheeded, his young friend wouldn't succeed. He also feared that the young man might not appreciate his suggestion that the loan be delayed for a few years.

Eventually Dad went ahead and wrote a letter after the loan officials promised it would never be shown to their client. But the officials went back on their word and did show Dad's letter to the young man. As Dad had suspected, the fellow took offense at my father's advice to wait. He proceeded to tell friends and neighbors uncomplimentary things about Dad's character.

In spite of this man's accusations, Dad's reputation remained intact. I have a feeling that it was due, at least in part, to his honest consistency with others.

Lord, I can't always keep my reputation spotless; I do make mistakes. But give me the courage to do the right thing whenever it is in my power. Thank You, in Jesus' name. Amen.

Instruction Manual

If I tarry long, that thou mayest know how thou oughtest to behave thyself in the house of God, which is the church of the living God, the pillar and ground of the truth (1 Timothy 3:15).

Scripture: **1 Timothy 3:8-15**
Song: "How Precious Is the Book Divine"

A tall man in dark garb walked through the English countryside. His face, one onlooker noted, appeared peaceful as he plodded on, glancing now and then at a thin book he carried in one hand. George Müeller was reading his New Testament, pondering each passage until a prayer of praise, thanksgiving, petition, or repentance came to his lips. Then he'd go on to the next verse, all the while enjoying the fresh air and early morning light.

Well-known for his orphanage program in Victorian England, Müeller made it a priority to seek God's counsel daily. He began several orphanages over the years and claimed he never started any new building project until he knew, for certain, exactly what God wanted him to do and how to do it. He also claimed the Bible contained everything necessary for knowing how to live as a Christian.

Paul wrote Timothy so the latter would know what to do even when Paul was not there to counsel him. Like Timothy, and like George Müeller, we have a gift from God to guide us each day: the Bible.

We are grateful, Father, for Your words of instruction at our fingertips even now. May we read and study so that we can know what to do in the daily situations we face. In Jesus Christ's precious name, we pray. Amen.

Follow the Map

Hear now, O Israel, the decrees and laws I am about to teach you. Follow them so that you may live (Deuteronomy 4:1, *New International Version*).

Scripture: **Deuteronomy 4:1-8**
Song: **"I Have Decided to Follow Jesus"**

I am definitely "directionally challenged"; I can get lost in a cul-de-sac. So when I took a recent trip to Nashville and had several appointments to keep . . . you can imagine my panic.

I searched the Internet and located a map Web site. As I uttered a prayer of thanksgiving, I downloaded the directions from where I was staying to every destination on my itinerary. Then, with maps in hand, I faced each day with confidence and with the assurance that I could find my way.

If only we knew the path ahead in our daily lives! We've heard Bible lessons since we were children, but when the time of crisis or conflict comes, we sometimes panic and don't know where to turn. I find assurance that God has gone before me. He knows all the pitfalls. His Word is loaded with just the guidance I need. When I follow His directions, I will gain wisdom and understanding. That is His promise!

Lord, prepare my heart for discernment today. I know I need to stay alert to Your presence in order to know Your leading. In Christ's name, amen.

January 16-22. **Jeannie Harmon** is a freelance writer and a mentor for the Christian Writer's Guild. She and her husband, Pat, live in Colorado Springs.

Blessings of Grandparenting

We will tell the next generation the praiseworthy deeds of the Lord, his power, and the wonders he has done (Psalm 78:4, *New International Version*).

Scripture: **Psalm 78:1-7**
Song: **"I Will Sing of the Mercies of the Lord"**

My favorite "occupation" is being a grandparent. It has helped me focus in two directions: (1) to remember the wonderful Christian heritage of my grandmother and (2) to see the dynamic potential set before me in reaching a new generation for God.

When all the dust settles in our busy lives, we come to realize that it is those who have gone on before that modeled for us the loving kindness of fruitful living and a deep passion for God. I would not be the person I am today if it weren't for a grandmother whose quiet spirit and loving heart reached out to me.

I want to do the same for the next generation. I want to tell of God's goodness, teach His ways, and help the youngsters commit their lives to His service. I want those who come after me to know Jesus as a friend and Savior. I know that by following Him they can find true riches in this life, and then pass the good news on to their children in turn.

Father, *thank You for teaching me Your ways all of these years. Help me to be a model of Your love to others, especially my children and grandchildren. Help them to know that all the answers they seek in this life, they can find in You. I pray in Jesus' holy name. Amen.*

Imitators of God

Be imitators of God, therefore, as dearly loved children (Ephesians 5:1, *New International Version*).

Scripture: **Ephesians 4:25–5:2**
Song: **"To Be Like Jesus"**

Working in a kindergarten allows me to watch kids in action. As students play on the playground, I am keenly aware that they are striving to be like adults. I watch little girls play in the sand, making cakes to bake in imaginary ovens. I observe the boys leading an army charge or mimicking some power hero they have seen on television.

Sometimes, because they are imitators and not the real heroes, they cannot anticipate how their models would react in certain situations. Relying on their instincts often leads them to overstep the boundaries of good behavior, causing hurt feelings, bruised bodies, and tears.

As a child of God, I too want to imitate my Father. I want to be like Him in every way. I want to show the world His love, compassion, and grace. But, because I am not God, I sometimes go beyond His perfect will and say or do things I shouldn't.

Thankfully, His discipline is fair, and His hand is ever ready to guide me in the right direction. Could I even say that God has faith in me and knows that with each error, I will learn to be like Him a little more each day?

Father, my prayer is to be like You. But don't spare me the lessons I need to learn in this endeavour. For in the process, I will also grow closer to You. In Jesus' most holy name I pray. Amen.

Abounding in Our Uniqueness

Just as each of us has one body with many members . . . these members do not all have the same function (Romans 12:4, *New International Version*).

Scripture: **Romans 12:3-8**
Song: **"The Family of God"**

Sarah Jones felt uneasy. She knew her minister wasn't gifted in organizing a dinner for a hundred people. However, her repeated offers to help seemed to fall on deaf ears. Now, an hour before the arrival of the guests, she ventured down the quiet hallway to the church kitchen. There stood the minister alone reading the back of a frozen lasagna box, one of many he had purchased at the last minute.

Arriving at the same time as another sister in the church, Sarah could see the handwriting on the wall. She and her friend quickly started to make beverages, cut salad, bake rolls, and set tables. The dinner was a success, but by a very narrow margin.

God created each person with different gifts. We are not all preachers or singers or cooks. We are gifted in different ways so that we all fit neatly together into the body of Christ. Therefore, appreciate your own giftedness today. And be alert for any opportunities to put those gifts to use for God's glory, whether in the pulpit or the kitchen.

Lord, thank You for the gifts and talents that You've given me. Help me to work together with those in Your family, without complaining, so that the world will see Your love flowing through us. In Jesus' holy name, amen.

Consecrated to God

Everything God created is good, and nothing is to be rejected if it is received with thanksgiving, because it is consecrated by the word of God and prayer (1 Timothy 4:4, 5, *New International Version*).

Scripture: **1 Timothy 4:1-5**
Song: **"The Love of God"**

Several years ago we visited Jamaica. We lounged on white sandy beaches, met the challenges of open-market shopping, and observed many interesting geographical and cultural wonders. One of the most memorable things we did was to worship with a small congregation of believers on the south side of the island.

As the congregation prepared their hearts to receive the Communion elements, the minister took the cup, blessed it, and passed it to his right for the next church member to drink from the cup. Immediately, my sensibilities were aroused. *We never do it this way in our church*, I thought.

Then I considered how Jesus might respond to me: "This has been consecrated unto Me and my memory . . . should it be rejected if it is received with thanksgiving?" By the time the cup reached me, my heart was settled. I partook, and later left the service blessed. Our creator God is so good!

Lord, give me a grateful heart for all the goodness of Your creation. I especially thank You in this quiet moment for the bread and the cup. How powerfully they recall to me Your eternal sacrifice on my behalf! Thank You for rescuing me, even from myself. In Christ's name I pray. Amen.

Training in Godliness

Train yourself to be godly (1 Timothy 4:7, *New International Version*).

Scripture: **1 Timothy 4:6-10**
Song: "It's My Desire"

Tom was the golden boy of his military high school. He'd been preparing for the coveted Battalion Commander position since his first days in the ninth grade. He quickly rose through the ranks, actively taking part in extra-curricular activities to make a good impression. He taught himself to be disciplined, look sharp, and be "in the know" about everything on campus.

Then during his junior year, he made some bad choices. He broke major conduct rules, which cost him the coveted position he wanted as a senior. He eventually left school, denying himself the prize he'd so longed for.

No matter what our goals in this life, true success requires training. We don't wake up one morning equipped to face real life. We must dedicate ourselves to the basic training of godliness, which the prophet Micah summarized nicely: "To act justly and to love mercy and to walk humbly with your God" (Micah 6:8). Yielding to God's training program and discipline will lead to the true prize in the end.

Dear Lord, may I always be in a state of training to be like You. Never let me forget that without You, I am nothing and have no future. Keep my heart right and my desire set on pleasing You with my life. Thank You for Your patience and Your willingness to train me with love. In Jesus' name, amen.

The Power of the Word

Until I come, devote yourself to the public reading of Scripture (1 Timothy 4:13, *New International Version*).

Scripture: **1 Timothy 4:11-16**
Song: **"Give Me the Bible"**

Ed and Sharon looked for ways to involve the entire congregation in the Sunday services. The senior minister carried a heavy load with teaching the adult class as well as preaching during the Sunday morning service. However, although faithful, the members did not seem to take an active role. With no personal investment, they took little away to strengthen them for the coming week.

Ed and Sharon had an idea. First, they approached the minister and asked if a few minutes each Sunday could be used for the public reading of the Bible. He agreed, so they asked people from the congregation to volunteer to read a few verses of Scripture on selected Sundays during the coming months.

As the weeks passed, a transformation occurred. The Word became alive. Each time someone rose to read the Bible, that person became God's oracle to the congregation. God was stirring hearts. Even those who were timid seemed to speak with strength and boldness. It brought confirmation to the minister's words, and blessed the congregation. A spiritual refreshing swept through them all.

Lord, remind me of the power that Your Word holds when read aloud—the power to build my faith as I hear it, and the power to change my life as I remember it throughout my day. In Your holy name I pray. Amen.

Offering the Best

Sing unto him a new song; play skilfully with a loud noise (Psalm 33:3).

Scripture: **Psalm 33:1-5**
Song: **"Lord, We Praise You"**

Papa understood what the psalmist wrote about music. He was the song leader for our small country church. We had neither piano nor organ, so Papa used a tuning fork for finding the proper pitch. In the evenings after supper, Papa would take his hymnbook and tuning fork and sit in a rocking chair, practicing the hymns. He never seemed to mind if I climbed up into his lap and nestled in his strong arms as he sang and rocked.

Despite the Depression and his heavy responsibility to provide for eight mouths on a small rented farm, and despite asthma that plagued his breathing most of his life, Papa took time to prepare well for each Sunday worship service.

Although I never inherited Papa's voice, to this day I instantly know whether someone is singing on key or not. And like that little girl who once nestled in her Papa's arms, I want to enter into a close fellowship with my Lord as I praise Him. I know that singing will go a long way toward producing that blessed result.

Heavenly Father, thank You for a godly earthly father. May I follow in his steps and offer praise that's worthy of Your name. In Christ, amen.

January 23-29. **Mary Ellen Gudeman** served for 26 years with the Evangelical Alliance Mission in Japan. She now works with international students in Indiana.

Manual for Life

He who conceals his sins does not prosper, but whoever confesses and renounces them finds mercy (Proverbs 28:13, *New International Version*).

Scripture: **Proverbs 28:4-13**
Song: **"Search Me, O God"**

Sometimes the book of Proverbs reminds me of a driver's license manual. Obey the law and there's no problem. Disobey it, and you will find plenty of trouble.

I had served in Japan for many years as a missionary. After I returned home to retire, the local Red Cross asked me to assist Japanese nationals with translation of the written driver's license test. (Recently, I almost memorized the driver's manual for Indiana!)

Of course, these folks need to pass a road test to demonstrate their understanding of the written laws. Some pass on the first try, and some don't. Ignore a stop sign or speed through a school zone, and you fail the test on the spot!

The law requires total obedience. Solomon seems to have understood this principle. Over and over again he compares the consequences of obedience and disobedience to the law. Passing a driver's test may help the driver understand the traffic laws, but he still must choose whether to obey or disobey the law. Some do and some don't.

Lord, help me not only believe Your laws but to follow the message that keeps me on the right path, walking with You each step. In Jesus' name, amen.

Children, Are You Clean?

Cleanse your hands, ye sinners; and purify your hearts, ye double minded (James 4:8).

Scripture: **Matthew 23:23-28**
Song: **"Are You Washed in the Blood?"**

Reading the Scripture for today, I recall scenes in Japan, where I served as a missionary. Shrines and temples dotted the countryside, and most were visited regularly, generation after generation.

I sometimes watched at a distance as the worshipers approached. They would lift a communal dipper to their lips, rinse out their mouths, and then wash their hands. Next they would ring a bell to get the god's attention before they prayed. Afterwards they threw their yen into an offering box, pressed their hands together, and bowed reverently. Witnessing this ritual reminded me of what my mother and father asked us every time we ate together: "Children, did you wash your hands?"

Despite the lack of indoor plumbing on our farm where I grew up during the Depression, a bucket of water drawn from the well always stood available in the kitchen. After washing, all eight of us would sit around the old oak table, heads bowed and hands folded, while Papa offered thanks for the food. That's really how I learned to worship, to come before Him with clean hands and, hopefully, a clean heart.

Dear Father, cleanse this heart each day so I may always worship You in spirit and in truth. In the name of Jesus I pray. Amen.

Free to Obey

Speak and act as those who are going to be judged by the law that gives freedom (James 2:12, *New International Version*).

Scripture: **James 2:8-13**
Song: **"Out of My Bondage"**

Few of us enjoy restraints. When I left for the mission field, seat belts were not yet the law in my state. Later, on one of my furloughs, they were required. After only using a bicycle in Japan, it took me a while to adjust to the confinement of a seat belt.

How grateful I was for that restraint on one trip many years later! I had spent a week at a conference in Michigan and had not slept well. Now as I headed south toward Indiana, the rhythmic swishing of windshield wipers, the overcast sky, and the unchanging roadside scenery lulled me into a stupor.

Alarm jogged my foggy state of mind when I saw I was heading toward the left lane. From that point I remember little more than total chaos, pain, intense thrashing about, darkness . . .

Later, an ambulance attendant wheeled me into the ER at a local hospital. "You could have broken your neck," the doctor said. "Be thankful you had your seat belt fastened!"

Now I'm (still) here to tell you: God's law, because of its wise constraints, brings true freedom.

Dear Lord, thank You for the freedom I experience when I obey Your law. Give me that faith and grace I need to follow it. In Jesus' name, amen.

Worthy of Honor

Treat . . . older women as mothers, and younger women as sisters, with absolute purity (1 Timothy 5:1, 2, *New International Version*).

Scripture: **1 Timothy 5:1-8**
Song: **"The Church's One Foundation"**

While I was serving in Japan, some fellow missionaries went on furlough, and I led the small congregation in their absence. After a worship service, a few of the women approached me, bowed, and said they faced a difficult decision. Two young people in the church planned to marry. The women wanted my advice about the color for decorating the church. I suggested my favorite colors, yellow and white. They again bowed.

The following week the same women approached me again, bowing deeply. Their grave faces convinced me something had gone wrong. "Sensei, the colors you suggested are funeral colors in Japan! We are so rude to ask again . . . but?"

"Oh, any color is fine!" I replied, relieved to know the problem had been so small. They suggested pink and blue, and I suppressed a smile recalling the occasion for using these colors in the USA. Later, when I considered Paul's advice to young Timothy, I thanked God for giving me insight into a sensitive issue in these women's culture.

Dear Father, thank You for Paul and Timothy, these models of godly men You have given as examples. Help us follow their lead in our relationships, with the goal of absolute purity. In Christ's name I pray. Amen.

Just an Ordinary Box

Devoting herself to all kinds of good deeds (1 Timothy 5:10, *New International Version*).

Scripture: **1 Timothy 5:9-16**
Song: **"A Beautiful Life"**

While Paul refers specifically to widows in this letter to Timothy, his qualifications make an excellent guide for all women. As I read his words, it seemed as if Paul were describing my Japanese friend Dote-san.

One job everyone avoided at church was cleaning the squat-type toilet. Time after time, I saw Dote-san emerging with cleanser and sponge in hand. Not many knew she replenished the flower vases and washed teacups while others chatted after meetings. They noticed only when she was absent.

Dote-san also filled a need in my life . . . maybe a phone call to see if my cold was better or a short visit to drop off some fresh fish or distributing church information in the neighborhood. Once while I was hospitalized, she ran errands, brought mail and fresh fruit, and prayed with me.

When it came time for me to end my missionary career, Dote-san shoved a slender box into my hands at the airport. The scent of sandalwood wafted through the wrapping. Inside lay a blue silk fan trimmed with delicate cherry blossoms. On the outside, just an ordinary box. On the inside, a gift no one could forget.

Dear Father, thank You for faithful friends who quietly see our needs and reach out to us. Help us follow in their steps. In Jesus' name I pray. Amen.

Am I Worthy?

The worker deserves his wages (1 Timothy 5:18, *New International Version*).

Scripture: **1 Timothy 5:17-25**
Song: **"Freely, Freely"**

A strong, self-reliant strain seemed to flow through me from childhood up. Perhaps by being the third of six children, I grew up with less reliance on parental care. Unlike my siblings, I remained single, only adding to an already decisive, independent nature.

After working for a number of years, I left the business world and went to Bible college, where God led me to prepare for the mission field. I graduated with no debts and no money, only God's call to "go." There was one problem. The thought of needing financial support hung heavily over my independent, self-sufficient lifestyle. A difficult task awaited me.

Then I remembered the Lord's words to ask Him for our needs. An amazing thing happened! Many friends and relatives reached out with their hearts and pocketbooks, and I was off to the mission field where I served for many years.

I cannot say I ever felt comfortable receiving support. But although the apostle Paul reserved the right *not* to receive support, he clearly believed and taught that a congregation didn't have the right *not* to offer it.

Dear Lord, thank You for the countless faithful who give and give and give so Your Word can be carried to the nations. In the name of Jesus, amen.

A Job Well Done

Great are the works of the Lord; they are pondered by all who delight in them (Psalm 111:2, *New International Version*).

Scripture: **Psalm 111**
Song: **"Great Is the Lord"**

"Good job, God!" my three-year-old grandson David exclaimed when he saw a fiery sunset one summer evening. The western sky over Colorado's Rocky Mountains blazed with the brilliance of gourmet colors—mango, plum, and watermelon. David's delight was obvious as he gave the creator credit for this glorious display.

The wonders of creation abound if we aren't too distracted by our hectic schedules to notice. Dancing leaves. Whirling snowflakes. Crocus blooms. Mountain peaks. Gentle streams. A newborn baby. God supplies endless evidence of His greatness all around us.

However, His greatest work is the transformation of hearts that have experienced the brilliance of divine grace and love. Changed lives are cause for great delight.

Regardless of how many years we may live on this earth, let us remember that God's wonders are worth a lifetime of pondering. May we experience endless pleasure as we keep our eyes and hearts attuned to His great works—and then share our delight in a job well done.

God, I delight in the works of Your hands and praise You with exuberance today! Through Your Son's almighty name I pray. Amen.

January 30, 31. **Marlene Depler** is a writer, teacher, and speaker living in Colorado. In her spare time she enjoys gardening, walking, and reading.

Rooted by a Stream

Blessed is the man who trusts in the Lord, whose confidence is in him. He will be like a tree planted by the water that sends out its roots by the stream (Jeremiah 17:7, 8, *New International Version*).

Scripture: **Jeremiah 17:1-8**
Song: **"Just Beyond The Rolling River"**

Countless times I've zigzagged across the Midwestern plains. Glancing out the car window, I sometimes notice a ribbon of trees in the distance, meandering their way across the prairie grasses. When I see the trees, I'm certain a river runs there out of my view. Trees in this part of the country can't survive the summer's heat without a constant source of water. A tree that grows by the river, though, doesn't rely on the unpredictability of rain.

Throughout history, towns and cities have sprung up on the banks of streams or along the shores of rivers and waterways. People recognize their reliance on the availability of water to sustain them—as well as to keep their crops and cattle alive and well.

It's much the same for us spiritually: we are more likely to grow if our lives are planted near the source of living water. When we send out our roots down by the stream, we will not only survive. Immersed in God's goodness, we will thrive.

Lord, we place our confidence and trust in You. Help us to see that the roots of our seemingly endless desires are thirsting for the water that only You can provide. In Jesus' name, we pray. Amen.

DEVOTIONS®

*F*rom a child thou hast known the holy Scriptures, which are able to make thee wise unto salvation.

—2 Timothy 3:15

FEBRUARY

Photo © Comstock

Gary Allen, editor

Get a Grip

Dear brothers, stand firm and keep a strong grip on the truth that we taught you in our letters and during the time we were with you (2 Thessalonians 2:15, *The Living Bible*).

Scripture: **2 Thessalonians 2:13-17**
Song: **"Hold to God's Unchanging Hand"**

We've all thrilled to those classic cliff-hanger scenes in books or films. Our heartbeats quicken as we follow our hero over the rocky ravine, as he dangles, perhaps clinging to a tree root by the fingertips. He looks down, and his grip tightens. Without a firm hold, death is inevitable. The saying, "Hang on for dear life!" takes on a literal urgency. We hold our breath, and our hero escapes in the nick of time.

We cling to whatever we value, don't we? At times I have held tightly to the hand of one of my young children as we crossed a busy street. My child's life depended upon my grip. Other times my children have clung to me like glue so they wouldn't get lost or feel afraid.

If we value what we have learned to be true about Christ, we will hold to these teachings with a firm grip. We must cling to the truth because our lives are at stake. If we are swayed by every new philosophy, we may forget just how deep is the dangerous canyon of misplaced loyalties.

God, I don't want to let go of the truth You've imparted to us. Help me to stand firm and hold tightly to Your teachings. I pray this in Your Son's holy and unfailing name. Amen.

February 1-5. **Marlene Depler** is a writer, teacher, and speaker living in Colorado. In her spare time she enjoys gardening, walking, and reading.

Use It or Lose It

The church grew daily in faith and numbers (Act 16:5, *The Living Bible*).

Scripture: **Acts 16:1-5**
Song: **"Faith Is the Victory"**

It's good for me! Just thirty minutes! I can do this!
With words like these, I prod myself to head out the door three times a week to exercise at a women's workout center. And in just a few short weeks, I have noticed a significant increase in the strength of my muscles, especially in my legs. I run up and down the stairs with greater ease. It has required exertion, but my stamina has increased.

Without exercise, muscles will shrink. Overexertion brings about exhaustion. But regular, moderate exercise produces increased muscle strength as well as endurance.

Isn't there something here to apply to our life of faith? As we act on the faith we already have, then our faith becomes stronger. Christianity isn't a sprint; it's a marathon. If we want our faith to take us the distance, we must regularly act on what we already possess, both individually and as a body of believers.

To grow stronger in faith—isn't that the desire of every believer and every congregation? These early fellowships grew stronger in faith and larger in numbers. So consider: Was their growing faith actually the catalyst for their increase in numbers?

Father, increase my faith muscles. May my growing faith keep me strong to the end and inspire others to grow as well. In Jesus' name, amen.

Something Worth Passing On

I have been reminded of your sincere faith, which first lived in your grandmother Lois and in your mother Eunice and, I am persuaded, now lives in you also (2 Timothy 1:5, *New International Version*).

Scripture: **2 Timothy1:1-5**
Song: **"Faith of Our Fathers"**

My dining room hutch displays a plate of Bavarian china, and I treasure its pastel roses and gold rim. I value this heirloom, not for its monetary worth, but because it belonged to my grandmother and then to my mother.

One day I too will hand down some of my treasures to my children and grandchildren. This plate will be given to one of my daughters, who will probably pass it to her daughter. With the passing of each generation, we celebrate our shared history and its mementos.

Faith may not be a tangible heirloom, but it is surely the best thing we can pass to the next generation. Modeling an authentic, growing faith in our own lives creates a generational legacy by which children are compelled to explore God's calling in their own lives.

I possess more than a plate that belonged to my grandmother. I'm fortunate to also have a legacy of faith from my mother and grandmother. This faith has become completely my own, and now I hold it out to my children and grandchildren, just as Lois and Eunice did with Timothy.

Lord, help me to be a living example of faith in You. And let my faith be a lasting legacy to the generations who follow. In Christ's name, amen.

Divine Remedy

God hath not given us the spirit of fear; but of power, and of love, and of a sound mind (2 Timothy 1:7).

Scripture: **2 Timothy 1:6-10**
Song: **"Safe in the Arms of Jesus"**

When a nasty cold hits, I scurry to find a remedy. It doesn't matter whether it's a home remedy or a prescription. I just want to feel better.

Any number of ailments cause us to seek remedies. We want a cure for everything from headaches to heartaches. And we'll buy almost any product that promises relief.

More importantly, we need a remedy for our deep-seated fears. Natural fear makes us instinctively alert to danger and helps protect us. However, if fear controls our lives, dictates our decisions, and leaves us paralyzed, it's no longer beneficial. Fear of this type keeps us from experiencing our full potential in Christ. It keeps us tethered to the familiar and makes us overly self-protective.

What are your deepest fears? Failure? Close relationships? Abandonment? Death? We desperately need a remedy for all the fears that hold us captive.

God's love is the antidote for fear. Only He is capable of a love that can replace fear with power. As we internalize God's love, allowing it to permeate the deepest places of our hearts, our fears subside.

Dear God, my spirit swirls with fear these days. Nevertheless, I now open my heart to Your love, the only remedy powerful enough to bring a peace beyond my understanding. In Christ I pray. Amen.

No Distortions, Please!

Retain the standard of sound words which you have heard from me, in the faith and love which are in Christ Jesus (2 Timothy 1:13, *New American Standard Bible*).

Scripture: **2 Timothy 1:11-18**
Song: **"Wonderful Words of Life"**

Safety standards. Emissions standards. The gold standard. Standardized tests. Standards of weights and measures. It seems there are standards for most everything. They insure consistency, accuracy, and safety.

We expect aviation safety standards to be carefully observed when we board an airplane. We expect a bushel of corn to be exactly 4 pecks, a gallon to equal 4 quarts, and a cup to be precisely 16 ounces.

We don't want these things to vary down through the years because without standards . . . *chaos!*

The same is true in our Christian journey. We want to avoid inaccuracies in what we believe and teach; therefore, we need to adhere to the standard of truth as set forth in the Scriptures. Paul admonished Timothy to make sure his words were accurate, reflecting the authentic message of Christ. In other words, "Timothy, don't distort the message. Make sure all that you teach accords with all that God has been teaching His people down through the years that have gone before you."

Dear Lord, help me to keep Your standard of truth in what I believe and what I teach. May our words be consistent and accurate as I proclaim Your love in a chaotic world. In the name of Jesus, our Savior, amen.

Faith as a Workout

He did not waver through unbelief regarding the promise of God, but was strengthened in his faith and gave glory to God (Romans 4:20 *New International Version*).

Scripture: **Romans 4:13-25**
Song: **"Higher Ground"**

To believe or not to believe? What were Abraham's thoughts when he heard that his aged wife Sarah would bring forth a child in their declining years? Distrust? Perhaps even some cynicism? Yet he was called to believe—and he did.

God asks us, as well, to believe Him to supply what we need. Just as the body thrives on consistent training, our spiritual lives are strengthened for the day's challenges as we push past the threshold of discomfort into a place of satisfied exhilaration. As we work our major muscle groups using weights, or push our body via aerobic exercise, we are training our physical bodies to use resistance as our ally and friend.

Similarly, God calls us to "work out" the muscles of our faith. It is the sure means of getting past the fears that paralyze us so we can move closer to Him.

Lord, we thank You for Your faithful support. In every way, You have graciously made up for our weaknesses with Your strength. Continue to build us up in faith, we pray, teaching us daily to exercise our spiritual muscles with the help of Your Holy Spirit. In Jesus' name we pray. Amen.

February 6-12. **Michele Howe** is a book reviewer, writer, and author of eight books for women. She lives in Michigan with her husband and four children.

Cast Off Disobedience

They stumble because they disobey the message—which is also what they were destined for (1 Peter 2:8, *New International Version*).

Scripture: **1 Peter 2:1-10**
Song: **"Victory In Jesus"**

When the rowing coxswain gave an order, the crew immediately followed his instructions. No discussion, no hesitancy, no holding back; the eight men were there to win. They knew that for their boat to take the prize, each individual had to give 100 percent. They also had to work as a team. Although this group of seasoned rowers prevailed and did actually win first place, it was a hard-earned victory.

During the season before, they lost time after time. Why? Because each of them, skilled in their own right, refused to listen to the coxswain's commands. Pride, self-sufficiency, and independence caused their downfall. Finally, at the close of a no-win season, they learned their lesson.

Is it any wonder that Peter, the impetuous, strong-willed disciple, would urge his fellow believers to stop, take heed, and obey Jesus' instructions? Peter, like us, learned his most memorable lessons through the school of hard knocks. But the important point is that Peter did, in fact, learn.

Dear Lord, like Peter, may I cast off any poor attitudes, habits, or mindsets that hinder me from living out Your plan and purpose for my life. I offer up my whole life to You now. In Christ, I pray. Amen.

Prayer: Essential Connection

Since the day we heard about you, we have not stopped praying for you and asking God to fill you with the knowledge of his will through all spiritual wisdom and understanding (Colossians 1:9, *New International Version*).

Scripture: **Colossians 1:3-10**
Song: **"'Tis the Blessed Hour of Prayer"**

Listening to the accounts of other believers' successes in sharing their faith does my heart good. I am especially heartened when I hear of a factory employee, for example, who prays and asks God to send him someone new, each and every day, to talk with about spiritual things.

I may not have his boldness, but I can pray for him. And I can continue to share my life and friendship with those in my world. As Francis of Assisi put it eight centuries ago: "Preach the gospel by all means; if necessary, use words."

Prayer prepares the scene for this kind of preaching that includes so many "means." Just as we need to lift up those around the world who are evangelizing, we can pray for any fellow believer who is doing the hard work of reaching out to neighbors on behalf of the kingdom. We hope others are praying for us, as well. As we intercede, we truly take part in one another's labors, for we are all part of one family . . . the family of faith.

Lord, light a fire within my heart to pray with fervency for those who work to share the good news of salvation. Let me make it my daily habit to spend time laboring in prayer for others. I pray in Jesus' holy name. Amen.

Under Orders

Endure hardship with us like a good soldier of Christ Jesus (2 Timothy 2:3, *New International Version*).

Scripture: **2 Timothy 2:1-7**
Song: **"Soldiers of the Cross"**

"Cheaters never prosper." Do we believe it?

According to Paul, if we join the army we should expect to follow our commander's directives to the letter. Similarly, God has given us principles and commands to insure our success as soldiers for Christ.

It's not always easy to follow those commands! Paul knew that Timothy would struggle, perhaps be tempted to cut corners for expediency or personal comfort. He therefore calls his young pastoral protegé to endure the difficulties and remain diligent in obedience to God.

As we pray for God's grace to keep us on task and focused on Him, we will suffer discomfort, perhaps even persecution. Yet, as we press on, living single-mindedly for Christ—careful to follow His lead—He promises that we'll also share in His success.

In our lifetime we might not see much outward evidence to support our efforts. But by faith we can press on day by day, faithfully carrying out our assigned missions under the greatest leader of all time: Jesus Christ himself.

Dear Lord, give me Your wisdom as I seek to understand Your will and Your ways. Help me to obey quickly and without hesitation. Let not doubt or distrust hinder me from being a soldier fit for service in Your kingdom. In the powerful name of Jesus I pray. Amen.

Someday Unchained

This is my gospel, for which I am suffering even to the point of being chained like a criminal (2 Timothy 2:8, 9, *New International Version*).

Scripture: **2 Timothy 2:8-13**
Song: **"In the Hour of Trial"**

Throughout history, countless philosophers have commented on life's injustices, upon the pain and suffering all around us. Some say that if this pain-ridden world is all there is, then why live for any purpose other than one's own advancement? These well-regarded sages are intelligent, educated, and often highly accomplished. Yet with all their diplomas and vocational successes, do they miss the point?

Have they considered Jesus and His message? "Remember Jesus Christ," Paul admonishes in his letter to Timothy. Remember how Jesus died and was raised from the dead. The miracle of Christ's resurrection speaks hope to every human heart. Indeed, as we keep our eyes fixed upon Christ's work, we discover that life does have purpose, and our choices have eternal consequences.

Yes, our work on earth will entail sacrifice; we are "chained" here to plenty of suffering. But this world is not the best of all worlds. We are not home yet; we're just passing through.

Lord, open my eyes to the Spirit's work all around me—and the glory that awaits us in the heavenly realm. Renew my resolve to live each day with eternity in mind. In Jesus' name, amen.

Handle with Care

Do your best to present yourself to God as one approved, a workman who does not need to be ashamed and who correctly handles the word of truth (2 Timothy 2:15, *New International Version*).

Scripture: **2 Timothy 2:14-19**
Song: **"Work for the Night Is Coming"**

If you've ever watched two college debate teams argue their respective positions, you've probably been amazed and impressed. Considering the number of hours each team member must spend memorizing key facts, developing possible strategies, and then orally debating against his own teammates in practice, it's no wonder these learned young adults come across as so knowledgeable.

Perhaps the most intriguing thing is that the debating position assigned to a team may not fall in line with what each individual actually believes. This does not matter, since the teams train themselves to respond to their opponents apart from any personal opinions they hold.

Just as teams of all sorts must train themselves to handle and overcome their opponents, so Paul encourages believers to be mindful of how they handle their words. He calls the early Christians to study the Word, understand it, and speak with care lest any foolish talk mislead and harm the church.

Lord, help me to stand firm on the foundation of Your truth. May I never give in to mindless arguing or silly debating but stay single-minded and on guard against false teaching. Thank You in Jesus' name, amen.

Polishing the Dross Away

If a man cleanses himself from the latter, he will be an instrument for noble purposes, made holy, useful to the Master and prepared to do any good work (2 Timothy 2:21, *New International Version*).

Scripture: **2 Timothy 2:20-26**
Song: **"Be Thou My Vision"**

Every morning the owner of a nearby antique shop meticulously polishes his beloved pieces of furniture until they gleam. Many shoppers stop at his display window to admire the beauty of these aged treasures.

It's no secret that this dealer knows how to present his goods to their best advantage. He takes the dirty, the worn, the broken, and transforms them into items of priceless value.

Similarly, Paul exhorts his fellow Christians to cleanse themselves from the dust and debris of the soul so that nothing can deter them from the noble purposes God has in mind for them. Lest others outside the faith look to believers and see immaturity, Paul speaks plainly: flee that which hinders you from serving Christ wholeheartedly. Don't bother with senseless pursuits, and turn away from foolish conversations.

So I have to decide: Will I turn to the Lord and allow Him to burn away the dross from my life? Will I let Him replace it all with that which lasts forever?

Today, Lord, I seek a pure and understanding mind and a servant's teachable spirit. Work Your will in me. Through Christ's name I pray. Amen.

Hidden Treasure

Thy word have I hid in mine heart, that I might not sin against thee (Psalm 119:11).

Scripture: **Psalm 119:9-16**
Song: **"I Hide Your Word Within My Heart"**

Valuable things are often hidden. Pirate treasures, extra keys, emergency cash. The reason? So they'll be there when we need them.

And what is more needed than a way to resist the temptation to sin? Temptations surround us: something to say that should not be said, something to eat that should not be eaten, something to see that should not be seen, something to do that should not be done.

But God has not left us defenseless. As the Spirit affirms: "There hath no temptation taken you but such as is common to man: but God is faithful, who will not suffer you to be tempted above that ye are able; but will with the temptation also make a way to escape, that ye may be able to bear it" (1 Corinthians 10:13).

The way? Jesus showed us when He went face-to-face with the tempter in the wilderness: resist the tempter with the Word. It's hidden treasure exhumed at the right moment to demonstrate its full value—and used to do what is urgently needed.

Praise You, Lord, *for the power of Your Word. Give me the deep desire to hide it in my heart. In the name of Your Son, the Word incarnate, amen.*

February 13-19. **Ronald G. Davis** is an editor, educator, and writer who lives in Cincinnati, Ohio, with his wife, Ruth.

Forever and Ever, Amen

Teach me, O Lord, the way of thy statutes; and I shall keep it unto the end (Psalm 119:33).

Scripture: **Psalm 119:33-40**
Song: **"Give Me Thy Heart"**

Solemn vows echo through time. "I do's" resonate for life. "I believe that Jesus is the Christ, Lord and Savior" directs choices made day to day. The psalmist declares, "I shall keep it unto the end (119:33) . . . with my whole heart" (vv. 33, 34). Such absolute decisions are both honorable and honored.

Thankfully, God's promises form the precedent and model for us. When He vows, He does what He vows. There is no need to doubt; we simply follow His example. In the hymn words of Frances Ridley Havergal:

Take myself, and I will be
    Ever only, all for Thee.

Golden wedding anniversaries, celebrations commemorating decades of ministry, memorial services for a faithful Christian—all are occasions that acknowledge and honor solemn vows uttered decades before, solemn vows kept no matter what life brought. That is the challenge for each of us: to find God's way, to vow to walk therein, and to do it . . . forever and ever, amen.

God whose way is true and worthy, give me the grace to walk therein. Help me in my effort to make Your way known to all. In Jesus' name, amen.

Free to Work

We hear that there are some which walk among you . . . working not at all (2 Thessalonians 3:11).

Scripture: **2 Thessalonians 3:6-13**
Song: "O Master, Let Me Walk with Thee"

What driver has not stopped at the end of a highway exit ramp to be greeted by the scribbled, hand-held sign, "Will Work for Food"? Yes, some individuals do go hungry for reasons beyond their own control. But just as many (or more) go hungry because of debilitating addictions.

Paul's handwritten "sign" never varies: a person is responsible for himself. From matters of life sustenance to matters of spirit salvation, each has personal responsibility. There is work to be done!

From the day of creation, each person has lived in the image of God, a creature given the highest gift God could grant: free personal will. But no one is free of the consequences of his choices. Being free in Christ does not free one from personal responsibility. In the first century and in the twenty-first, some Christians behave otherwise. "Let George do it" is their motto.

God says to His kingdom workers: *"You* do it!" It is always true: when each Christian fulfills his or her personal responsibility, the church will thrive. Each Christian faces the question, "Am I doing my share?"

God who blesses us with the choice to have personal freedom from sin, give me the wisdom and the will to work Your will. In Jesus' name, amen.

Hang Around Whom?

He that walketh with wise men shall be wise: but a companion of fools shall be destroyed (Proverbs 13:20).

Scripture: **2 Timothy 3:1-9**
Song: **"God's Wonderful People"**

Who wants to hang around people like those Paul describes in today's Scripture passage? They are an ugly lot, disfigured by sin and its consequences. The world is densely populated with such as these.

Each one started the process in the manner Paul lists first: each one began to love self more than anything or anyone else. A lover of self will covet, boast, blaspheme, disobey parents, reject thankfulness, and revel in all the other behaviors Paul lists. Such behavior springs from being completely self-centered, a lover of self.

One of the true blessings of being part of Christ's church is the company and companionship of those seeking righteousness in their lives. To be among those who truly wish to love others as they love themselves is one of God's most precious gifts. As the Spirit works in their lives, coveting will be replaced with mutual rejoicing. Boasting will be swallowed up in humility. Disobedience will be forgotten in submission. Every evil passion will be missing. Every holy intention will be gloriously present. Who wants to hang around such people? Only the wise.

God, who will put a stop to the perilous days of wickedness, thank You for the hope of an eternity of blessed fellowship with You and those wearing the white robes of righteousness. In the name of Christ, amen.

Does the Bible Matter?

Thou hast known the holy Scriptures, which are able to make thee wise unto salvation through faith which is in Christ Jesus (2 Timothy 3:15).

Scripture: **2 Timothy 3:10-17**
Song: **"God Has Spoken by His Prophets"**

In many churches, and with seeming intent, fewer disciples gather in study groups to give focused attention to Scripture and its meaning. Elaborate worship assemblies with carefully chosen songs and diligently crafted sermons, do expose all who gather to scriptural truths. But it seems that fewer Christians these days seek a daily time in the Word or a weekly classroom of study. What a tragedy!

Timothy—and Paul, his mentor in the gospel—never fell into thinking that the written Word didn't matter. In fact the apostle can't resist listing the life-changing values that culminate in a life of satisfying service.

The person of God who cannot exclaim with the writer of Psalm 119 the marvels of the Word has not given the Word its opportunity to change his or her life. The one who walks in the shallows of divine water will have only tingling toes. Until we immerse ourselves in the depths of God's life-giving flow, we will never know the joy of complete exhilaration. Paul knew. He wanted Timothy to know. He wants me to know.

God of revelation, I marvel in Your wisdom. Give me the joy of knowing Your Word as I diligently study. Through Christ I pray. Amen.

His Appearing

[Christ] shall judge the quick and the dead at his appearing. . . . Henceforth there is laid up for me a crown of righteousness, which the Lord, the righteous judge, shall give me at that day: and not to me only, but unto all them also that love his appearing (2 Timothy 4:1, 8).

Scripture: **2 Timothy 4:1-8**
Song: **"We Shall Behold Him"**

Certain events change the direction of history. Noah's flood. Marathon. Pearl Harbor. World Trade Center. Only one event can finalize history's progression.

Christ's appearing will end temporal history. The creator of time will end it also. The destiny of both the living and the dead will be eternally fixed. Therefore, only one personal event matters. That is the occasion when each commits to the lordship of Jesus and begins submission to Him in the waters of baptism. For the one who loves Him, His appearing will be joyous.

Imagine the ecstasy of the moment when Christ gently sets a crown on the believer's head, and says, "Come, ye blessed of my Father, inherit the kingdom prepared for you from the foundation of the world" (Matthew 25:34). That vision kept Paul going. That vision was all Paul needed to finish his course. And isn't that vision all any Christian needs?

God of beginning and end, give me the grace to say with Paul, "I am now ready" for Your Son's appearing. I praise You for being the righteous judge who will do the right thing for Your children. In Jesus' name, amen.

Paul and Psalm 23

The Lord shall deliver me from every evil work, and will preserve me unto his heavenly kingdom: to whom be glory for ever and ever. Amen (2 Timothy 4:18).

Scripture: **2 Timothy 4:9-22**
Song: **"The Lord Is My Shepherd"**

If Paul had written Psalm 23, would it have been worded in different phrases? Would he have written, "He maketh me to lie down in dank prisons" or "He leadeth me into raging seas"? Of course not. Paul's sentiments would mirror the conclusions of David. Paul would write, "The Lord shall deliver me from every evil work and will preserve me unto his heavenly kingdom."

The shepherd's leadership and care lasts. Day to day in earthly life, eon to eon in heavenly life. David knew that. Paul knew that too. Though David knew dank caves and Paul knew dank prisons, both knew about the glories of Heaven. Though both David and Paul knew human thirst, both knew of divine waters of life. Though both David and Paul knew treacherous friends, both knew the friend who stays true.

Our attitude can reflect the here and now, or it can reflect God's future. Neither David nor Paul chose to dwell in the difficulties of the day. Both chose to ponder the day of His coming. That choice makes all the difference.

God, preserve me unto Your heavenly kingdom. Help me by Your Spirit to see the end beyond the journey. All honor and glory to the Son; amen.

Unique Gifts

Under his direction the whole body is fitted together perfectly, and each part in its own special way helps the other parts, so that the whole body is healthy and growing and full of love (Ephesians 4:16, *The Living Bible*).

Scripture: **Ephesians 4:11-16**
Song: **"Gifts that Last"**

Jesus' challenge to the apostles was great, but they were filled with the Holy Spirit and the unique gifts that God gave to each. So it is today. Our challenge to be disciples today is also great, but He provides what we need. We have each been given unique gifts that become evident as we mature. But how do we know what our gifts are? One thing that helps is feedback from other believers.

"I gained a lot from that class you taught, John!"

"Melissa, you sure know how to help people in need."

"Juan, I've seen so many coming to Christ through your testimony."

As we get involved in ministry, we can listen to His people for feedback. Yet, when our gifts are revealed, we won't cling to them. Rather, with thankful hearts, we'll use them in works of love and service to promote a growing church. The ultimate test of effectiveness is whether the Holy Spirit brings fruit from our prayerful efforts.

Father, show me my gifts that I may serve others as did Your Son. Let me be an encouragement to someone today. In Christ's name I pray. Amen.

February 20-26. **Alex Bienko** has been married to Angela for 40 years. Living in Houston, Texas, they have two remarkable sons and one joy of a grandson.

February 21

Knowledge That Unites Us

As you know him better, he will give you, through his great power, everything you need for living a truly good life (2 Peter 1:3, *The Living Bible*).

Scripture: **2 Peter 1:3-12**
Song: **"I Will Be with You"**

"Friendship is one mind in two bodies," said the quipster with a twinkle in his eye. But was he really very far from the truth? Perhaps you've noticed that, down through the years of the relationship, you and your close friend tend to become more and more alike. Doesn't your conduct often imitate his or hers? And don't you find yourself frequently thinking along the same lines?

How wonderful that this same "friendship phenomenon" occurs in our deepening relationship with God. As we open ourselves, His mind becomes our mind. And while a close friend can provide comfort and counsel, none can compare with the God who can give us everything we need. With each new level of intimacy, we bind with Him so we can bear His fruit. "Yes, I am the Vine; you are the branches. Whoever lives in me and I in him shall produce a large crop of fruit. For apart from me you can't do a thing" (John 15:5).

In what ways has your mind, and your whole life, been influenced by Christ lately? This great friendship has all the potential of a beautiful oneness that will last forever.

Jesus, lead me into greater friendship with You today, for You alone give me all that I could possibly need. In Your powerful name I pray. Amen.

Why Crash Around in Darkness?

If we are living in the light of God's presence, just as Christ does, then we have wonderful fellowship and joy with each other, and the blood of Jesus his Son cleanses us from every sin (1 John 1:7, *The Living Bible*).

Scripture: **1 John 1:5-10**
Song: **"The Lord Is My Light"**

I arose at night, half awake, to stumble my way through an unlit room. The outcome of my sleepy little adventure: a painfully stubbed big toe, a broken glass table top, a smashed Limoge vase, and a howling Schnauzer limping on a bruised paw.

Now these are not desirable outcomes when one simply wishes to move from one room to another in his own safe and peaceful domain! But, clearly, some things are much better done in the light.

In our spiritual walk, the light of God's presence provides guidance so we can see and avoid destructive obstacles in our lives. Jesus put it like this: "I am the Light of the world. So if you follow me, you won't be stumbling through the darkness, for living light will flood your path" (John 8:12). As we draw closer to this light, our vision improves dramatically. Best of all, our confidence in Him, and our relationship with Him, give us reason to want to be seen in the full light. For now, those who notice may well see a glimmer of the Savior in our faces.

Lord, I pray to walk always the lighted path and avoid the disaster of eternal darkness apart from You. Through the name of Jesus, amen.

Excellent Helping

Dear friend, you are doing a good work for God in taking care of the traveling teachers and missionaries who are passing through (3 John 5, *The Living Bible*).

Scripture: **3 John 2-8**
Song: **"All You Who Pass This Way"**

Mother would insist on hosting the entire family for the holidays. Days in advance, she'd begin cleaning, decorating, and baking. All must be ready before the guests arrived. Hard work, but very much appreciated.

Similarly, John praised the friend who welcomed "family"—fellow Christian teachers and missionaries—into his home. It is something we are all called to do. As the apostle Paul wrote, "When God's children are in need, you be the one to help them out. And get into the habit of inviting guests home for dinner or, if they need lodging, for the night" (Romans 12:13).

Most of us would gladly welcome a missionary or other minister into our homes. But is it not an even grander idea to demonstrate our Christian hospitality to whomever we meet, wherever we are in this world? Those who believe always need love and encouragement. And our own hospitality can draw those who have not yet heard of the Lord's banquet and His loving hospitality to His warm hearth and shelter.

Father, I ask to be of warm heart and kind hospitality to all I meet today. Let me be ready to open my heart and home, as You have opened to us all the riches of Your grace. In the name of Jesus, our Savior and Lord, amen.

Elderly Influence Required

These older women must train the younger women (Titus 2:4, *The Living Bible*).

Scripture: **Titus 2:1-5**
Song: **"Happy Are Those Who Follow"**

"But Mom, it wasn't my fault! I know Sammy took his parents' car, but I just rode along with him." To which Mom asked: "Alex, if Sammy jumped off a bridge, would you jump off after him?"

Who hasn't heard that show-stopping parental rejoinder at least once in his young life? It seemed to ring in my ears once or twice a week! If only older Sammy had been a better example. . . .

But, of course, that was no excuse.

It is valid, however, to expect the older believer to train the younger, as the apostle Paul tells us. Yes, as Christians we have a special responsibility to mentor the spiritual growth of others by instruction and example. The great thing is that everyone benefits. When we influence others with our conduct and offer a Christ-like example, we too experience growth.

And remember: example is often more effective than words alone. To make that point stick, I'll just leave you with an ancient Chinese proverb: "Not the cry but the flight of the wild duck leads the flock to fly and follow."

We ask, Lord, that You strengthen us to lead others to You by our loving example. Let the older pay attention to the younger—and vice versa. In the name of Jesus, our greatest mentor, I pray. Amen.

You Can Go Either Way Here

Here you yourself must be an example to them of good deeds of every kind. Let everything you do reflect your love of the truth and the fact that you are in dead earnest about it (Titus 2:7, *The Living Bible*).

Scripture: **Titus 2:6-10**
Song: **"How Good It Is"**

"Do as I say, not as I do." A parent may say it in jest, but the humor is often lost on the child. If we are to convince our own children, or any young person, of the truth found in the Word, then we must present evidence of our own conviction through our obedient behavior.

Not an easy task! And we can go either way with it: "Adam caused many to be sinners because he disobeyed God, and Christ caused many to be made acceptable to God because he obeyed" (Romans 5:19). With an understanding of Christ's life and teachings, we see the power of His example to influence others to obey.

There was no deviation between what our Lord *said* and what He *did* during His earthly life. When we accept Christ as Lord of our lives, and we demonstrate our obedience to Him, we hasten the day when others will come to know Him.

By loving the truth we demonstrate our love for Him. By living the truth in our daily lives we demonstrate His love to others.

Lord, please help me show my love by obedience, just as Jesus did with the Father. In Jesus' precious name, amen.

Multiply the Kindness

[He] died under God's judgment against our sins, so that he could rescue us from constant falling into sin and make us his very own people, with cleansed hearts and real enthusiasm for doing kind things for others (Titus 2:14, *The Living Bible*).

Scripture: **Titus 2:11-15**
Song: **"Come to Set Us Free"**

In the year 2000, the film *Pay It Forward* considered what the world might be like if each of us performed a truly selfless act for the benefit of three other people. Likewise, those three people would do the same for three others, and on and on. How the kindness multiplied!

Typically, a gift is something we put in a box and wrap in colorful paper. But have you learned that, as in the film, gifts of self bring greater joy—and for longer duration?

That is the kind of gift Christ offered to us on the cross: the gift of an eternal, perfect self. He set us free from the control of sin and only asked us to trust Him and follow His guidance for living our earthly lives.

"It is God himself who has made us what we are and given us new lives from Christ Jesus; and long ages ago he planned that we should spend these lives in helping others" (Ephesians 2:10). His was the ultimate gift, an unconditional and complete love. When we are in Him and He is in us, we can't help but pay that love forward to each person we encounter each day.

Lord, help me to lose myself in Your infinite love and share that love with others. I pray in the name of our Savior, Jesus Christ. Amen.

Created for God

God created man in his own image, in the image of God he created him (Genesis 1:27, *New International Version*).

Scripture: **Genesis 1:26-31**
Song: **"This Is My Father's World"**

We know from the Bible that our bodies were made from the dust of the earth. But God says He is "spirit," so how could it be that He created us in His own image? After all, we aren't all-powerful as God is. We aren't perfect in wisdom and love, and we are certainly limited by our bodies as to where we can go and what we can do. Yet God is unlimited by space and time. He can see into the past and knows what the future will bring.

But consider three aspects of human nature that surely demonstrate God's image: we have personality, emotions, and will. We are unique persons, we experience feelings, and we can make choices. This is the essence of personhood, which is what God has conveyed to us in the way He made us.

I find it very interesting that God has feelings! He can be happy, sad, angry, or please. In fact, we can please Him or make Him sad. And He has will, which He chose to use when He created us. He wanted beings to love who would love Him back. Am I exercising my will to do that?

Dear Lord, thank You for creating each of us in Your own image. Help us walk with You today and every day. In Jesus' name, amen.

February 27, 28. Beverly Bittner enjoys reading in her retirement, especially biographies. She has also found time recently to write a Bible study on angels.

Complete—but Not Finished!

The Lord God said, It is not good that the man should be alone; I will make him an help meet for him (*Genesis 2:18*).

Scripture: **Genesis 2: 7, 15-25**
Song: **"Happy the Home When God Is There"**

Can you find the Tigris and Euphrates Rivers on your Bible map or atlas? The Euphrates begins in Turkey and flows south, hundreds of miles, to the Persian Gulf. The Tigris joins the Euphrates about forty miles north of the Gulf. The Bible mentions the meeting place of these rivers, and two others, as the site of the Garden of Eden. When the northern snows melt in the spring, the rivers flood the land, making a lush, fertile plain as the waters recede. Some call this area the "cradle of civilization," and we can hardly imagine how beautiful it must have been.

God finished creating the animals, Adam named them, and mists from the rivers watered the Garden so Adam could keep it flourishing. All seemed to be well. Yet something was missing: It remained for God to make a companion for Adam. Then he would be complete.

Many happily married men today will tell you of this kind of marital completeness. They will NOT go along with the old joke: "A man isn't complete 'till he's married; then he's finished."

Father God, may we make our homes as pleasant as the garden home of Adam and Eve. Bless our marriages and families today! This I pray in the precious name of Jesus. Amen.

My Prayer Notes

_____

_____

_____

_____

_____

_____

_____

_____

_____

_____

_____

_____

_____

_____

_____

_____

_____

My Prayer Notes

My Prayer Notes

DEVOTIONS®

*W*hen I consider thy heavens, the work of thy fingers, . . . What is man, that thou art mindful of him?

—Psalm 8:3, 4

MARCH

Photo © Digital Vision

Gary Allen, editor

God Makes a Promise

I have set my rainbow in the clouds, and it will be the sign of the covenant between me and the earth (Genesis 9:13, *New International Version*).

Scripture: **Genesis 9:8-17**
Song: **"Standing on the Promises"**

Remember the childhood promises you loved to hear? Maybe Mom said, "If you're good, we'll go to the zoo on Saturday." You'd say, "I promise," putting on your best behavior. But it could rain on Saturday, or Mom may have to work, or someone in the family might become sick. Many things can keep promises from fulfillment.

God's promises will come to pass, however. When His promise or covenant is unconditional, it means He demands nothing from us to fulfill it. The beautiful, seven-color rainbow that arches across the sky after a rain signifies God's first unconditional covenant with all the people of the world.

No doubt Noah and his family were happy to step onto dry ground after riding out the flood for so many months. But deep in their hearts they may have shivered with fear: what if God sends another terrible downpour? So God sent a visible sign to remind them (and us) of His promise never to destroy all life again by flood.

Lord, we often make promises we can't keep. How thankful I am that Your promises are true and endure forever! In Jesus' name, amen.

March 1–5. **Beverly Bittner** enjoys reading in her retirement, especially biographies. She has also found time recently to write a Bible study on angels.

A Dry and Weary Place

My soul thirsts for you . . . in a dry and weary land where there is no water (Psalm 63:1, *New International Version*).

Scripture: **Psalm 63:1-8**
Song: **"How Firm a Foundation"**

David knew what it was to be thirsty. In the dry, barren desert of Judah, with only a few followers, he camped in a hot and dusty cave. Israel's enemies, the Philistines, occupied Bethlehem. "Oh, that someone would give me a drink of the water from the well of Bethlehem," David lamented.

Three of his bravest soldiers heard him and broke through the Philistine defenses to draw a flask of water from the well by the city gate. David cherished their bravery and devotion, but he would not drink the water. He poured it on the ground as a love offering to God.

Once I wasn't allowed to eat or drink for 12 hours in preparation for a medical test. As I grew more and more thirsty, I was sure I was suffering terribly from this deprivation. Later, I drank greedily of the cool water given to me. But did I stop to thank God for this wonderful blessing?

How often we take God's provision for granted! Many early Christians would recite Psalm 63 as a daily prayer. Perhaps we should do the same.

Father, I do thank You. You not only created us, but You provided everything necessary on the earth to sustain life. May I remember to give thanks and to share my abundance with others. In Christ I pray. Amen.

Always There: His Strength

My flesh and my heart faileth: but God is the strength of my heart (Psalm 73:26).

Scripture: **Psalm 73:21-28**
Song: **"Living for Jesus"**

I recently attended a missionary conference. How pleasant it was to get acquainted with so many servants of God whom I knew only through pictures, prayer cards, and an occasional letter! I came away with a new appreciation of missionary families. They have heard a call from God and have gladly obeyed.

One young couple stands out in my mind. They wore the colorful dress of Uruguay, where soon they would be returning. They were eager to go, even though it might be several years before they would return to their homes in their native country again. They were eager to go, though surely some of the days ahead would test the strength of flesh and heart. I resolved to remember them in daily prayer.

We have a common bond in the Lord, who gives us strength wherever we are. When any of us believers must be apart, He knows where each of us is at all times. Our fellowship remains strong. And the all-powerful God remains with us to uphold our hearts in His will.

Lord, I thank You that we are never out of Your sight. I pray You will help me live as a bright light even when the world seems dark and troubled. May You always be the strength my heart turns to in time of need. In the name of Jesus I pray. Amen.

See, and Serve!

We see Jesus . . . that he by the grace of God should taste death for every man (Hebrews 2:9).

Scripture: **Hebrews 2:5-10**
Song: **"Calvary Covers It All"**

I recently wrote a story called "The Smallest Cherub." It's about an angel who wanted more than anything to serve God. Many angels had been called to do special work for the Great Creator, but the little angel was not summoned. Was it because he was small and shy and easily frightened?

God's voice thundering from His throne sent the little cherub flying to his hiding place. He watched eagerly as angels were chosen to announce Jesus' birth. He practiced saying "Glory to God in the highest," but he was not chosen to go. He then hid among the strong angels who stood ready to deliver Jesus from the cross. But Jesus did not call them. The little cherub watched in sorrow as Jesus died and was buried. What rejoicing in Heaven and on earth when Jesus rose from the dead!

Do you desire to serve God but feel too small and insignificant? Just think, God created human beings for a special place in His kingdom. He loved each of us so much that He sent Jesus from Heaven to die for our sins. No one is too big or too small to serve Him. At the cross we see Jesus. And there we all stand on level ground.

Father, thank You for loving us enough to send Your Son to taste death on our behalf. I love Him so much, the One in whose name I pray. Amen.

Care for This!

You made us only a little lower than God, and you crowned us with glory and honor. You put us in charge of everything you made, giving us authority over all things (Psalm 8:5, 6, *New Living Translation*).

Scripture: **Psalm 8**
Song: **"Heaven Came Down and Glory Filled My Soul"**

When God placed humans in their first home, His instructions were, "Tend and care for this place." Adam, with the help of his wife, Eve, was to keep the home clean and orderly. They were not to waste the resources God gave them. They were not to destroy or neglect their beautiful dwelling place.

As descendants of Adam and Eve, we can take that instruction to heart. It was God's pleasure to make His earthly creation special in all the universe. Now it will please Him if we take care of His world.

As I write this, it is spring where I live. My window is open, and the aroma of new-mown grass wafts through the room. Well-tended flowers brighten my neighbors' yards with bright colors and sweet odors. Your home and surroundings may be much different from mine, but isn't it grand to know that we are neighbors in God's world? As we take care of our homes, together we are serving God. Let us be the best of caretakers!

Lord God, I thank You for all You have allowed me to use. Help me appreciate Your goodness to me. May I be generous, too, in sharing with others what even I do not truly possess. In Christ I pray. Amen.

Glory, in Word and Deed

The heavens declare the glory of God (Psalm 19:1, *New International Version*).

Scripture: **Psalm 19:1-6**
Song: **"Morning Has Broken"**

I often hear my friends saying nice things about their loved ones. They will talk about projects accomplished, awards won, or services performed. Grandparents, parents, and friends beam with pride in their loved ones.

I have two children. When the older one became a member of his school's academic honor society, I certainly let my parents, friends, acquaintances—and anyone else who would listen—know I was quite pleased with his accomplishments. (And after all, didn't he inherit those brains from his father?) Then there's my younger son, nine years younger, who also is making good grades. If you have a few days to spare, I can tell you all sorts of interesting things about both of these great guys.

We like to proclaim wonderfully good things about our loved ones. In today's Scripture, the Bible says that the "heavens declare the glory of God." God is so wonderful that the heavenly beings want to share the glories of God with all creation. As children of God, may we too declare the wonderful love of our Lord in all we say and do.

Lord, help me contribute to the work of the heavens today, in proclaiming Your glory by the way I live my life. In Christ's name I pray. Amen.

March 6–12. **Peter Anderson** is minister in Ocala, Florida. His hobbies include playing with his computer and taking overseas mission trips.

Those Throw-Away Pages

All of you people, come praise our God! Let his praises be heard (Psalm 66:8, *Contemporary English Version*).

Scripture: **Psalm 66:1-9**
Song: **"Praise Him! Praise Him!"**

I'm a college football fan. I just enjoy the sport. It doesn't matter whether I'm sitting in front of the television or attending the game in person, I love watching football. I have a favorite team, of course, and I'm quite passionate about its success.

When I'm at a game, it's clear to me that we fans are really pumped up about "our" team. When our guys score a touchdown, we all holler and give each other high fives. If the other team is moving with the ball, we shout out "De-fense!" We are passionate about the sport.

I remember a song I used to sing when I was growing up. It included the words: "I'll shout it from the mountain top. [Praise God!] I want my world to know; the Lord of love has come to me, I want to pass it on." ("Pass It On," Kurt Kaiser, © 1969 Lexicon Music, Inc. Used by permission.)

We can be passionate about sports, but more we should be thrilled about our God. In fact, we are invited to come praise our God, everywhere and at all times. And why not? He is eternal; the sports pages land in the wastebasket after only a single day.

Father God, I praise You today and every day. And may I always be more enthused about Your eternal kingdom work than thrilled with yesterday's fading box scores. In the precious name of Jesus I pray. Amen.

An Enduring Love

Give thanks to the Lord of lords: His love endures forever (Psalm 136:3, *New International Version*).

Scripture: **Psalm 136:1-9**
Song: **"Give Thanks"**

Did you happen to notice that, in Psalm 136, each verse includes the same repeating phrase? The first part of each verse states something God has done and then concludes with: "His love endures forever." Why do you think the psalmist wrote this way?

Although my children think of me as being quite old, I certainly wasn't around when these words were first composed. But I can guess why the writer ended each verse with "His love endures forever." It's just my personal opinion, but I think he wanted his readers to know one basic fact about God: "His love endures forever!" That fact is so important that it leaps from the pages 26 times in this chapter.

Do you feel lonely? "His love endures forever." Feel thankful? "His love endures forever." Do you wonder whether God loves you? "His love endures forever." Do you feel stressed out? "His love endures forever." As you go about your business today, remember that "His love endures forever!" God loves you, and His love will always uphold you.

Although I may take Your love for granted, **Lord,** *You never take me for granted. Help me to remember this week that You hold me always in Your unfailing love. In the name of Your Son, my Savior, I pray. Amen.*

Setting Foundations

You built foundations for the earth, and it will never be shaken (Psalm 104:5, *Contemporary English Version*).

Scripture: **Psalm 104:1-13**
Song: **"For the Beauty of the Earth"**

For the moment, let's not debate evolution. Let's not debate exactly *how* God created the world. Let's just marvel at the magnificence of God's creative abilities! Today's passage speaks of God's building the foundations for the earth and covering the earth with the ocean. Yet God has set limits for the waters so there will never be a world-wide flood again. God's majestic and orderly work has foundations and built-in boundaries.

In raising my children, I know the importance of setting boundaries. The boys may do certain things and *not* do other things. They know the punishments and rewards related to their treatment of behavioral strictures.

God created the foundations for the earth as well. I'm not a builder, but I do know the importance of a solid foundation. With the sand and sinkholes so prevalent in my native state of Florida, we can't afford to skimp on this component of construction. But to think that God has created the foundations and the boundaries of our entire world . . . What an awesome almighty God we serve!

*All of creation proves there is a God, **O Father**! Help me to appreciate the world You created and to enjoy the fruits of Your creation. And, yes, thank You for the beauty of the earth I see out my window this very moment. In the name of Jesus, Lord and master of all, I pray. Amen.*

God Keeps It Growing

The trees of the Lord are full of sap; the cedars of Lebanon, which he hath planted (Psalm 104:16).

Scripture: **Psalm 104:14-23**
Song: **"Fill My Cup, Lord"**

Some people are gifted in working with green things. They plant and water—and then watch their lush landscape blossom with life and color and all manner of fruit.

I do not have that gift. Give me a thriving, healthy plant, and within a few days I can make it wilt and die. I seem to have been born with this dubious talent, so I envy those with green thumbs. Apparently all of my digits revert to a dusty shade of brown as soon as I reach for a seed packet. (You don't want to know what happened to my vegetable garden last year.)

God not only created the earth, but He continues to be active in His creation. Even the trees are full of sap because the Lord sends the rain and tends to them. Yes, "April showers bring May flowers." God's caretaking hand makes it all possible.

But consider this: Are you being watered by the truth of God's Word? Plants need water to grow, and people need food, water, and air to grow. Christians need the Word of God to grow into full maturity in Christ. Open your heart to God's Word. He knows how to grow things.

O Lord, I'm overflowing with the truth of Your love. Allow others to see the Spirit of truth living and thriving in me today. And keep me growing in the knowledge of who You are. In Christ I pray. Amen.

Satisfied!

When you open your hand, they are satisfied with good things (Psalm 104:28, *New International Version*).

Scripture: **Psalm 104:24-30**
Song: **"Praise God, from Whom All Blessings Flow"**

When I was still a child, my dad would travel with his college choir to various parts of the country. When he came home, he often brought little gifts to give to my siblings and me. I looked forward to his return, not only because I wanted to see him again, but because I'd likely receive a small souvenir from the places he had visited.

God provides for His creation, opening His hand to us and revealing great and good gifts. In the Old Testament, He held manna for the children of Israel during their wilderness journeys. In the New Testament, Jesus spoke about the Father providing birds of the air with food. God provides for all His creation. When He opens His hand, we are blessed with His goodness.

Good things come from God. But do you ever name all the blessings you have? Like me, you are no doubt aware of the problems in your life, some of which may be quite serious. But don't forget the blessings. God's hands are big, and His hands overflow with love. He is the one source of lasting satisfaction in all the universe.

Dear God, today I will take a moment to name and appreciate the blessings You have given me. Let me practice giving You thanks while I am here on earth, for I know this will be my high privilege throughout eternity. In the name of the Father, the Son, and the Holy Spirit, I pray. Amen.

Worthy Singing

As long as I live, I will sing and praise you, the Lord God (Psalm 104:33, *Contemporary English Version*).

Scripture: **Psalm 104:31-35**
Song: **"I Could Sing of Your Love Forever"**

Imagine a world without music and songs. No Beach Boys, no Beetles . . . no Beethoven! And while the world would be without their music, there would be no gospel hymns either.

I'm glad there is singing; it makes the world a better place. It gives us a glorious means, too, of lifting our praises to God. But sadly, we also can use our vocal chords for sin. While we might honor God with lofty words in one moment, we might hurt someone in cutting tones a moment later. Have you heard the expression "sticks and stones may break my bones, but words will never hurt me"? That expression is not true in my opinion. Words *do* hurt.

Let us use our tongues not for hurt or for singing lyrics of dubious morality, but for high praise to God, employing our voices to sing His greatness. Even if we are not good singers, we can make a joyful noise to Him, proclaiming His love and goodness every day of our lives. Others will hear and learn of this Lord who wants to love them too.

*Today I worship You, **Lord**, in word and in song. When I am tempted to use my tongue to hurt another person, remind me that Your Son died for that person as well. You are worthy of all praise—not just with my tongue, but with my whole life. In the name of my Savior, Jesus Christ, amen.*

An Obvious Name

Worship the Lord with gladness; come before him with joyful songs (Psalm 100:2, *New International Version*).

Scripture: **Psalm 100**
Song: **"Jesus Saves"**

The Sicilians call it "the Happy Church." The small, but growing, congregation began four years ago after Al and Beth Barone sold everything they had and left their home in Whitefish, Montana. They moved to Al's native Sicily, an island off the coast of Italy.

Life is hard there. Unemployment looms at 42 percent. Religion tends to be legalistic and joyless. Perhaps it's the Barones' background that equips them to minister in such a challenging field. As a child and teenager, Beth suffered severe illness. She ministers to others so powerfully because she's been saved from so much.

In addition, she and Al have adopted three sons from orphanages in Bulgaria. Each adoption redeemed a young boy from neglect and abuse, from places where children stayed in bed all day and never ventured outside their rooms. The Barone family inspires hope in a culture steeped in hopelessness. The joyful songs and genuine love flowing from their missionary endeavor quickly earned a cheerful name for the church where they serve.

Lord, thank You for the opportunity to approach You with joy today. I worship You for Your great salvation! In Christ's name, amen.

March 13–19. **Patty Duncan** teaches fifth grade at a Christian school in Eugene, Oregon. She and her teenage son often provide foster care for lost kittens.

Nighty Night!

Indeed, he who watches over Israel will neither slumber nor sleep (Psalm 121:4, *New International Version*).

Scripture: **Psalm 121**
Song: **"The Steadfast Love of the Lord"**

My son and I share our home with two cats (with their permission, of course). While these domesticated animals might seem dependent on us as their keepers, they actually provide many useful services in our household. The feline sisters entertain us when they bat a tiny cat-food biscuit around the kitchen floor or chase a flashlight beam up the wall. They provide stress relief when they curl up on our laps for petting. They decorate the window sills when it's sunny outside.

I've discovered they're also excellent watchcats. Before you picture them hissing threateningly at strangers, let me assure you that they do not act like watch*dogs*. In fact, when they hear a car drive in, they both rush to hide under my bed. However, in the middle of the night recently, I woke from my slumber to find one cat snuggled beside my pillow and the other sitting up next to her, apparently watching me sleep! I laughed at the prospect of being guarded by my nocturnal pets, but the psalmist says I can take great comfort in knowing God watches over me, every minute of my days and nights.

Heavenly Father, I'm so glad You never sleep! The thought gives me peace as I lie down to rest. I know You're watching over me in Your great love and care. Good night, Lord, I pray, in Your holy name. Amen.

Showing God's Care

He protects the immigrants, and cares for the orphans and widows (Psalm 146:9, *The Living Bible*).

Scripture: **Psalm 146**
Song: **"Make Me a Blessing"**

"Carolyn's going to Hawaii!" a fellow teacher shared with me at school. "A friend she's known since kindergarten is paying her way—and another lady friend's expenses too. They'll be gone for 10 days."

"Oh, that's wonderful!" I replied. After school I slipped into Carolyn's classroom to celebrate with her and hear more about her coming trip.

She told how her friend's husband had succeeded in his business as a building contractor in San Francisco. Although they became wealthy, the couple continued to live the lifestyle of their earlier years. They remodeled their modest house instead of buying a bigger one, and they frequently open their home in hospitality. They constantly serve by giving of their means in creative ways.

For Carolyn, the trip offered a much-needed rest. While raising her children as a single mom for 20 years, she had endured a lot of hardship and learned to depend on God's provision. For her, this was just like the Lord—using wonderful friends—to shower her with blessing.

God, You have a special concern and tender care for fatherless children and women who are widows. Thank You for watching over these who need Your help and for touching the hearts of people to be a channel of Your blessings. In the precious name of Jesus I pray. Amen.

20 Questions

You know when I sit and when I rise; you perceive my thoughts from afar (Psalm 139:2, *New International Version*).

Scripture: **Psalm 139:1-6**
Song: **"Search Me, O God"**

Did you ever play the guessing game 20 Questions? One person thinks of an object, and the opponent may ask 20 yes-or-no questions to discover the mystery word. God doesn't need 20 questions—or even one question—to guess what we're thinking. He already knows. Because of this, I decided many years ago to be honest with God when I pray.

It just seemed logical. Why try to hide a thought when He already knows it? While my theology was sound, my understanding of human nature was limited. Since childhood I've seen myself as a "good girl," so I often deceive myself to protect my self-image. I could not possibly think an impure thought, indulge in jealousy or hatred, or have selfish motives.

Ha! Think again! As each decade slips by, I understand more deeply my inability to be honest with myself. It's a scary and comforting idea that God perceives my true heart. Scary because He's holy, and I'm certainly not. Comforting because through His incarnate Son He empathizes with the thought processes of human beings. He understands me, even when I don't have a clue.

Lord, You know me like no other. Today, help me relax my control and welcome Your loving meddling in my mind. In Christ's name, amen.

No Escape

Where can I go from your Spirit? Where can I flee from your presence? (Psalm 139:7, *New International Version*).

Scripture: **Psalm 139:7-12**
Song: **"Where the Spirit of the Lord Is"**

In the middle of the night, my friend's sister, distraught because of her difficult marriage, drove several hours from her home in southern California to Yosemite National Park. She then hiked to the top of Half Dome, the park's famous glacier-carved, half-sphere rock formation. The final ascent up the curved back of the granite mountain is challenging in daylight but filled with risk after dark. When she reached the peak, she hiked back down, got in her car and drove home.

Pondering the dramatic story, I wondered what she was feeling and thinking. Was she hoping she'd fall off the giant rock? Was she running away from her problems—then somehow found enough strength to go back and face them? Was she angry? Was she crying?

All of us would like to escape at times. The psalmist has good and bad news for us: we can't run away from God. While I don't know whether the frustrated wife found peace in her marriage, I do know that even the night sky at the top of Half Dome was not dark enough to hide her from God's presence and love.

Dear Lord, *like Adam and Eve in the garden, we run away to hide our shame, our sin, our pain. Forgive me, and help me come out of hiding to acknowledge Your abiding presence. Through Christ I pray. Amen.*

Care Before the Beginning

You saw my bones being formed as I took shape in my mother's body (Psalm 139:15, *New Century Version*).

Scripture: **Psalm 139:13-18**
Song: **"Turn Your Eyes Upon Jesus"**

"Look!" McKenzie cried as she hurried into our classroom. Setting her backpack down, she handed me a small black-and-white photo. "It's my little sister, Elly," she explained joyfully.

"Oh, it's an ultrasound," I said. "How exciting! I see her little face. Isn't it wonderful to see your baby sister before she's born?"

We can do amazing things with technology these days. Sound waves bouncing off a tiny baby in the womb now create an image on a screen to be printed onto paper. Doctors and eager parents can study the little person who will make his or her appearance months later.

Of course, God doesn't need a sonogram machine to see prenatal development. He's been weaving together tiny limbs and organs in mothers' wombs for as long as humans have inhabited the earth. He cares for each of us, even before we take our first breaths. Even if parents consider a pregnancy an accident, God does not goof up. What a comforting thought!

Father God, You are amazing. If I really understood and believed how involved You have been in every second of my life, I'd surely live differently. May I rest more secure in Your love today—a love that began before I began. I pray in Jesus' name. Amen.

Constructive Correction

See if there is any offensive way in me, and lead me in the way everlasting (Psalm 139:24, *New International Version*).

Scripture: **Psalm 139:19-24**
Song: **"Change My Heart, O God"**

I committed a major blunder at school. Several parents of my fifth-grade students went to the principal and complained, and I was summoned in for a conference. My principal didn't mince words as she communicated the parents' concerns. Clearly, I was wrong.

I apologized. Inwardly, though, I defended my action, justifying what I'd done and excusing myself. Later, alone with the Lord, I was able to see the incident from the parents' viewpoint . . . and I was devastated. I felt incompetent, unworthy to care for the precious charges entrusted to my care. Truly, the Lord pointed out an "offensive way" in me that day.

Thankfully, He didn't leave me there. While my principal dealt with the problem directly, her correction came wrapped in encouragement. She makes room for mistakes because I'm new to teaching. She mentors me and leads me to improvement.

Isn't this how God works with us? Unlike the enemy's condemnation, which creates despair, God's way of correction sets us back on the path, on the "way everlasting."

Lord, I'm so glad You refuse to leave me as I am, even using people around me to help me change and grow. You are direct and merciful all at once. Thank You. In Jesus' name, amen.

Face the Face

Look to the Lord and his strength; seek his face always (Psalm 105:4, *New International Version*)

Scripture: **Psalm 105:1-11**
Song: **"The Solid Rock"**

As a child I often rode my bike on sweltering summer afternoons to the local swimming pool. Enormous potholes and jagged rocks littered the bumpy dirt road. Towel draped around my neck, hands slippery with sweat and sunscreen, I struggled to steer a path around the obstacles in my way.

One day I noticed a large rock in the road just ahead. I determined to keep it in sight, so I wouldn't run over it. Strangely, the harder I stared at the rock, the more my tires seemed drawn to it. I couldn't turn away. I couldn't do anything but watch in horror as the seemingly inevitable happened. My bike crashed into the rock, and I flew over the handlebars, landing in a bruised and bleeding heap.

What rock looms in your path right now? Is it a sin you're struggling with? a difficult circumstance? a painful relationship? Take your eyes off that potential disaster and fix them instead on the Lord's face. While He may not remove the obstacle, He'll help you rise above it. And that beats crashing any day.

Dear Lord, *when I am distracted by obstacles in my life, take my chin in Your hands and lift my face up to Your face. In Christ I pray. Amen.*

March 20–26. **Becky Fulcher,** mother of two, lives and writes in scenic Monument, Colorado.

Whose Dream?

The Lord will fulfill his purpose for me (Psalm 138:8, *New International Version*).

Scripture: **Psalm 138**
Song: **"Take My Life, and Let It Be"**

"I just signed a book contract with ABC Publishing!" My friend's voice bubbled with excitement at the thought of seeing her name in print—again. Part of me felt happy for my friend. Another part wanted to kick her in the shins.

Familiar doubts and questions flooded my mind: "What's wrong with me? Why can't I seem to make this happen? Maybe I should just give up." For years I'd dreamed of becoming a writer, but other things always got in the way: my parents' expectations, making a living, and now the consuming demands of motherhood. Though I longed to write, I couldn't seem to get my dream off the ground. But *why?*

My answer came through Psalm 138:8. The Lord will fulfill *His* purpose for me. Instead of pursuing God's purpose, perhaps I'd been chasing my own skewed ideas of what it meant to be a writer. God showed me that my writing isn't mine at all, it's His—a tool in His hands to be used according to His design.

What is your dream? Is it God's dream too?

Dear Father, give me Your perspective on my dreams. Help me see beyond my self-made purposes to pursue the plans You have for the whole world. In the name of Jesus, Lord and Savior of all, I pray. Amen.

Delighted Dad

For the Lord takes delight in his people (Psalm 149:4, *New International Version*).

Scripture: **Psalm 149**
Song: **"Jesus *Likes* Me, This I Know"**

Have you ever noticed how even the most humble, unassuming people go a little overboard when it comes to their kids? People who'd never dream of bragging about themselves will shamelessly crow about their children as if they were the most remarkable creatures ever born. I recently overheard my husband, ordinarily a modest man, brazenly boasting to a friend about our wondrously gifted 11-year-old daughter's extraordinary accomplishments on the piano. (See there? I just did it myself.)

That's just how parents are about their kids. And that's how God is about *you*. He delights in you. He not only loves you, He *likes* you. He likes to be with you, to listen to you, to talk with you. The thought of you makes Him smile. As someone once said, "If God had a refrigerator, your picture would be on it."

This realization—that we are thoroughly liked by the God of the universe—can permeate our whole perspective on life. No longer must we measure up to other people's expectations. No longer must we try to be perfect on our own. Though He is growing us, God loves us, this moment, just as we are.

Dear Father, teach me to walk every day in the remembrance that You delight in me as one of Your beloved people. Through Christ I pray. Amen.

Singing and Weeping

Let everything that has breath praise the Lord. Praise the Lord
(Psalm 150:6, *New International Version*).

Scripture: **Psalm 150**
Song: **"Shout to the Lord"**

Musty air blew cold on my face, the car's air conditioner competing against the stifling Dallas heat. "I'll check us in," my husband said, hurrying into the lobby. We were not on vacation. We were here for a funeral. My sister had committed suicide two days earlier.

As I huddled on the front seat, terror—cold and black—washed over me. The days ahead loomed unbearable: facing my family, attending the memorial service and burial, and then what? What do people do when their world falls apart? Suddenly I knew I couldn't do any of it.

I teetered on the brink of an all-consuming darkness. And then the opening phrase of a psalm came to my mind: "Praise the Lord, O my soul; all my inmost being, praise his holy name" (Psalm 103:1, *NIV).* I forced myself to continue, reciting the words softly under my breath. As I did, the blackness receded as if beaten back by the words themselves; peace took its place.

Praise is powerful, isn't it? It envelops us in the deepest truth: God is enough, no matter what. Barbara Lee Johnson wrote, "Praise to You has overruled the sorrow of the world and has made me sing, even while I weep."

Almighty God, may Your Spirit put words of praise in my mind and my mouth in every situation I face. In Your holy name I pray. Amen.

Watery Witness

One generation will commend your works to another; they will tell of your mighty acts (Psalm 145:4, *New International Version*).

Scripture: **Psalm 145:1-7**
Song: **"I Love to Tell the Story"**

One Sunday afternoon, my brother's 5-year-old son Will approached him: "Daddy, you know when we were singing all those songs to God in church this morning?" My brother, sensing that something spiritually significant may have occurred, responded eagerly, "Yes, Will, I remember. What about it?"

"Daddy, you were just spitting all over me."

Ouch! As believers, we are to commend God's works to the next generation. How do we do this? How do we help our kids understand who God is and what He has done in our lives? While accidentally spitting on them won't help much, my brother was definitely on the right track. He wasn't just *telling* his son about God, he was giving him a glimpse into his own relationship with Him. He was showing him what it looks like to praise the Lord with all one's heart, to exalt Him as God and King. He was letting Will in on his own deep-seated conviction that God truly is great and most worthy of praise.

I think Will got the message. In spite of the spit.

__Dear God,__ may my relationship with You be so intimate and genuine that the next generation can't help but see You in me. May I proclaim Your great deeds by all my actions. In Jesus' name, amen.

Relax: No Chads Here!

Thy kingdom is an everlasting kingdom, and thy dominion endureth throughout all generations (Psalm 145:13).

Scripture: **Psalm 145:8-13a**
Song: **"Our God Reigns"**

Who could forget the USA's presidential election of 2000? For 35 days our country lingered in a state of limbo, not knowing who its next leader would be. Tensions ran high as votes were counted, chads examined, and court battles raged. A profound sense of turmoil and uneasiness settled over the entire nation, a single question churning in each person's mind: how will it all turn out?

Every four years in our country, we face this same question. And with it comes apprehension and anxiety. What kind of person will our next president be? Will he make wise decisions? Can he be trusted? What impact will he have on our future?

As believers, we know that the identity of our heavenly leader is never an issue. We have a God whose kingdom lasts forever, whose dominion endures through all generations. He is one we can trust without limit.

In other words, we can relax. We don't have to wonder and worry about who is in control. Our God reigns— today, tomorrow . . . forever.

Dear Lord, *help us to remember that You are God. You rule over all the earth, and You are good. Give us wisdom in selecting our earthly leaders, but give me the assurance that You are the one who is ultimately in control. Through Christ I pray. Amen.*

Yes, You're Okay

Thou openest thine hand, and satisfiest the desire of every living thing (Psalm 145:16)

Scripture: **Psalm 145:13b-21**
Song: **"You're All I Want"**

Hot tears soaked the front of my shirt as sobs wracked my 11-year-old daughter's body. Her shoulders shook as she poured out her grief. When finally she could speak, her words came out in shuddering gasps: "You don't understand. Piano is my *thing!* If I don't have piano, I don't have anything!"

The phone call had come just minutes before, relaying the results of the morning's piano competition. Everyone, including her highly competent teacher, thought our daughter would win. She didn't even place.

There will be more opportunities down the road, of course, many great experiences, win or lose. But on a deeper level my daughter made a mistake so common to us all: She'd counted on something other than God to make her feel okay at the center of her being. Can anything do that for God's creatures except the creator himself?

Even our heralded accomplishments lose their luster after a time. Our attempts at lasting status always fall short. Only the Lord, with unconditional love, satisfies the cry of our hearts: Let me know that I really am *okay!*

Dear Father, what am I counting on to give me lasting satisfaction? Teach me to draw life and fulfillment from You alone. In Christ's name, amen.

A Blessed Man

In the land of Uz there lived a man whose name was Job. This man was blameless and upright; he feared God and shunned evil (Job 1:1, *New International Version*).

Scripture: **Job 1:1-5**
Song: **"Now Thank We All Our God"**

Do you know someone who seems to lead a charmed life—happy marriage, loving family, good health, financial success, sterling reputation, scores of friends? Job was that type of person. In fact, verse 3 *(NIV)* describes him as "the greatest man among all the people of the East." But Job wasn't just a person of fortunate circumstances. He was, above all, a godly person. He knew that everything he had came from God. And as we see later in this chapter (v. 21), Job knew that whatever God gave could be taken away.

It's all too easy to fall into the I-did-it trap. Of course, we are responsible to develop and use our gifts and talents. But who gave those gifts to us? We can work hard, but who gave us our health? We can be brilliantly creative, but who crafted our minds? Many people use *blessed* as a synonym for *lucky* or *successful*. Job had the correct perspective. He knew that if he was blessed, it was because God was blessing him. And this same God has blessed us too.

Dear heavenly Father, *thank You for Your blessings: food, shelter, family, and friends. May my life display my gratitude today. In Jesus' name, amen.*

March 27–31. **John Conaway,** writer and editor, lives with his wife, MaryEllen, in Colorado. Their favorite activity is enjoying their two young grandsons.

Holy Hedge

Hast not thou made an hedge about him, and about his house, and about all that he hath on every side? (Job 1:10).

Scripture: **Job 1:6-12**
Song: **"Savior, Like a Shepherd Lead Us"**

This passage raises puzzling questions about the relationship between God and Satan. But instead of trying to wrestle with the loftier theological issues, I'd like us to consider a single word: *hedge.* From the time we knew our daughter was expecting, our Sunday school class prayed for her and her baby.

When Jonathan was born severely premature at 2 pounds, 5 ounces, the prayer intensified. Another baby in the neonatal intensive care unit contracted a serious infection, so Jonathan was tested. He didn't have the same condition; but the tests revealed a different infection. Treatment began before any symptoms appeared! He was protected from a deadly disease.

The prayer continued after he came home because he was at risk for many developmental disabilities. Today he is a healthy, bright 6-year-old.

When we pray for the health and safety of people we love, we are asking God to place a hedge of protection around them. Have you experienced God's hand of protection? Thank Him for His hedges of safety.

Dear heavenly Father, *thank You for Your loving care. Thank You for hearing and responding with love when Your children cry for help. I pray through our deliverer, Jesus. Amen.*

Restraint in Sorrow

In all this, Job did not sin by charging God with wrongdoing (Job 1:22, *New International Version*).

Scripture: **Job 1:13-22**
Song: **"Have Thine Own Way, Lord"**

In times of great agony, no one expects us to be in control. We've seen TV reporters shoving microphones into the faces of those who've just lost loved ones to some tragedy. Whether the event affects hundreds of others (as in a natural disaster) or only one or two are involved (as in a drive-by shooting), we've become used to seeing people lose composure. And we're forgiving of the way these survivors behave, whatever they say or do.

In contrast, we have Job. He suffered great loss, and the rest of the book makes it clear that he lived in mental and physical agony. Yet Job didn't think his loss gave him clearance to let loose with careless words. Somehow, even in this time of intense misery, he remembered that he belonged to God. In fact, verse 21 affirms his belief that God was sovereign over his life, even in this extreme situation: "The Lord gave, and the Lord hath taken away."

Job's response mattered because it expressed his heart-deep attitude toward God. But how do we respond to bad news? What do our reactions reveal about our faith?

Dear heavenly Father, thank You that because of the suffering of Your Son, You understand the depths of my suffering. Help me to honor You in the way I respond to my experiences of pain and despair. In the name of Jesus, the suffering servant, I pray. Amen.

Active Acceptance

Shall we accept good from God, and not trouble? (Job 2:10, *New International Version*).

Scripture: **Job 2:1-10**
Song: **"Like a River Glorious"**

I've known several people who have experienced the one-two punch of back-to-back tragedies. One woman was diagnosed with cancer, and then her husband filed for divorce. A couple lost a son to cancer, and then a daughter died in a car accident. A man lost his job (and his health insurance), and then suffered an injury, with costly hospitalization and rehabilitation to follow. It seems tragedies seldom come in manageable doses; while we're still reeling from one blow, another hits. Job had already lost his children and possessions. Now he lost his health.

His response? Acceptance. But his declaration to his wife (v. 10) wasn't a statement of defeat, fatalism, or resignation. He knew God was still in charge. In Philippians 1:12, Paul voiced this reaction to his imprisonment: "The things which happened unto me have fallen out rather unto the furtherance of the gospel." Paul's storm cloud had a silver lining.

Job didn't know why he was suffering, but he surely knew God had a reason for allowing it. But what about us? Do we really believe that, for those who love God, all things work together for the good (Romans 8:28)?

Father, when I'm walking in the darkness of despair, help me recall the truths You've taught me in happier times. In Jesus' name, amen.

Honestly!

May the day of my birth perish, and the night it was said, "A boy is born!" (Job 3:3, *New International Version*).

Scripture: **Job 3:1-10**
Song: **"Nearer, My God, to Thee"**

Do you have trouble being completely honest with God? I do. Even when distressed, defeated, or discouraged, I've found myself crafting "theologically correct" prayers. I might express my feelings to some extent, but I hasten to assure God that my theology is still orthodox. It's almost as if I'm afraid that God can't handle my honest expression of feelings!

Not so with Job; he didn't hold back. And others in the Bible approached God with similar candor. David voiced his deepest emotions: "How many are my foes! How many rise up against me!" (Psalm 3:1, *NIV*). Jeremiah even went so far as to attribute his troubles to God: "He has filled me with bitter herbs and sated me with gall"(Lamentations 3:15, *NIV*).

When I was a child, I argued with my father. But did I have to assure him that I loved him? Did he have to remind me that he loved me? No, that issue was settled; therefore, I could say what I really thought. If we belong to God, if we've trusted in His Son, if we have a relationship with Him . . . shouldn't we be honest with Him?

Our heavenly Father, when I'm at my lowest point, I come to You. Thank You for the freedom to tell You whatever is on my heart. In the name of my Savior, Jesus Christ, amen.

DEVOTIONS®

I **know that my redeemer liveth, and that he shall stand at the latter day upon the earth.**

—Job 19:25

APRIL

Photo © Brand X Pictures

Gary Allen, editor

Father Knows Best

Why died I not from the womb? (Job 3:11).

Scripture: **Job 3:11-19**
Song: **"God Moves in a Mysterious Way"**

A friend began his ministry life in a fairly ordinary way. After graduation from a Bible college, he became involved in youth ministry. After a number of years, he attained a position of church leadership. As he became well known, he began writing articles. Eventually he became an influential writer.

But amidst all these normal things, tragedy struck. Within a few years, two of his children died. He found himself drawn to those who mourn, helping many survivors through the painful process of grief recovery. Before his own death, he said, "I never would have chosen this ministry. Nor would I have chosen the way God prepared me for it. But as I look back, I can see God's hand on my life, even in the most painful experiences."

Faced with his own tragedy, Job said, in effect: "If it had been up to me, I wouldn't have chosen to be born." He knew his life had a plan; it just wasn't the plan he would have chosen. Our Father in Heaven doesn't consult us before allowing difficult days into our lives. But in time I believe we'll discover that He does, indeed, know best.

Lord, thank You for Your plan, though I may dimly understand it. Help me continue to follow You faithfully, nevertheless. In Jesus' name, amen.

April 1, 2. **John Conaway,** writer and editor, lives with his wife, MaryEllen, in Colorado. Their favorite activity is enjoying their two young grandsons.

It's Not About Me

Why is light given to those in misery, and life to the bitter of soul? (Job 3:20, *New International Version*).

Scripture: **Job 3:20-26**
Song: **"A Charge to Keep I Have"**

"If I'd rather be dead, why does God keep me alive?" That's the question Job asks in this passage. In verse 26 *(NIV)* he says, "I have no peace, no quietness; I have no rest, but only turmoil." If life is not worth living, why continue?

It might help us to look at Paul's perspective on this issue. In Philippians 1:23, 24 *(NIV)* we read, "I am torn between the two: I desire to depart and be with Christ, which is better by far; but it is more necessary for you that I remain in the body." Paul would rather have been dead too—not because his earthly life was so horrible, but because life in Heaven would be so much better.

But Paul knew there was more at stake than his own preference. God had put him here and given him a commission that involved great blessing for others. He needed to stay and be faithful to his task until he completed it.

Sometimes we wish we were somewhere else, doing something different. Let us choose to look at things differently. We are here on assignment—for God's glory, not for our own gratification. And we'll find our ultimate satisfaction in pleasing Him.

Our heavenly Father, help me to see my life as an assignment from You. Thank You for the privilege of serving You, right where I am. I pray this prayer in the name of Jesus, my Savior and Lord. Amen.

Only One Life

Man's days are determined; you have decreed the number of his months and have set limits he cannot exceed (Job 14:5, *New International Version*).

Scripture: **Job 14:1-6**
Song: **"Only One Life"**

Edwin suffered from a lung condition that caused him to become short of breath with the slightest exertion. His legs and ankles were grossly swollen. He asked God to allow him to die . . . then realized there were reasons for his extended life. In fact, there was at least one clear purpose: God wanted him to pray for the salvation of children in his community.

Flowers and shadows appear for a time, then fade. So with our lives. Job observed in today's verse that God has allotted each person a specific time of existence—no more, no less than what is given by a divine timetable. The quantity of our days is not as important as our life's quality, however. People may live long, yet be hateful and greedy. On the other hand, a young mother dies and leaves children who model their lives after her godly example. Whether our stay on earth is brief or long, let us live every day for the glory of God.

Father, thank You for our lives and the purposes You have for us. Whether my life is long or short, help me accomplish Your will. In all I do, may I work in the strength and wisdom You provide. In Jesus' name, amen.

April 3–9. **Jewell Johnson** lives in Arizona, where she enjoys walking, reading, and quilting. She and her husband have six children and seven grandchildren.

A Covering for Sin

My offenses will be sealed in a bag; you will cover over my sin (Job 14:17, *New International Version*).

Scripture: **Job 14:7-17**
Song: **"Grace Greater Than Our Sin"**

"At the end of the day, I think of all the bad things I've done and how displeased God must be with me," Bonnie shared with the Bible study group.

"But an unhappy Christian is no benefit to herself or anyone else, Bonnie," a friend responded. "Could you accept Christ's forgiveness and move on to the joy of the Lord?" It seemed Bonnie focused only on her misdeeds.

Job's friends were quick to point out that Job's afflictions must have resulted from his sins. And from his place on an ash heap, covered with painful sores, he could have pondered that possibility. But for Job the question of sin was settled. He had a glimmer of a loving God's provision for his transgressions; they were covered by the eternal (time-transcending) sacrifice of Jesus.

Yes, God is aware of our sins (Psalm 69:5). He knows each one that binds us, yet He sent a Redeemer who paid the ransom for our freedom. No need for the hounding thought, "You've sinned too much; God can't pardon you." The forgiveness of God is as wide as the sky and as vast as an ocean. Jesus' blood is sufficient.

Father, we are sinful and need a redeemer. Thank You for Your loving provision in Christ. I accept His blood as the covering for all my transgressions—and take Your joy as my daily strength. In Jesus' name, amen.

A Peace to Guard Us

As water wears away stones and torrents wash away the soil, so you destroy man's hope (Job 14:19, *New International Version*).

Scripture: **Job 14:18-22**
Song: **"Rock of Ages"**

Life circumstances broke upon Job much as uncontrollable floodwaters crash over the shore. In one gigantic sweep, his family, property, and health were swept away. Only ruins remained.

Life circumstances broke upon Bryan too. He'd hoped for a scholarship to play college football. But between his junior and senior years in high school, he became ill with a muscle disease that left him walking with a cane. He eventually recovered, but by then football was not an option.

Bryan's dreams and plans slipped away, and he struggled to find acceptable alternatives. Like Job, he discovered that life has a way of raining on our ambitions, crushing our aspirations, and shattering our hopes. Some turn from God at this point, becoming cynical and negative. They complain and shake their fists at Heaven.

There is another way to handle the low places in life. We can turn them over to one bigger than ourselves and look for His working amidst our pain. He promises His unending presence, and as we open our hearts to Him, He brings a peace that "transcends all understanding" (Philippians 4:7, *NIV)* to guard our hearts and minds.

Father, because of disastrous situations, some friends have lost hope. Revive them through Your Word! I pray this in the name of Jesus. Amen.

The Fresh Breath of God

It is the spirit of a man, the breath of the Almighty, that gives him understanding (Job 32:8, *New International Version*).

Scripture: **Job 32:1-10**
Song: **"God Is So Good"**

I was especially stressed during our worship service. Our daughter was suffering with an eating disorder, and that morning I felt angry and confused as I lingered in the church vestibule hoping someone would speak to me. A friend put her hand on my arm. "How are things going?"

"Not good. Our daughter has a problem. It's terrible."

"Let's sit down and talk," she said. As I shared my burden, the load became lighter. I felt God's peace, and I walked away knowing I could make it through another day. My friend discerned the essence of my need and quietly listened. Just listened, with all her heart. In contrast, Job's friends gave him pat answers and philosophical speeches that left him feeling bewildered and alone.

When people share problems with us, what do they need most at that moment? An answer? A planned-out solution? What about a gentle spirit that hears and empathizes? When we listen—*really* listen—to our friends' needs, we can feel with them, speak encouraging words, and assure them of our prayers. This will be to them the fresh breath of the Almighty.

Lord of All, thank You for Your wisdom, Your breath within us. Help me use it to listen and encourage when others tell me of their needs. In the precious name of Jesus I pray. Amen.

Justice and Mercy

He repays a man for what he has done; he brings upon him what his conduct deserves (Job 34:11, *New International Version*).

Scripture: **Job 34:11-15**
Song: **"At Calvary"**

As a young man, Augustine abandoned the faith of his mother, pursuing a worldly lifestyle. He knew he deserved God's judgment, but he remained unconcerned. His mother continued to pray for him.

One day when he was in his 30s, he heard a voice tell him to "take and read" the Scriptures. Augustine appealed to God's mercy, and his life was transformed; he became a great church leader. Although he died in A.D. 430, his book *Confessions* is still read today and continues to influence people to place their trust in God. Augustine deserved judgment, but he accepted mercy.

Job, on the other hand, was known as a righteous man. Yet he lost his children and property. His wife spiritually abandoned him, and his body oozed with sores. Elihu, his friend, concluded that Job was reaping God's justice for past evil deeds.

Was Elihu right? Of course not! We know God allowed Job's suffering for a higher purpose. But whether you are an Augustine or a Job as you live your days, please be assured: through His Son, God extends mercy, something essential to every human being.

God, we don't deserve mercy, but we do receive it. As I know Your love, may I extend it even to the unlovable around me. Through Christ, amen.

Ultimately Not Chance

How great is God—beyond our understanding! The number of his years is past finding out (Job 36:26, *New International Version*).

Scripture: **Job 36:24-33**
Song: **"How Great Thou Art"**

The woman glanced at the door of her prison cell and saw a book wedged between the bars. Opening it, she let the words speak to her heart, which eventually led her to the waters of baptism. But how did the book get stuck between the bars? It remained beyond her understanding.

Job's friends tried to make complete sense of his life. They explained the whys within the framework of their own experiences. But much of what happens to us defies explanation, right? We may conclude, "It just happened." And, yes, certain laws of nature make for a probability in the world. "Time and chance happen to . . . all" (Ecclesiastes 9:11, *NIV*). Yet God created the laws and rules them all, including the laws of probability! "The lot is cast into the lap, but its every decision is from the Lord" (Proverbs 16:33, *NIV*). He is great, and we can trust Him.

Our finite minds can't fully comprehend an infinite God. One person who escaped the Twin Towers disaster on September 11, 2001, said slow turnpike traffic saved her life. She gives thanks for that traffic, hardly understanding why she was blessed to be in the slow lane while in such a hurry.

God of greatness, God of power, thank You for Your mighty acts on my behalf. I praise You for weaving all the events, whether trivial or weighty, to make my life meaningful and pleasing to You. In Jesus' name, amen.

Knowledge of God

Do you know how God controls the clouds and makes his lightning flash? (Job 37:15, *New International Version*).

Scripture: **Job 37:14-24**
Song: **"This Is My Father's World"**

Sitting in a garden drinking tea one day, Isaac Newton saw an apple fall from a tree. Curious about the forces at work within the universe, he questioned why the fruit fell straight down. Why not sideways—or up? From these and other observations, this 18th-century scientist developed the theory of gravitation.

We can learn much by observing nature. Consider Elihu, for instance. If traditional dating for Job is correct, then he had no written Scripture. What he knew of God came from stories passed from generation to generation, dating back to men like Noah, to whom God spoke. And he looked to the sky and earth for knowledge.

While nature can't provide a complete revelation of the creator, it can at least offer hints of intelligent design and purpose. What Job's friend saw in clouds, rain, and soil surely helped in their pursuit of truth.

We live in a new day. While we continue to see God's hand at work in nature, we also have a greater revelation of Him through the written Word. We don't know exactly *how* the Lord controls His universe. But we do know that He chooses to make His home in our hearts.

Almighty God, thank You for dwelling within Your creation—and in me, Your beloved creature. In the name of my gracious Redeemer, Jesus, amen.

Humbling!

Who is this that darkeneth counsel by words without knowledge?
(Job 38:2).

Scripture: **Job 38:1-7**
Song: **"God, the Omnipotent!"**

When I read today's Scripture, I had an instant flashback to my childhood. In my mind's eye, I could see my mother, arms akimbo, confronting me when I had overstepped myself. She would say, "Just who do you think you are, young lady?" Once again, I had—as my grandfather would put it—"gotten too big for my britches." Mother would remind me that, although she loved me dearly, I was not in charge of our household.

Job was feeling pretty sorry for himself. Bad things had been happening to him, and he was complaining loudly. But God took him to task for speaking "words without knowledge." God reminded Job of who was in charge by asking whether Job could explain all the intricacies of creating and maintaining the universe. How humbling!

When adversity strikes in my life, I too sometimes crave understanding, seeking the reason for my suffering. Like Job I want to know, "Why is this happening to me?" It's not always possible to understand. It's then I have to remind myself to accept God's sovereignty over my life.

God, forgive me when I make petulant or strident demands. Help me move forward, trusting your unfathomable goodness. In Christ I pray. Amen

April 10–16. **Doris Mueller** has been a teacher all her adult life. In addition to writing devotionals, she writes for children. She also likes to travel.

Dark Night of the Soul

Their light is withholden, and the high arm shall be broken (Job 38:15).

Scripture: **Job 38:8-18**
Song: **"The Kingdom of God on Earth"**

Have you ever felt as if you were all alone in a hostile world? When you believed your friends and your family had abandoned you or even turned against you? When you felt unjustly maligned, although you were innocent of any wrongdoing? Or, worst of all, when you tried to pray and sensed no response, no relief?

This is how Job must have felt—as if God were absent. His possessions and his family had been taken from him. He was suffering intense physical pain. Then, to add insult to injury, his so-called friends pelted him with judgment and condemnation.

What can we learn from Job to help us when we are going through this dark night of the soul, with the light of faith seemingly withdrawn? What are we to do? Even when we feel so empty, so barren, we can continue to hold fast to the God we knew in the light. Perhaps we can also take up a new way of praying for a while. Suppose we simply come before the Lord with our arms outstretched, saying: "Here I am, Lord; see me hurting . . . ," and wait patiently before Him?

Dear heavenly Father, *sometimes I cannot sense Your presence, and I feel so alone. Help me to survive these times of estrangement. Deepen my faith, I pray. In Your Son's precious name, amen.*

Humility: Road to Reconciliation

Surely I spoke of things I did not understand, things too wonderful for me to know. . . . Therefore I despise myself and repent in dust and ashes (Job 42:3, 6, *New International Version*).

Scripture: **Job 42:1-6**
Song: **"Have Thine Own Way"**

While Job was undergoing his many travails, we can see him struggling to understand what was happening to him and trying to rely on his relationship with God. Yet he eventually responded with bitterness and resentment over his woes, with protests of his innocence, with self-justification and self-pity—even defensiveness when his friends rebuked him—and finally, with repentance and humility.

Does any of this strike a familiar chord in our lives? Of course it does. When a crisis comes, aren't we prone to plead or demand that God resolve the problem? If He does not do so instantly, we may then strike out in anger or simply sulk and pout. We feel abused, even abandoned, alone and miserable—estranged from God.

But then we reach the point that Job reached (usually at rock bottom) when he said, in effect: "I spoke without understanding. Please forgive me!" It is hard to do, to let go and give over to God. But is it something you need to do at the moment?

Lord, even if I'm not in dire circumstances now, I know that hard times are always a possibility in the future. Prepare my heart with discernment and humility, that I might please You in all my responses. In Jesus' name, amen.

The Rest of the Story

The Lord blessed the latter end of Job more than his beginning (Job 42:12).

Scripture: **Job 42:10-17**
Song: **"Just as I Am"**

The rest of the story, as told in the last part of the final chapter of this ancient book of Job, reads like the traditional happy ending. Job forgave his judgmental friends, no doubt foreshadowing how Jesus would love and forgive even His cruelest enemies. Then God heaped blessings upon Job for the rest of his days, giving him a new family, great wealth, and long life.

So what is here for us to apply to our own lives? Certainly, Job's stoic acceptance of suffering and his steadfast integrity in the face of great adversit, present a challenging example for us. His constant avowal of faith in God throughout his trials, his acknowledgement of sin, and his prayer of repentance point the way to a closer relationship with God.

Job is often cited is an exemplar of patience. However, the name *Job* actually comes from an Arabic word meaning "repentance." He lived up to his name!

For twenty-first-century Western Christians, whose culture promotes independence and self-assertiveness, the lesson of humility before the Almighty, as modeled by Job, may be one of the most difficult for us to learn.

Awesome Lord, I bow before You, confessing my sins. I make no excuses, praying through our merciful advocate, Jesus. Amen.

Too Good to Be True?

Trembling and bewildered, the women went out and fled from the tomb. They said nothing to anyone, because they were afraid (Mark 16:8, *New International Version*).

Scripture: **Mark 16:1-8**
Song: **"Christ Arose"**

Three heavyhearted women took spices and journeyed, just after sunup, to the tomb of Jesus to anoint His body. In addition to their gut-wrenching grief, they were troubled by a more practical concern: who would roll away the stone from the tomb's entrance?

Imagine their amazement upon seeing the huge stone already rolled back! Timidly they entered. But instead of seeing the body of Jesus, they saw a young man robed in white, who proclaimed that Jesus was alive.

Did they believe it? No, it was simply too good to be true. Instead of responding with joy and thanksgiving, the terror-stricken women fled, telling not a soul of their "close encounter of the third kind."

We may marvel at the lack of faith demonstrated by these close associates of Jesus, who had surely heard Him foretell not only His death but also His resurrection. But wait! Can we be so sure we would have reacted differently? And how much would we lose? For, as Shakespeare put it: "Our doubts are traitors, and make us lose the good we oft might win by fearing to attempt."

Dear God, help me be sensitive to Your messages, ready to accept the truth and all its blessings. I pray in the name of the living Christ. Amen.

Flabby Faith?

Afterward he appeared unto the eleven as they sat at meat, and upbraided them with their unbelief and hardness of heart, because they believed not them which had seen him after he was risen (Mark 16:14).

Scripture: **Mark 16:9-14**
Song: **"Only Trust Him"**

The disciples, mourning the loss of their beloved master, were so overcome with guilt and grief that when they received the good news that Jesus was alive . . . they just couldn't believe it. They must have been filled with self-recrimination for not standing by Jesus in His hour of need.

In addition, they likely feared for their own safety now that Jesus was gone. At any rate, their minds were closed to the resurrection message. Only when Jesus appeared to them in person were they finally able to take in the joyous news.

Can you identify with the doubts of these early disciples? We too suffer periods of doubt, and our faith muscles sometimes go flabby. But suppose we were to practice trusting in God so that our faith became stronger? We can achieve that by acting as if we believe and stepping out in faith. Then, as we see what trusting God can accomplish, our faith becomes even more muscular.

Dear God, may my doubts spur me to keep seeking the truth. Help me open my heart and mind to Your Word and to Your still, small voice within. In the holy name of Jesus, our Lord and Savior, I pray. Amen.

Faith Alive!

Go ye into all the world, and preach the gospel to every creature (Mark 16:15).

Scripture: **Mark 16:15-20**
Song: **"Ye Christian Heralds"**

The great Christian apologist G. K. Chesterton (1874–1936) once said, "The Christian ideal has not been tried and found wanting; it has been found difficult and left untried" *(What's Wrong With the World)*. Yes, it is difficult to believe and to live in faith. Some do give up. But in our Scripture today, the doubters at last became strong believers again.

Having seen the living evidence of their Lord's resurrection, their faith was finally—and firmly—restored. Newly emboldened, they were ready to hear Jesus' final command: share the good news wherever you go.

They took His words seriously and dedicated their lives to carrying out the mission. When people tried to silence them, they responded, "We just can't help witnessing to all the things we have seen and heard."

Should less be expected of us? The clarion call resounds: go and preach. And we can do it with confidence, knowing the message will live forever. For, as Chesterton also said: "At least five times . . . with the Arian and the Albigensian, with the Humanist sceptic, after Voltaire and after Darwin, the Faith has to all appearance gone to the dogs. In each of these five cases it was the dog that died" *(The Everlasting Man)*.

Lord, nothing can thwart Your plan for the gospel to spread throughout the world. Let me be a part of the mission! In Christ I pray. Amen.

Darkness and Dawn

The sun rises and the sun sets, and hurries back to where it rises (Ecclesiastes 1:5, *New International Version*).

Scripture: **Ecclesiastes 1:1-11**
Song: **"Where He Leads Me"**

On that appointed Friday, when the sun set on those who had once been faithful to Jesus, they must have echoed the Teacher's words from Ecclesiastes: "All is meaningless." They had lost their Lord and were afraid enough to hide. They had abandoned their confessions of commitment to Him, made as recently as the night before.

Even though Jesus had prepared them for the events, they had forgotten or ignored His words in the horror of what had happened at Golgotha. Their ministry must have seemed like nothing because their plan had been destroyed when Jesus died.

But when the sun rose on the first day of the week, they found their meaning again. Jesus was alive!

It all reminds me of a Christian song popular several years ago (by Carman, 1973). It spoke of how Satan's plan to keep Jesus locked in death forever looked so successful on Friday evening. But the repeating refrain (and title) of the song reminded the evil one—and all of us who face deadly troubles at week's end: "Sunday's on the way!"

Heavenly Father, *remind me of the cross and the empty tomb when I'm tempted to feel defeated. The Son is risen! In His name I pray. Amen.*

April 17–23. **Laura Wasson Warfel** writes from her home base in southern Illinois. Fifteen years ago, she dedicated her life to full-time Christian ministry.

Finding the Joy

I devoted myself to study and to explore by wisdom all that is done under heaven. What a heavy burden God has laid on men! (Ecclesiastes 1:13, *New International Version*).

Scripture: **Ecclesiastes 1:12-18**
Song: **"My Life Is in You, Lord"**

Like the writer of Ecclesiastes, author Rick Warren has done a lot of studying and exploring. God placed him where he could experience both riches and poverty as he ministered in one of the largest churches in the United States. While working to win more souls for the kingdom, Warren also helped those with many "under heaven" problems—addictions, divorce, grief, illness, and so much more. He saw their sense of meaninglessness firsthand.

To find answers and direction for his ministry, he began studying the things of Heaven in the Bible and then applying them to life under Heaven. Thus he discovered joy. In his book *The Purpose-Driven Life,* Warren provides the answer that the Teacher of Ecclesiastes sought: "The purpose of your life is far greater than your own personal fulfillment, your peace of mind, or even your happiness. . . . You were born *by* His purpose and *for* His purpose." Claiming that purpose moves us beyond the meaninglessness described so well in Ecclesiastes. As believers, we are resurrection people, living in the light of God's Son.

Lord, You have created us for an eternity of meaningful work and praise. Whatever I have here under Heaven, whatever I am, I give back to You. In Christ's precious name I pray. Amen.

Seek God's Wisdom

I became greater by far than anyone in Jerusalem before me. In all this my wisdom stayed with me (Ecclesiastes 2:9, *New International Version*).

Scripture: **Ecclesiastes 2:1-11**
Song: **"All I Need"**

During his years as a prisoner in Hitler's Germany, Lutheran minister Dietrich Bonhoeffer (1906-1945) dedicated himself to sharing God's wisdom. Through letters and other writings, he often emphasized that his wisdom was nothing; God's wisdom was everything. In his wisdom, Bonhoeffer had joined the secret resistance movement and participated in several failed attempts to eliminate Hitler. In God's wisdom, he spent the remainder of his life behind bars.

Here, in the most unlikely place, Bonhoeffer's faith grew strong. Through God's divine wisdom, he devoted his final days to studying the Scriptures, writing, teaching others, and continuing his ministry from behind bars. As the days and weeks passed, he realized that his time on earth probably was drawing to a close. Just a few months before his execution, he wrote: "If Jesus had not lived, then our life would be meaningless, in spite of all the other people whom we know and honor and love." Jesus is the hope and promise we cling to, the true wisdom.

Creator, Redeemer, and Teacher, come to me in my weakness and make me strong in You today. My shield and my fortress, surround me with Your love. Guide and guard me so that I may live for You in all I do. I offer this prayer in Jesus' name. Amen.

Thankful for Life

So I hated life, because the work that is done under the sun was grievous to me. All of it is meaningless, a chasing after the wind (Ecclesiastes 2:17, *New International Version*).

Scripture: **Ecclesiastes 2:12-17**
Song: **"Come, Ye Thankful People"**

Ask Gianna Jessen whether life is meaningless. Born to an unwed, 17-year-old mother in the early morning hours of April 6, 1977, Gianna weighed just 2 pounds at birth. Because of oxygen deprivation, she has dealt with the effects of cerebral palsy each day of her life. Through the efforts of her foster mother, she learned to sit up, crawl, stand—and finally walk, with the assistance of leg braces—just before her fourth birthday. On that day she was adopted by her foster mother's daughter.

Eventually Gianna underwent four surgeries and extensive physical therapy so that today she can walk without assistance. "I am happy to be alive," she says. "Every day I thank God for my life." She has committed her life to serving God through singing and sharing her faith. She believes that all life is valuable and a gift from our creator.

It would be easy for this child of God to take the opposite view. Gianna lived when she was supposed to die. She survived her mother's saline abortion of April 5, 1977.

Holy Lord, giver of life and meaning, I pray for all who are seeking Your light today. Help me to be a beacon in their darkness and to draw them closer to You and Your eternal purposes. I pray in the name of Jesus, the one who makes living worthwhile. Amen.

Legacy from Jesus

For a man may do his work with wisdom, knowledge and skill, and then he must leave all he owns to someone who has not worked for it. This too is meaningless and a great misfortune (Ecclesiastes 2:21, *New International Version*).

Scripture: **Ecclesiastes 2:18-26**
Song: **"I Know that My Redeemer Lives"**

It was time for me to compose a new will. My husband had died, and my situation had changed dramatically. I resisted getting it done, though. After all, wasn't once in a lifetime enough to deal with this distasteful task?

And what obstacles I encountered! The computer crashed while the document was being prepared, my witnesses had a flat tire and were late to the meeting with my lawyer, and my hand shook while I signed the papers. But on the way home, with my completed will in hand, I began to visualize those whom God was allowing me to bless after my death. What a comfort!

I wondered whether Jesus had felt like this as He gave all He had for us on the cross. Even though He wasn't going to be with them, He left all He had done on earth in the care of His disciples, with the legacy of go, make disciples, baptize, teach (Matthew 28:19, 20). We have that same legacy. He gives us everything we need to serve Him and build His kingdom—a blessing that keeps on giving.

Lord, *thank You for leaving Your Spirit within us as a testament to Your living reality until You come again for us. Help me to honor Your legacy today by telling others about You. In Your precious name, amen.*

It's No Secret!

You are witnesses of these things (Luke 24:48, *New International Version*).

Scripture: **Luke 24:36-48**
Song: **"It Is No Secret (What God Can Do)"**

One of the most popular movies of 1985 was *Witness*, which received eight nominations and two Academy Awards. It tells the story of a young Amish boy who sees a murder take place while he and his mother wait in a train station. What he doesn't realize is that he has seen more than a murder; he has witnessed evidence of corruption in the police department of a major city.

When a detective puts the pieces together, he goes into hiding with the boy and his mother in their cloistered community. They share a terrible secret. If they reveal what they know, they will surely be killed.

As Christians, our witnessing ought hardly be a secret! We have wonderful news to share with the entire world. The Bible gives us eyewitness accounts from Jesus' disciples about His ministry, death, and resurrection. We are also direct eyewitnesses to the power, glory, and grace of the Savior in our daily lives. His love and salvation are not a secret for us to keep, though it may sometimes be safer to stay quiet. But can we overcome our fear? Will we share the best news of the day with a neighbor who needs it?

Dear Lord, may Your love and salvation motivate me each day to tell others the good news. I want to honor You by bringing more into the kingdom before Jesus returns. In His name I pray. Amen.

Where Is the Peace?

Jesus came and stood among them and said, "Peace be with you!" (John 20:19, *New International Version*).

Scripture: **John 20:19-23**
Song: **"I've Got Peace Like a River"**

My sister gave me a unique gift: an acoustic relaxation machine. Advertised as a "sound spa," this disk-shaped appliance generates sounds of nature at the touch of a button. She hoped it would calm my restless nights by helping me relax and sleep more soundly. Recovering from the death of my husband and then, three months later, the death of our mother had not been easy for me. Disturbing mental slideshows crowded my mind each night.

Eagerly I plugged in the machine and pushed the first button, labeled "Spring Rain." Soon I realized this sound wasn't peaceful to me. So I pushed the next button, then the next, until I had pushed all six. I was looking for peace. Where was the button for *peace?*

Then, instead of pushing a button, I opened the Book. In the Gospels alone, I found peace mentioned more than 30 times. Maybe instead of a sound spa, I will make more use of my "soul spa"—a deliberate attuning of my heart to God's presence, learning to relax in all His promises for my life. "Ocean Waves" can bring some relaxation, but Christ is the prince of peace for my deepest anxieties.

God of all peace, draw me closer to You today as I seek the peace that passes all understanding. Whether life is wonderful or life is difficult, You are always with me. Thank You in Jesus' name. Amen.

Fear Not

I sought the Lord and he answered me; he delivered me from all my fears (Psalm 34:4, *New International Version*).

Scripture: **Psalm 34:1-8**
Song: **"The Lord I Will at All Times Bless"**

I love films with characters who overcome fear to perform courageous acts. *Braveheart* is one of my favorites. Mel Gibson plays William Wallace, who fights to free Scotland from England in the 1200s. After leading a revolution that brings the Scots to the brink of freedom, Wallace is caught and sentenced to death. On the morning of his execution—which he knew would involve torture—he prayed for God to give him the courage "to die well."

And God did indeed deliver him from his fears. With his last breath, he shouted "Freedom!" That word spread, and more people joined a cause that eventually prevailed.

In our Scripture verse today, King David also faced the possibility of death, at the hands of the Philistines. When the ordeal was over, he wrote Psalm 34, testifying that God delivered him from his fears. Of course, we know that God doesn't always keep our fears from becoming reality. And some of us struggle with anxiety throughout our lives. But His abiding presence is our guarantee that someday fear will have no existence at all.

Lord, I know that You are bigger than my fears. Thank You, too, for bringing an end to fear forever when You return. Come, Lord Jesus! Amen.

April 24–30. **Lee Warren,** of Omaha, Nebraska, has written a singles' devotional book called *Dinner for One.*

Avoiding Extremes

There is not a righteous man on earth who does what is right and never sins (Ecclesiastes 7:20, *New International Version*).

Scripture: **Ecclesiastes 7:15-22**
Song: **"He Ransomed Me"**

Sometimes I've felt pretty good about my Christian character—only to have God reveal an improper attitude or motivation that I'd clearly ignored. Every time that happens, I am moved by God's mercy. How patiently He moves me along the path of spiritual growth!

In Ecclesiastes 7:18 *(NIV)*, King Solomon said that "the man who fears God will avoid all extremes." In the preceding verses, he tells us what those extremes are: over-righteousness and over-wickedness. We know that we are supposed to live holy lives, so finding out that we need to avoid the extreme of over-wickedness is hardly a surprise. But are we really supposed to avoid over-righteousness?

Perhaps. Especially if *over-righteous* describes that feeling we get when we think we've "arrived" on our Christian journey. With that feeling ee mistakenly sense that we actually have achieved holiness, some form of sinless perfection. In reality, such holiness can never be achieved in our lifetime. It can only be "credited" to us through faith in Jesus Christ (see Romans 4:1-8).

Father, thank You for showing us mercy when we deserve only judgment. Thank You for not giving us over to our improper attitudes, motivations, and actions. I acknowledge that holiness comes only through Your Son and His magnificent work on the cross for us. In His name I pray. Amen.

Comfort in Letting Go

No man has power over the wind to contain it; so no one has power over the day of his death (Ecclesiastes 8:8, *New International Version*).

Scripture: **Ecclesiastes 8:2-8a**
Song: **"He Will Carry You Through"**

My high school tennis team once traveled to play at a school that had built their courts in an open field with nothing to block the wind. Most schools with similar set-ups have wind screens (made of a thin canvas material) built into the fencing surrounding the courts. Not this one.

As I struggled to keep the ball on the court, I kept wishing I could stop the wind until my match was finished. Of course, I have no more power to stop the wind than I have power to decide the day of my exit from this life.

King Solomon tells us that godly wisdom "brightens a man's face and changes its hard appearance" (v. 1, *NIV*). In other words, remembering that God controls all things—including the weather, our life spans, our leaders, and even our next few moments—ought to bring comfort and peace to our souls.

I don't know why it was so windy that day. But I do know it would have made more sense to stop battling the wind and concentrate more on my worthy opponent.

Father, I confess that I have enough to battle each day without adding the weather to my worries. I acknowledge Your sovereignty in all things and, with this prayer, willingly submit the rest of my day to Your will. In Jesus' awesome name I pray. Amen.

Love . . . While You Can

Enjoy life with your wife, whom you love (Ecclesiastes 9:9, *New International Version*).

Scripture: **Ecclesiastes 9:1-12**
Song: **"Abide with Us, the Day Is Waning"**

President William McKinley (1843-1901) was known for dearly loving his wife, Ida. She often had epileptic seizures and was considered to be chronically ill. He did not want to leave his wife at home while he campaigned for president in 1896, so he conducted a "front porch campaign" in his hometown. Over 750,000 people came to hear him speak, and he won the election. In 1900 he won re-election.

Shortly after the start of his second term started, McKinley attended an event in Buffalo, New York, where he was shot twice. After the shooter had been tackled, McKinley's concern was only for his wife. "My wife—be careful, Cortelyou, how you tell her—oh, be careful," he said to his secretary. Nine days later, the president died.

President McKinley's wife meant everything to him. That was evident both before he won the election and after he was shot. Yet all of us share a "common destiny," according to King Solomon (v. 2, *NIV*). I have to ask myself, am I using the days I have left to love, love, love?

Father, help us to set our priorities straight in all our relationships, whether married or single. Help me to value the people around me, recognizing that my days are numbered. And give me a heart that takes pleasure in the simple things of life that flow from Your gracious hand. In Jesus' name, amen.

Let It Alight!

There is a time for everything, and a season for every activity under heaven (Ecclesiastes 3:1, *New International Version*).

Scripture: **Ecclesiastes 3:1-8**
Song: **"There Is a Time for Everything"**

In the late 1980s, you couldn't avoid hearing a song called *Don't Worry, Be Happy* by Bobby McFerrin. It was blaring everywhere—at baseball parks, in supermarkets, on radio, and on television. If you somehow avoided it in all of those places, your next-door neighbor would surely be whistling the tune within earshot.

The song was an anthem for a nation of people who, for several decades, seemed to make happiness their most important pursuit. But hasn't that attitude always existed among us humans?

In our Scripture today, Solomon gives us a much different picture of the meaningful life. There is a time for *everything*—including weeping, mourning, hating, and dying. Hardly things to be happy about, but God intended all of them to be part of the human experience.

God never promised us perpetual happiness, and He certainly never called us to make it our life's goal. I like the way the great writer Nathaniel Hawthorne once put it: "Happiness is a butterfly, which when pursued, is always just beyond your grasp, but which, if you will sit down quietly, may alight upon you."

Father, often we pursue only experiences we hope will bring us happiness. Show me that Your joy is so much better. Through Christ I pray. Amen

Deserved Reverence

I know that everything God does will endure forever; nothing can be added to it and nothing taken from it. God does it so that men will revere him (Ecclesiastes 3:14, *New International Version*).

Scripture: **Ecclesiastes 3:9-15**
Song: **"Great and Marvelous"**

I have a friend who is married with children. He faithfully writes in a journal that he intends to give his children when they are older. He doesn't treat the journal as a diary. Instead, he records his insights about how God works in his family members' lives.

I told my friend recently that he couldn't give his daughters any earthly treasure more valuable than that journal—which now spans three huge volumes. For generations to come, people will read it and thrill to the ways God worked in their family before they were even born.

Sadly, a generation probably will come along that will put the journal into storage or maybe even accidentally destroy it. Long after it is gone and forgotten, however, God's actions will stand. Everything God does, in never-ending abundance, calls us to revere Him.

But God doesn't *need* us to revere Him! He simply *wants* us to. Remembering the big and little things that God does in our lives will glorify His name.

Father, we know of Your goodness by the Words of Scripture and through the compassion of Your Son in our lives. I adore You, worship You, revere Your holy being. In the name of Jesus I pray. Amen.

Inevitability of That Day

I thought in my heart, "God will bring to judgment both the righteous and the wicked, for there will be a time for every activity, a time for every deed" (Ecclesiastes 3:17, *New International Version*).

Scripture: **Ecclesiastes 3:16-22**
Song: **"God Gives His Mercies to Be Spent"**

If you read the newspaper often, you know that every day overflows with predatory crimes. Murder, abuse, assault, slander, theft—the list goes on and on. The stories we read are about people who've been caught in these criminal actions. But how many get away with it? For them, crime may seem to pay great dividends.

Yet the "interest" on every crime will come due eventually. Then the criminal himself will have to pay. In our verse for today, Solomon said there is "a time for every deed." In light of the context, we realize that he spoke of God's bringing judgment on both the righteous and the wicked. Some will see that happen on earth, and some will see it only at the final judgment day.

This verse indicates that, when a person commits a crime and escapes earthly authority, God merely allows it for a time. We may never know or understand His timing in such matters, but we should both rejoice and tremble at the knowledge that judgment is inevitable.

Father, I confess that I am often disheartened by the evil I see. I also confess that at times I question why You allow it. Nevertheless, keep my eyes focused on Your coming day of total justice. In Jesus' name, amen.

My Prayer Notes

DEVOTIONS®

*T*rust in the Lord with all thine heart; and lean not unto thine own understanding.

—Proverbs 3:5

MAY

Photo © Brand X Pictures

Gary Allen, editor

Riches Within Reach

If thou seekest her as silver, and searchest for her as for hid treasures; then shalt thou understand the fear of the Lord, and find the knowledge of God (Proverbs 2:4, 5).

Scripture: **Proverbs 2:1-5**
Song: **"I'd Rather Have Jesus"**

Have you ever said "I'll know it when I see it"? Perhaps it was a gift you sought for a friend. Perhaps it was property you wanted to buy. Maybe it was a decorating touch for your home that would set in motion an entire renovation project. Governed by an instinct deep within, you set out on your quest, like a bird certain of its destination though on its maiden migratory flight.

Our verse today is good news for anyone seeking to know God. He is knowable. His wisdom is available, His mercy is accessible, His love is receivable. Though sometimes hidden, Heaven's riches remain within reach.

This is the essence of Solomon's counsel: when we hunker down and listen to God, we start becoming wise. When our highest joy is to seek the counsel of the Almighty, something begins to click. In other words, wisdom is a choice, a goal reached only by those who truly pursue it.

The process can take a lifetime. But, oh, the blessing!

Lord, Your wisdom is pure, and I seek it. Your paths are true, and I want them. I give You my heart, for I treasure Your name. In Christ I pray. Amen.

May 1–7. **Brian Dill** is a minister and writer in Orlando, Florida, who enjoys composing hymns and developing creative Bible studies.

Mirrors and Ears

Discretion shall preserve thee, understanding shall keep thee (Proverbs 2:11).

Scripture: **Proverbs 2:6-15**
Song: **"We Are One in the Spirit"**

Do you ever wonder why a visit to Disney World in Florida is such a happy event for most people? It's more than mouse ears and castles. It has to do with the entire Disney philosophy and how employees live it out. When you stroll the Disney grounds, you're not a customer but a "guest." If you work at the theme park, you're not an employee but a "cast member."

Everything has a purpose, and behind every purpose is a singular company philosophy. Founder Walt Disney said he wanted to create an atmosphere like no other place on earth, where people could enter a land of enchantment, where dreams really do come true.

God's kingdom magnifies this principle, being built, not on "make believe," but upon discretion, understanding, and truth. Guided by a singular purpose, God's people live remarkable lives. Filled with buoyant hope, they create an atmosphere in which faith can flourish. When we follow God's Son, we have the privilege of casting His shadow on our world today. Those who are blessed by it find more than a brief escape; they find eternal redemption.

Lord, whose ways are good and pleasant, help me to bear Your name before the world so that others might see and follow with discretion and understanding. Keep me close, as I pray in Your Son's name. Amen.

High Cost of Low Living

[Wisdom] will save you also from the adulteress, from the wayward wife with her seductive words (Proverbs 2:16, *New International Version*).

Scripture: **Proverbs 2:16-22**
Song: **"O Jesus, I Have Promised"**

What $28 billion-a-year industry hurts some 1.5 million American children? If you answered "adultery" or "divorce," you are correct. Marital disharmony is costly. Legal fees alone take a considerable chunk of our time and money. We could support the entire country of Bolivia on what it costs us each year to be unfaithful! Our children deserve better, and so do we.

Adultery is a luxury few can afford and even fewer survive. Proverbs makes this clear in today's Scripture, cautioning against the perils of straying from the path. While we have softened infidelity with words like *consenting adults* and *mid-life crisis*, the bottom line is the same. Sex outside marriage destroys us, and we must avoid it.

God designed marriage to reflect the love He has for us all. Faithful in His ways, He wants us to be faithful in ours as well—not because He wants to stifle us, but because He wants to free us. He designed us to live in harmony.

Just as a single slip on an icy sidewalk can kill, so can a single indiscretion in marriage. If you think not, just remember that $28 billion price tag.

Lord Most Holy, *keep us faithful to one another and faithful to You. In the name of Your faithful Son I pray. Amen.*

By the Way

Trust in the Lord with all thine heart; and lean not unto thine own understanding. In all thy ways acknowledge him, and he shall direct thy paths (Proverbs 3:5, 6).

Scripture: **Proverbs 3:1-12**
Song: **"Walking in the King's Highway"**

If there were a hall of fame for wisdom, it would not be complete without this counsel from Proverbs. I long ago lost track of the number of times I've heard believers extol, from memory, the power of Proverbs 3:5, 6. "In all thy ways acknowledge him," they emphasize, almost leaning into the words as they say them.

It is true: God meets us at every turn. On the road to Emmaus, Jesus went with the two disciples all the way—to their village, their home, their dinner table, their meal, to the very disclosing of His soul. Such is the life of faith. Christ, who travels with us, knows the route. He came from Heaven to earth. Who better knows the way?

Years ago my wife and I became lost while driving through a large park in western Pennsylvania. Roads meandered in every direction, uphill and down. Just as we resigned ourselves to spending the night in our car, a motorist came along, sensed our predicament, and said, "Follow me!" Follow we did . . . to freedom!

Lord of All Wisdom, I often lose my bearings and follow the wrong paths. Thank You for Your offer of guidance! Lead me through each day so that, should I stray or die, You won't have to look far to take me home. I pray through our deliverer, Jesus. Amen.

How Thoughtful!

[Wisdom's] ways are pleasant ways, and all her paths are peace (Proverbs 3:17, *New International Version*).

Scripture: **Proverbs 3:13-20**
Song: **"O Lord, You're Beautiful"**

Have you ever noticed how the truly wise are also truly gracious? I have never met a person I considered wise who wasn't also affable and kindhearted. The two seem to go together, don't they?

This is because wisdom means not just knowing *what* to do; it is knowing *how* to do it.

Suppose you have a houseguest who seems constantly underfoot. The two of you are fast friends, but you are neat and she is messy. As you prepare for a dinner party in her honor, she insists on being helpful—something she is *not!* What do you do?

Wisdom suggests several options. Send her out for the day with a mutual friend, making sure they are back soon enough to freshen up? Occupy her with a task she would enjoy (arranging flowers, polishing silver)? Or just arrange in advance to cater the whole meal, so both of you are free to enjoy your time together.

Oh, how our world needs common sense and peace! Oh, how a little thoughtfulness can go a long way! Never for a moment think that wisdom is just being smart. More often than not, wisdom is just being kind.

Lord, so fill my heart with love that I will ever prefer wisdom to knowledge, graciousness to greatness. Through Christ I pray. Amen.

Wisdom from A to Z-z-z-z

When you lie down, you will not be afraid; When you lie down, your sleep will be sweet (Proverbs 3:24, *New International Version*).

Scripture: **Proverbs 3:21-30**
Song: **"It Is Well with My Soul"**

Have you ever awakened feeling wonderfully refreshed? Perhaps the enticing aroma of breakfast cooking over a campfire did the trick. Maybe it was the brief power nap you took before going out for the evening. Or maybe, when you were a child, it was simply because you knew your mother and father were in the next room.

Sleep is one of God's greatest gifts. We relax, our pulse rate slows down, we slumber, and the body quietly repairs itself in preparation for a new day. What a remarkable process! The stresses we feel at bedtime frequently vanish after a good night's sleep, as if angels come during the night and take them away.

Sleep that is deep and sweet often results from the way we live. More than one repentant sinner has said, "On the night I gave my life to Christ, I slept like a baby." This is because wisdom produces holiness, and holiness produces wholeness. David declares that God "giveth his beloved sleep" (Psalm 127:2).

Yes, God wants to give us life. But He also wants to grant us rest. How sweet the sleep of those who walk wisely, day by day.

Lord, grant that whether I wake or sleep, I shall rejoice in Your care. And let my sleep be sweet this night, in the name of Jesus. Amen.

Shy or Shine?

Withhold not good from them to whom it is due, when it is in the power of thine hand to do it (Proverbs 3:27).

Scripture: **Proverbs 3:31-35**
Song: **"Reach Your Arms Around the World"**

Suppose some week the sun doesn't rise, the stars don't shine, the wind doesn't blow, and the rain doesn't fall? Do you celebrate? Hardly. We've grown accustomed to living in a world governed by a generous God who loves to bless us with daily gifts. How miserable we would be if this ever stopped!

Proverbs 3:27 challenges us to be as benevolent as we are blessed. Some of us are blessed financially. Some of us are blessed emotionally and spiritually. Some have talent to burn—and money to burn, as well. Whatever our gift, wisdom says don't waste it because someone out there needs it.

Somewhere a child needs a parent.

Somewhere a parent needs a hug.

Somewhere a prisoner needs a visit.

Somewhere a visitor needs a friend.

Successful living means cheerfully doing what we can for others simply because it's in our power to do so. Jesus called this kind of good-works outreach "shining" (see Matthew 5:16). It's not just a good idea; it's the only authentic way to live.

Lord, help me focus more on giving than on receiving, more on consoling than on controlling. Through Christ I pray. Amen.

Wisdom as a Guidance

Hear; for I will speak of excellent things; and the opening of my lips shall be right things (Proverbs 8:6).

Scripture: **Proverbs 8:1-9**
Song: **"Lead on, O King Eternal"**

Patricia craned her neck, looking up at the long rope, feeling anything but confident. She was to perform some difficult feats on this high rope, while being spun around at rapid speed. You see, our small town was known far and wide for its amateur circus. Townsfolk, ages 7 to 21 performed the acts, some at significant heights.

They all had to try out to be chosen, though, and Patricia wanted very badly to do this act. But at her try-out, she became frightened. The trainer came over and put her arm around Patricia. "Climb up the rope, and I'll guide you through it." Patricia scaled the rope, hooked her foot in the loop, and got ready—now with more confidence. Later, she told her mom, "I wasn't afraid with the trainer there; her words were so encouraging."

We all need guidance and can find it through others who have wisdom. Ultimately, though, according to Solomon, we find it in God. He is always there, extending His hand to us.

O God, let me not forget to turn to others who have wisdom and encouraging words for me. Let me also speak "excellent things" at all times. I pray in the precious name of Jesus. Amen.

May 8–14. **Pat Stackhouse,** formerly an elementary schoolteacher, now serves as a CASA (Court Appointed Special Advocate) for the juvenile courts.

Wise to Get Wisdom

Wisdom is better than rubies; and all the things that may be desired are not to be compared to it (Proverbs 8:11).

Scripture: **Proverbs 8:10-21**
Song: **"Trust and Obey"**

High school was over, and sleeping until noon was a favorite luxury of my 19-year-old son. He hadn't found a summer job and was, in general, living a life of leisure. He ran around with his friends, ate lunch at fast-food restaurants, and cruised in his car. He had few responsibilities and . . . life was good!

Then fall rolled around, along with 8:00 A.M. college classes. It was a tough adjustment. I recall these words at one point: "My life is over." The carefree existence had ended. In its place came studying, writing papers, and listening closely to complicated lectures. Imparting my wisdom as a mother, I said, "Son, your life is only beginning. It's what lies ahead that counts."

What lies ahead for any of us depends much upon our relationship with the wisdom that flows from God. One of the most wonderful promises in the Bible is that we don't have to rely purely on our own intelligence or skill as we face tomorrow. We can ask for something as precious as fine jewels—something *better:* "If any of you lack wisdom, let him ask of God, that giveth to all men liberally, and up-braideth not; and it shall be given him" (James 1:5).

***Lord,** please help me turn to You as my guide for the future. In Your precious wisdom, You have prepared the way. Through Christ I pray. Amen.*

Why Am I Here?

When he appointed the foundations of the earth: Then [wisdom] was by him (Proverbs 8:29, 30).

Scripture: **Proverbs 8:22-31**
Song: **"One More Day's Work for Jesus"**

The great question pondered by human begins down through the ages goes something like this: "How did I get here, and what is my purpose?" We realize through Solomon that God's wisdom preceded the creation of all things, including ourselves. We don't understand the miracle of our creation; it is one of God's mysteries. But we do know that we must have been placed on this earth for a wise, meaningful purpose.

Created in God's eternal wisdom, we can live each day looking to Him for direction. What does this mean to you?

Frederick Buechner (1926–) applied it to our search for a life's vocation in his book *Wishful Thinking:* "The kind of work God usually calls you to is the kind of work (a) that you need most to do and (b) that the world most needs to have done. If you really get a kick out of your work, you've presumably met requirement (a), but if your work is writing cigarette ads, the chances are you've missed requirement (b)."

God created you, in His infinite wisdom, for a meaningful mission in this life. Open your heart to His leading, and you will find the perfect place for you.

Dear Lord, I want to do the work You have made me to do. Help me discern my gifts and use them in Your service. Through Christ I pray. Amen.

Understand, and Do!

Hearken unto me, O ye children: for blessed are they that keep my ways (Proverbs 8:32).

Scripture: **Proverbs 8:32-36**
Song: **"In the Garden"**

Solomon tells us to listen to wisdom. I was raised by a college professor, a man quite comfortable with imparting wise advice, in the classroom as well as at home. Mother used to say, "Listen to your father; he's an expert."

Indeed, as a little girl, I always found my father to be very wise. Then I grew up, left home, and eventually began raising my own family—of seven children. As they grew older, I did not always seem as wise to them, and my advice wasn't always taken seriously. As Mark Twain once said: "When I was a boy of 14, my father was so ignorant I could hardly stand to have the old man around. But when I got to be 21, I was astonished at how much the old man had learned in seven years."

This great American writer offers a lot of down-to-earth wisdom, though his relationship with God seemed quite lacking. Nevertheless, as I think about the clear and simple challenge coming to me from Proverbs 8:32, another of Twain's quips hits the mark: "Most people are bothered by those passages of Scripture they do not understand, but the passages that bother me are those I *do* understand."

Dear Lord, open my heart to Your precious wisdom. Let me look to Your Word for the guidance I'll need today. I pray in the name of Jesus. Amen.

Eaten Yet?

[Wisdom] hath also furnished her table. . . . Come, eat of my bread, and drink of the wine which I have mingled (Proverbs 9:2, 5).

Scripture: **Proverbs 9:1-6**
Song: **"Let Us Break Bread Together"**

Karla, a foreign exchange student from Costa Rica, came to live in our home for the school year. She was anxious to meet other young people right away, so we decided to invite someone to dinner. Another foreign exchange student seemed like a reasonable choice. In fact, a boy from Costa Rica was also attending her school for the semester. We invited him and his host family to our evening meal.

Karla fixed spaghetti because she makes an excellent sauce. She prepared the food, set the table with care, and after prayer we dined together. We became acquainted, sharing cultures. Soon Karla was laughing, and she and the young man began speaking their native language. During that meal, they started what would become a solid friendship over the year to come.

An invitation to eat is one of the great joys of human life. It speaks of hands and hearts opening in friendship. To eat together, we must lay down our fear or mistrust and accept a gift. No wonder the Scripture shows us God's wisdom as a fine meal! Have you eaten yet today?

Dear Lord, I know when I'm hungry. Help me recognize, as well, when I'm famished for Your wise direction in my life! Through Christ I pray. Amen.

Learn? Or Be Taught?

Give instruction to a wise man, and he will be yet wiser: teach a just man, and he will increase in learning (Proverbs 9:9).

Scripture: **Proverbs 9:7-12**
Song: **"Show Me Thy Ways, O Lord"**

When I graduated from school with my master's degree, I thought I was wise indeed. I had earned the degree through long hours of hard work. In other words, I thought I had the "world by the tail on the downhill pull."

I walked around the campus on graduation day feeling ever so proud. I thought my diploma had earned me the right to whatever I wanted or needed. After all, hadn't I "arrived"?

Soon I realized that I still had a lot to learn. And lots of people wanted to give the new graduate advice about the future. Some said, "Be thrifty." Others said, "Follow your dreams." But one wise soul told me, "Keep learning." In other words, growth doesn't stop with a master's degree. In fact, it ought never to stop. The wise person can become even wiser.

I began to realize that, in order to keep growing, I did indeed need to keep learning. The challenge comes in something British statesman Winston Churchill once said about his own attitude: "I am always ready to learn, but I do not always like being taught." How is it with you?

Dear Lord, I need You at the helm of my life to guide me today. I like learning; help me also to appreciate being taught. Through Christ I pray. Amen.

A Bit Sick . . . and Wiser

Honor your father and mother (which is the first commandment with a promise) (Ephesians 6:2, *New American Standard Bible*).

Scripture: **Proverbs 9:13-18**
Song: **"Open My Eyes That I May See"**

My high school drama club was quite a social clique as well. I never was accepted as one of the inside group—not really. I was shy and never played one of the main characters in any of the plays. I usually worked on building the stage, sewing the costumes, painting background scenery, and setting up props.

The club's director was a young teacher who socialized with the in group of students. I thought it was wrong for him to be so biased, but I did envy from afar that special little group of the cool kids.

Surprisingly enough, they invited me to one of their parties. I was thrilled; however, Mom had some misgivings about my going.

Naturally, I begged. Eventually, she relented.

The party wasn't all I'd expected. I was a loner the whole time, spending most of my time at the snack table. I also drank punch until I noticed it actually tasted pretty strange. Feeling lightheaded, I finally realized that bright red concoction had been spiked. I called Mom to come after me, a kid who felt a little sick but also a little wiser.

O Lord, help me to listen to those who are wiser than I am. And no matter our age, may we honor our parents always. In Jesus' name, amen.

Room of Refuge or Ruin?

The way of the Lord is a refuge for the righteous, but it is the ruin of those who do evil (Proverbs 10:29, *New International Version*).

Scripture: **Proverbs 10:27-32**
Song: **"Constantly Abiding"**

Choosing a hotel for a week of vacationing on the beach is no small task. First there are considerations related to location: Is the hotel *directly* on the beach? What restaurants and attractions are located nearby? Are the swimming pools large enough to accommodate the crowds? (And is there an indoor pool for rainy days?)

Assuming that the rooms are clean, there's the issue of price. Many people simply stay at the hotel with the cheapest rates. Sure, they might save 10 bucks by taking a room facing the street, but they will miss waking up to the indescribable beauty of the sun rising over the ocean. Or they'll use up their savings in gas and parking fees.

In the same way, the wicked choose to do what comes naturally to the sinful nature rather than paying the cost of obedience. In so doing, they miss out on many of God's best blessings: joy, protection, guidance, forgiveness. In the end, their failure to invest in eternity leads to ruin.

Dear God, we know that the choices we make in life affect the eternal room reservations You are booking for us. Help me to understand that the price of discipleship is worth the cost. Through Christ I pray. Amen.

May 15–21. **Brian J. Waldrop** is a freelance writer and professional copy editor living in Cincinnati, Ohio. He enjoys vacationing on the beaches of Florida.

Integrity for Sale: 25 Cents

The Lord abhors dishonest scales, but accurate weights are his delight (Proverbs 11:1, *New International Version*).

Scripture: **Proverbs 11:1-5**
Song: **"More Precious Than Silver"**

Deception and dishonesty have come to be expected from used car lots and TV infomercials, but are they now to be expected at Mrs. Jones's garage sale too? Someone told me about purchasing a used shirt that looked to be in excellent condition, only to get it home and find a stain hidden underneath the huge, glued-on price tag.

In two other cases, hopeful garage-salers asked whether the appliances they were buying actually worked. "Yes, it runs," came the standard reply from each seller. Upon bringing the items home, the buyers discovered that the small appliances did indeed "run," but they didn't "work." The microwave wouldn't heat anything, and the toaster burnt the bread, regardless of the selected setting.

Shouldn't integrity be worth more than a quarter or two? Whether a quarter or a quarter of a million dollars, "wealth is worthless in the day of wrath" (v. 4, *NIV*). The liars and deceivers will indeed someday be "brought down by their own wickedness" (v. 5, *NIV*). In contrast, "the integrity of the upright guides them" to eternal life (v. 3, *NIV*).

Heavenly Father, You never cheat us but graciously give us all things—even the promise of eternal life. May my treatment of others be a reflection of Your generosity towards me. In Christ's name, amen.

Do You Have a Joyful Effect?

When the righteous prosper, the city rejoices; when the wicked perish, there are shouts of joy (Proverbs 11:10, *New International Version*).

Scripture: **Proverbs 11:6-10**
Song: **"Make Me a Blessing"**

From westerns to sci-fi thrillers to murder mysteries, the movies illustrate today's Scripture text well: Most of us still root for the good guys and sneer at the villains. A real-life illustration of this became apparent to me as I watched televised reports of coalition forces rolling into Baghdad at the beginning of the second Iraq war. In celebration, Iraqi civilians shouted and cheered, toppling giant statues of their wicked dictator.

Each of us has the potential for great good as well as enormous evil. One of the saddest commentaries on a human life is when a death row inmate is executed because it's been determined the world would be a better place without him or her.

If we think our choices affect only ourselves, we are wrong. Most successful people can point to a mentor who believed in them and encouraged them. In contrast, most criminals would cite an absence of such a positive influence. You never know who's watching—your children, your coworkers, a non-Christian friend. When others look at me, get to know me, I pray they feel a little more joyful.

Dear God, empower me to alter areas of my life that need refining, so that others will see me as a cause for rejoicing. I pray in Christ's name. Amen.

Watch Those Words!

A man who lacks judgment derides his neighbor, but a man of understanding holds his tongue (Proverbs 11:12, *New International Version*—all citations on this page are from the *NIV*).

Scripture: **Proverbs 11:11-15**
Song: **"Wonderful Words of Life"**

There are words we all want to hear: *I love you. Will you marry me? Congratulations. You win!* Then there are words we dread: *You're fired. Good-bye. Your account is overdrawn. But we can still be friends.*

Often it's hard to know the right words to say in a given situation. And when we're angry, it's even harder to hold our tongues and not say what's really on our minds. James gives the following advice: "Everyone should be quick to listen, slow to speak and slow to become angry" (James 1:19). And Proverbs 18:7 wisely notes that "a fool's mouth is his undoing."

Many of us who would never consider throwing a punch don't think twice about slicing up someone with our words. On the flip side, "Pleasant words are a honeycomb, sweet to the soul and healing to the bones" (Proverbs 16:24). The ability to use our words wisely is a mark of spiritual maturity. Like David, we need to earnestly pray, "May the words of my mouth . . . be pleasing in your sight" (Psalm 19:14).

Lord God, empower me to know when to speak and when to remain silent. For I long to hear Your words someday, "Well done, good and faithful servant!" (Matthew 25:21). Through Christ I pray. Amen.

Cornfield Common Sense

Be sure of this: The wicked will not go unpunished, but those who are righteous will go free (Proverbs 11:21, *New International Version*).

Scripture: **Proverbs 11:16-21**
Song: **"Is Your All on the Altar?"**

Growing up in central Illinois, I watched each summer as college students worked the cornfields, pulling off the tassels from the tops of corn plants to prevent if from pollinating any of the corn in the field. Tassels from other corn grown nearby would pollinate the entire field. Later the harvested corn would be be sold as quality hybrid seed to farmers. Seed corn companies know that the better the seed corn, the better the yields for farmers. In other words, you reap what you sow.

It's a common-sense principle that we can apply to many different areas of life. For example, people who eat nutritiously and exercise are usually going to be healthier than those who regularly feed on junk food. This same principle of reaping and sowing applies, generally, to spiritual life. Those who plant seeds of faith and repentance in their lives will reap eternal life. In contrast, one who arrogantly ignores God's offer of salvation through Christ cannot expect to receive His blessings, for such a one "brings trouble on himself" (v. 17, *NIV*). What are you planting? What kind of yield will your life produce as a result?

Lord, thank You that because of Jesus, I will reap the blessings of eternity rather than the punishment I deserve. In His name I pray. Amen.

Gold-Studded Swine

Like a gold ring in a pig's snout is a beautiful woman who shows no discretion (Proverbs 11:22, *New International Version*).

Scripture: **Proverbs 11:22-26**
Song: **"Jesus Breaks Every Fetter"**

Those who have been forgiven by the precious blood of the sinless Son of God have received a gift of immeasurable worth. Yet many Christians have cheapened God's grace in the eyes of nonbelievers through corny clichés and inconsistent living. As Jesus noted in Matthew 7:6, we have become guilty of tossing our pearls to pigs.

One of our most common "pigpens" these days has become the backsides of our cars, in the form of religious bumper stickers and emblems. I used to have the popular dove symbol on my car, but when trading vehicles, I decided not to replace the symbol. Although I have a clean driving record, I didn't feel that my driving could live up to the perfect example that Christ's magnificent salvation deserves.

Christ's gift of eternal life is anything but ordinary. Therefore, in gratitude, let us live our lives in extraordinary ways that reflect an appropriate discretion. Let us never carelessly treat our salvation as if it belonged in a pigpen; let's treat it as something worthy of a palace.

Heavenly Father, You placed Your Spirit in my heart. Forgive me when I bring shame to Your name by carelessly treating my salvation as commonplace. Forgive me when the wickedness of my life hides Your worth from those who don't know You. I ask this in the name of Jesus. Amen.

Time to Leap?

He who seeks good finds goodwill, but evil comes to him who searches for it (Proverbs 11:27, *New International Version*).

Scripture: **Proverbs 11:27-31**
Song: **"Seek Ye First"**

What is the driving force behind your life? What floats your boat and billows your sails? If your life were a boat, what kind would it be?

Maybe your life is like a pleasure cruiser: you have lots of luxury and fun but little concern for your eternal destiny. Or maybe your life is a pirate ship: you grab all the prestige and wealth you can get with no thought for others. Then again, are you a lifeboat—just trying to stay afloat and survive the demands of everyday living?

Believers are commissioned by Christ to serve as His representatives, and they are equipped with His provisions to do so. We are, therefore, like explorer ships, always seeking the good. And Jesus says we don't have to worry about our daily needs when we put Him first: "Seek first his kingdom and his righteousness, and all these things will be given to you as well. Therefore do not worry about tomorrow, for tomorrow will worry about itself" (Matthew 6:33, 34, *NIV*).

Is your life on the wrong boat? Take a leap of faith and jump overboard.

Father God, I know that living for mere pleasure keeps me from preparing for eternity. Help me to be content seeking the good things of Your Kingdom until Jesus comes again for us. In His name I pray. Amen.

The Cost of Education

Wisdom is supreme; therefore get wisdom. Though it cost all you have, get understanding (Proverbs 4:7, *New International Version*).

Scripture: **Proverbs 4:1-9**
Song: **"Christ Is Made the Sure Foundation"**

At first glance, this passage sounds like a commencement speech encouraging high school graduates to go to college (especially the phrase, which rings true for many parents, "though it cost all you have"). Yet there is quite a difference between seeking knowledge and gaining wisdom, isn't there?

Knowledge involves understanding gained through experience, whereas wisdom adds the ability to discern what is true or right. No wonder the proverb writer recommended getting wisdom at all cost! Nevertheless, discerning truth and knowing the right thing to do can be difficult. Life seems so full of shades of gray. As we come before the Lord, seeking His wise guidance, it is well worth it to put all our concentration, effort, and creativity into listening for His quiet voice.

And we need not worry about classes or exams or grades. Our teacher, Jesus, always has our best in mind. He is truth (John 14:6) and the best source of wisdom.

Heavenly Father, You have told us that Your ways are not our ways. Guide me into a more complete understanding of Your ways so I may discern the paths You have chosen for me. This I pray in Jesus' name. Amen.

May 22–28. **Shelia Watson** has written several devotional books and guides. She lives with her husband and three daughters in Charleston, South Carolina.

A Serious "Game"

I guide you in the way of wisdom and lead you along straight paths (Proverbs 4:11, *New International Version*).

Scripture: **Proverbs 4:10-15**
Song: **"He Leadeth Me"**

Remember playing Follow the Leader as a child? Do you recall the funny things the leader often had his followers do? When I played the game with my friends, we'd often try to outdo each other in silliness: one would have everyone hop on one foot, the next would have everyone hop on one foot while flapping one arm and closing one eye . . . and so on.

Which was more fun for you, following or leading? Sometimes it is easier (or preferable) to lead than to follow. I admit that most times I would rather be the one who knows which way we're going—including when, where, and how. But being a follower can be both challenging and rewarding. Following can take just as much dedication, skill, and fortitude as leading, and it brings with it the critical task of discerning whom to follow and *why.*

Today's passage reminds us of whom we are following. Our leader is God, creator of all wisdom, whom we know in the person of Jesus Christ. Having Jesus as our guide brings certainty and safety to this serious "game" of Follow the Leader, all the way from earth to Heaven.

Dear Father, continue to make my heart attentive to Your perfect instructions, each step of the way. In Christ's precious name I pray. Amen.

Spiritual Nourishment

The lips of the righteous nourish many, but fools die for lack of judgment (Proverbs 10:21, *New International Version*).

Scripture: **Proverbs 10:18-23**
Song: **"Eat this Bread, Drink this Cup"**

Look at a food pyramid and see the varieties of nutrients we can choose to feed ourselves. Without the proper combination of fruits, vegetables, proteins, and assorted vitamins, our bodies would soon begin to feel the effects of malnourishment.

Just as our bodies need food, our spirits need nourishment as well. And it can come from several sources, with worship, fellowship, Bible reading, and prayer being at the heart of our soul-diet.

Today's Scripture mentions the nourishment found in "the lips of the righteous." This is another way of describing the encouragement that comes to us from caring, compassionate persons, the kind of people Jesus has called us to be.

So think about a time when you were supported by someone with nourishing kindness. Did you feel your inner spirit strengthened, as if you'd been fed an enriching meal? Could you offer today, with your own lips and actions, a similar kind of spirit-enriching meal to a friend or neighbor?

Dear Lord, *it is my privilege to feed others Your nurturing Word. Grant me grace sufficient for the preparation of such a meal, and bestow on me the ability to sustain others with heavenly kindness. In Jesus' name, amen.*

Voice for the Voiceless

Speak up for those who cannot speak for themselves, for the rights of all who are destitute (Proverbs 31:8, *New International Version*).

Scripture: **Proverbs 31:1-9**
Song: **"Lord, Speak to Us that We May Speak"**

Consider some of those who cannot speak for themselves: victims of trauma and abuse, some of whom are young children and the elderly. They aren't necessarily mute in a physical sense, but often they are afraid or confused, which leaves them voiceless.

The biblical directive to us is clear. We are to speak up for those who cannot speak for themselves, and the ways to fulfill such a mandate are many. The Guardian Ad Litem program, for instance, trains volunteers in helping and caring for abused children as their court proceedings unfold. Trauma and survivor centers can always use volunteers. Even a simple "I'd rather not hear" to a gossipmonger sends a loud message on behalf of the one being maligned (who, being absent, cannot speak).

Speaking for others is easier when we remember we're not alone in the task. As we look around at the many voiceless ones in our society, we do well to rely on the eternal advocate. Ultimately, it is God who speaks compassion, and we are merely the vessels of His choosing.

Father, give me the words You would have me speak on behalf of those who cannot find a voice. Show me where and when my words may help, bringing only justice, comfort, and love. In the name of Jesus, amen.

Noble Character

A wife of noble character who can find? She is worth far more than rubies (Proverbs 31:10, *New International Version*).

Scripture: **Proverbs 31:10-15**
Song: "Shine, Jesus, Shine!"

The comparison in today's passage is an interesting one: noble character is worth more than rubies. Rubies are precious stones—sparkling, brilliant, dazzling—and quite valuable, in biblical times as well as in today's market. A noble character, according to the dictionary, is "having or showing qualities of high moral character, such as courage, generosity or honor." Are such characteristics really more valuable than jewels?

Rubies are beautiful, and money (along with other things of value) is a necessity. Yet there is no contest when these things are placed against the examples of Helen Keller's courage, Mother Teresa and her generous nature, or the honor of Dietrich Bonhoeffer, the German minister who was executed for speaking against the Nazi regime.

Where can one find such noble character, worth far more than rubies? It is being formed in us through the power of the Holy Spirit. In God's eyes, we are already worth far more than precious stones. (And if you happen to need a wife, you know what to look for, right?)

Heavenly Father, I thank You for the knowledge that we are of great value to You, worth everything, even the death of Your Son. Keep working in me through Your Spirit to conform me to His image in every way. For I pray in His precious, holy name. Amen.

Why, If Not to Help?

She opens her arms to the poor and extends her hands to the needy (Proverbs 31:20, *New International Version*).

Scripture: **Proverbs 31:16-23**
Song: **"I, the Lord of Sea and Sky"**

After a friend had helped me through a rather rough time, I told her how much her efforts had meant to me. She responded by opening her arms, hugging me, and saying, "Why are we here, if not to help one another?"

What a marvelous question to ponder! The woman mentioned in today's passage is a shining example of why we are here. She opens her arms to all in need. How does she find them? Does she get names from an agency? Does she take names off the yearly angel tree at Christmas? Does she donate money or work at the soup kitchen, or invite people into her home?

The passage doesn't answer these questions. Perhaps it was the intention of the writer to leave the how and where vague enough for us to follow the example without force-fitting ourselves into specifics. After all, we'll know the how and where if we listen closely for the guidance of the Holy Spirit. It's the why that matters so much. Why are we here, if not to help one another?

Dear Father in Heaven, I thank You for the opportunity to be Your arms and hands in the world to help the poor and needy. Guide me to where I can be most useful in serving Your purposes. And help me to remember that all I am and have comes also from Your hands. In the holy name of Jesus, our Lord and Savior, I pray. Amen.

True Beauty

Charm is deceptive, and beauty is fleeting; but a woman who fears the Lord is to be praised (Proverbs 31:30, *New International Version*).

Scripture: **Proverbs 31:24-31**
Song: **"All Things Bright and Beautiful"**

Beauty is "skin deep." It's probably no surprise that the cosmetic advertising industry would likely agree! Most ad campaigns are geared toward promising amazingly youthful looks if one only buys the skin product—a message difficult to believe.

Today's passage reminds us that it's what's inside that counts. In fact, looks are, according to the Proverbs writer, "deceptive" and "fleeting"—ineffective marketing images for today, but true nonetheless. Instead, the praiseworthy characteristic is to fear the Lord. In this sense, fear of the Lord means to have reverent, devout awe of Him, to be humble and obedient to His will. To live in such a way is to be worthy of praise.

Thankfully, God sees beyond whatever charm and beauty we possess and into our souls—where the fear of the Lord is praiseworthy. But what will that mean for you today, in practical terms? What particular sins will you have to avoid? Which people will you need to love a little deeper, and which hard choice will you finally have to make? Let the fear of the Lord guide you in all things.

Dear Father, *here I am. See in me all my desire for Your life to blossom within me as true beauty. This I pray in the name of Christ. Amen.*

Impossible to Let Us Down

As the scripture says, "Anyone who trusts in him will never be put to shame" (Romans 10:11, *New International Version*).

Scripture: **Romans 10:9-13**
Song: **"I Know Whom I Have Believed"**

"Every emotion I have seems to turn immediately into shame," said Susan to her counselor. "I can't say I've ever really been angry, sad, or afraid for very long. Immediately, I just start feeling ashamed."

"I'm thinking you may not feel much joy, either," the counselor responded. And he was right. Because of parental abuse in Susan's childhood, a false sense of shame saturated her being. It was false because none of the abuse was her fault. But still it was powerful because she had no one to tell her she was innocent.

The truth of today's Scripture verse can help Susan—and any of us suffering shame—if we can let the message of forgiveness sink deep down into our hearts. The gospel tells us that if we trust the Lord, we need never be ashamed (no matter what we've done—or had done to us). This doesn't mean we'll never succumb to false guilt while here on earth. However, when we stand before the Almighty at the last day, and point to Jesus as our only Savior, it will be impossible that He should let us down.

Dear Father in Heaven, I place all my trust in You. I know there is no shame in clinging to Your eternal promises. In the name of Jesus, amen.

May 29–31. **Gary Allen** is editor of *Devotions.* His favorite hobby is singing in a barbershop harmony chorus with forty other men.

God, or Just Great?

God was pleased to have all his fullness dwell in [Jesus] (Colossians 1:19, *New International Version*).

Scripture: **Colossians 1:15-20**
Song: **"Jesus, the Very Thought of Thee"**

Jesus is quite popular among the masses of people these days. Just listen to a few typical comments:

"He was one of the greatest teachers of all time."
"He showed us how to love all people."
"He was so tolerant; He never judged anybody."

"What a great man!" they will say. But then some small voice in the back of the room ventures this statement about our great teacher: "He was God in the flesh."

Stand back as the outrage flows. In fact, such a claim may evoke outright hatred in no time at all. Yet, the simple statement of Scripture is that in this great exemplar we also have a Savior, the only God-man, deity in the flesh.

Now the crowds back off: "Let's keep Jesus in the best-of-humans category, where He can remain harmless. That way, we can take Him out whenever we need to show we're tolerant of religion. But bow our knee to this Lord by whom 'all things were created'? No, we really can't go that far." But how far do you go with Jesus? Right up to His eternal existence?

Father, Son, and Holy Spirit, I bow my knee to You in all things. You are more than just great. In You all things hold together. In Jesus' name, amen.

Always in Style

There is one body and one Spirit . . . one Lord, one faith, one baptism (Ephesians 4:4, 5, *New International Version*).

Scripture: **Ephesians 4:1-6**
Song: **"Make Us One"**

I'm not exactly a "fashion hound." In fact, on Father's Day last year, my college-age sons gave me a card that showed a 1970s father on the cover. He was dressed in too-short bell-bottom pants, an ugly paisley tie, a gross over-the-ear haircut, and those horrible platform shoes. The caption said: "Part of being a great father is making sure the entire family is never one degree behind the fashion curve. Thanks, Dad, for showing us the way."

Talk about tongue-in-cheek! I was almost embarrassed enough to remove my pastel green leisure suit on the spot. However, no one will convince me to give up the one-size-fits-all section of any clothing store. Especially when it comes to expandable waistline pants or those hats with adjustable headbands.

In God's kingdom, believers come in a variety of languages, cultures, worship styles, and ministry approaches. However, aren't you thankful that one size fits them all when it comes to the basics of Christian doctrine? As different as we may look from the outside, all true believers cling to one Lord, one faith, one baptism. It's just something that will never go out of style.

Dear God, the faith once delivered is the same faith we hold today. Let me never waver from the truths that make us one. In Christ's name, amen.

DEVOTIONS®

Where is the wise? where is the scribe? where is the disputer of this world? hath not God made foolish the wisdom of this world?

—1 Corinthians 1:20

JUNE

Photo © Digital Stock

Gary Allen, editor

Bless, and Be Blessed

Grace and peace to you from God our Father and the Lord Jesus Christ (1 Corinthians 1:3, *New International Version*).

Scripture: **1 Corinthians 1:1-9**
Song: **"Let There Be Peace on Earth"**

One of my coworkers hails from New Orleans. On his desk hangs a little cellophane-wrapped voodoo doll with a pin stuck through its wrapper. He thinks it's cute. But I wonder: Why is it so easy to make light of the true power of evil or the strength of a verbal curse? And why do we appear to struggle with the idea that blessings, too, exist— and more powerfully so than their counterparts?

When someone sneezes these days, less and less do we hear "God bless you!" Surely in our current day of anxiety, we could eagerly invoke the blessing of peace and grace on friend and foe alike.

In Scripture, how often Christ hails His followers with "Peace!" And the apostle Paul rarely closed a letter without a prayer that the receiver know God's peace. This is a wonderful thing for us to do as well because I believe the one who offers a blessing also shares in that blessing.

So . . . may the blessing of grace and peace fill your life with God's goodness this day.

Gracious God, I need Your peace in my life. And may Your grace and peace touch every person I meet today as well. I pray this in the name of my Lord Jesus Christ. Amen.

June 1–4. **Phillis Harris-Brooks** writes from Denver, Colorado. She and her husband, Darryl, have one son.

Being Better Off

I appeal to you, brothers, in the name of our Lord Jesus Christ, that all of you agree with one another so that there may be no divisions among you and that you may be perfectly united in mind and thought (1 Corinthians 1:10, *New International Version*).

Scripture: **1 Corinthians 1:10-17**
Song: **"When We Gather in His Name"**

During World War II a Dutch family hid Jews living in their community. At one point, with five people hidden in their home, the family members learned about an older asthmatic woman also needing a place to hide. Since getting to the hiding place meant climbing stairs, sheltering her would increase the danger to all. Suppose the woman took too much time getting up those stairs when Nazi soldiers knocked at the door? But when the group of refugees and their protectors cast secret ballots to decide on the woman's acceptance, all nine voted yes.

Difficulty puts tremendous stress on character, doesn't it? Though most of us won't face life-or-death decisions calling for self-sacrifice, we will be challenged regularly to put aside our pure self-interest for the good of all. In the church it means that, before speaking our disagreement, we remember our unity through the name of our Lord Jesus Christ. We may not be able to control a decision, but we need not infect others with our discontent.

Lord, let my words flow from Your Spirit within me, that I might contribute to the unity of Your church in all I say. In Jesus' name, amen.

No Two Ways Here!

Where is the wise man? Where is the scholar? Where is the philosopher of this age? Has not God made foolish the wisdom of the world? (1 Corinthians 1:20, *New International Version*).

Scripture: **1 Corinthians 1:18-25**
Song: **"I Am Not Skilled to Understand"**

Why is common sense so uncommon? As a child growing up, I often heard: "Oh yes, that guy is as smart as a whip, but he doesn't have enough common sense to come in out of the rain."

Then I tried to imagine why someone would want to remain standing in a downpour! What if a firefighter were trying to douse the flames of a burning house? Or suppose a farmer had to bring in a harvest without delay? It was just a matter of looking at things from both sides.

Not so with the wisdom of Scripture. There is only one wisdom, even though those who look at it from the world's perspective might think it foolishness. Yet never will the wise man without God be wise. Never will the scholar without God be informed. And never will the philosopher without God have a grip on life's ultimate meaning. As they also used to say in my childhood: "There are no two ways about it."

To love God with all our hearts and minds is the height of wisdom. And if we are wise in this way, every other form of knowledge will seem foolish in comparison.

Lord, I rejoice in Your all-encompassing wisdom! Allow me to rely on that wisdom so that I may joyfully obey You. Through Christ I pray. Amen.

Exactly What He Did

As it is written, "Let him who boasts boast in the Lord" (1 Corinthians 1:31, *New International Version*).

Scripture: **1 Corinthians 1:26-31**
Song: **"Ye Servants of God, Your Master Proclaim"**

As the apostle Paul demonstrates, the memory of God's redeeming goodness leads us to gratitude and praise. Even if I cannot say "He has done such and such for me," I've still witnessed God's movement in others' lives. Perhaps He turned around a wayward child, healed a medical condition for which professionals held no hope, breathed life into a dying marriage. I remember it all, and I "boast" in the Lord's marvelous goodness.

For me, He made a way where there was no way. Having given up on my childhood dream to write, I nevertheless devoured books as though I'd authored them myself. But an energy-sapping career coupled with motherhood left few moments for a military wife to write. Soon professional writing had dropped off my horizon.

Or so I thought. Then, while I was in hot pursuit of God, a writing opportunity came to me. I never dreamed God would tune the strings of my disillusioned heart to the key of thankful adoration. However, in His good time, in His own way, that's exactly what He did.

Lover of my soul, You reached down through the heavens to bless me. I adore You—yes, even boast in You—as I recall Your wonderful ways in my life. I give all the praise and glory to You through my precious Lord and Savior, Jesus Christ. Amen.

How Will I Interpret?

Consider it pure joy, my brothers, whenever you face trials of many kinds, because you know that the testing of your faith develops perseverance (James 1:2, 3, *New International Version*).

Scripture: **James 1:2-8**
Song: **"Through It All"**

Joy eluded me when my husband contracted pneumonia. Five hours after he landed in the emergency room, nurses wheeled John into intensive care and hooked him up to more gadgets than I could count. He needed oxygen and constant monitoring. All I knew was fear.

We certainly didn't enjoy that trial, but God taught us valuable lessons through it. Listening to the groans of the patients around him, my husband expressed gratitude for his normally good health. He could easily stop whining about minor irritations. He developed a deeper appreciation for the many friends who came to cheer him.

And I learned a little more about trusting God's love in a stressful situation—and about letting Him care for us through other people. Through it all, we both learned that testing can produce perseverance . . . or not. We always have the option to give in to our fear, to let despair win the day. It's always my choice: How will I "consider" this tough time? What will my interpretation be?

Father, thank You that nothing happens without Your knowledge and permission. Help me persevere in the midst of trouble. In Jesus' name, amen.

June 5–11. **Bonnie Doran** works as a bookkeeper for her church in Littleton, Colorado. Besides writing, she enjoys reading, cooking, and scuba diving.

The Envy Monster

If you harbor bitter envy and selfish ambition in your hearts, do not boast about it or deny the truth (James 3:14, *New International Version*).

Scripture: **James 3:13-18**
Song: **"Heart of Worship"**

That old green-eyed dragon reared its ugly head again. Wasn't I beyond such petty emotions? But I couldn't ignore the nettles of rage as I heard one more writer gushing about his phenomenal success. Why him? I write just as well. When would I win a contest, sell an article to a prestigious magazine, or land a three-book deal?

I'm a slow learner, but the emerald steam coming out of my ears was tough to ignore. I finally confessed my jealousy. And as I look back, it seems that God has reshaped my attitude so I don't turn chartreuse in the presence of rejoicing friends. Usually I can actually say "That's wonderful! Congratulations!" And mean it.

God also gently reminded me that success usually requires an awful lot of hard work. Applying the seat of my pants to the seat of my chair will propel me in my writing career much better than a fit of envy. I need to do the work before me and leave the results to God. He will orchestrate my success, whether it takes the form of a published novel or a "well done, good and faithful servant." In the meantime, I'll let sleeping dragons lie.

Lord, thank You for revealing my envy and selfish ambition. Keep working to make me more like Your Son, in whose name I pray. Amen.

Power Paupers

That power is like the working of his mighty strength, which he exerted in Christ when he raised him from the dead (Ephesians 1:19, 20, *New International Version*).

Scripture: **Ephesians 1:15-21**
Song: **"I Sing the Mighty Power of God"**

I work part-time in a church office. One day a young man came in and blurted: "I want to talk to somebody about salvation."

I kept my jaw from dropping to the floor. Barely. "Let me see whether the minister is in," I said. No minister. No administrator, no children's minister . . . no janitor! Before I became a puddle of panic, I prayed, "Help!" Then I turned to the man and said, "I'm not a trained counselor; I'm the bookkeeper. But you can talk to me."

I listened and comforted. I found a Bible, newsletter, and visitor's pamphlet. The administrator finally came to my rescue and offered additional materials. (She gave him a bag so he could carry it all!)

The man returned to the office the next day and talked with our youth minister. Together they contacted the man's former minister, who invited him back with open arms.

God's power was at work there. Although I was a small conduit of the power line, I do believe God used me. But how will He use you today? Are you open?

Father, I so often forget the mighty strength You offer as I carry on Your Kingdom work. Praise to You for Your resurrection power! In the name of the risen Christ I pray. Amen.

Invitation to the Party

To them God has chosen to make known among the Gentiles the glorious riches of this mystery, which is Christ in you, the hope of glory (Colossians 1:27, *New International Version*).

Scripture: **Colossians 1:24-29**
Song: **"Let the Lower Lights Be Burning"**

Have you ever driven by a house and seen people inside through the open drapes? Sometimes as I go by, I pause to wonder who those people are and what they are doing. I usually picture them enjoying a scrumptious feast and stimulating conversation.

Of course, I'd never go up to a stranger's home, bang on the door, and ask, "May I join in the fun?" The owner of the house would think I was crazy. And he'd be crazy if he let me in, having no idea what kind of person I am.

When I knocked at God's house, however, He opened the door wide. He sent me an invitation, you see, delivered in person by Jesus. Even though He knows all my faults, He welcomes me as His own.

Each of us believers has once been on the outside looking in. Now we are guests in Christ's home, getting to know Him better and being introduced to new friends like peace, hope, and joy—all the glorious riches of His indwelling. We don't need to wonder any longer what it's like inside. The mystery is revealed, and we ourselves enjoy fellowship in the bright light of His presence.

Lord, let the light of Your glorious love shine through my life, so I attract others to You. In Jesus' name, amen.

Fame Not Needed

My message and my preaching were not with wise and persuasive words, but with a demonstration of the Spirit's power, so that your faith might not rest on men's wisdom, but on God's power (1 Corinthians 2:4, 5, *New International Version*).

Scripture: **1 Corinthians 2:1-5**
Song: **"There Is Power in the Blood"**

In 1970, Judy Collins made an a capella recording of "Amazing Grace." This old hymn, sung simply, sold a million singles in Great Britain and the United States, an amazing feat for a song written by a man who had once been a slave trader. In fact, fellow sailors had nicknamed John Newton the Great Blasphemer because of his pre-conversion reputation for profanity, coarseness, and debauchery.

The song has endured for over 200 years because of its plain but profound message: "I once was lost, but now am found."

In a Hollywood-dominated culture, we often think we must have professional musicians or famous speakers even for our church programs. But it's the message, not the messenger, that has the power of God behind it.

How wonderful it is to be able claim that message! Each of us, no matter how ethical we were before coming to Christ, were "dead in [our] transgressions and sins" (Ephesians 2:1, *NIV)?* What powerful grace that saves!

Thank You, Lord, that Your salvation doesn't depend on human wisdom. My Your Spirit's power be evident in me today! Through Christ, amen.

Party Hearty

No eye has seen, no ear has heard, no mind has conceived what God has prepared for those who love him (1 Corinthians 2:9, *New International Version*).

Scripture: **1 Corinthians 2:6-10**
Song: **"When We All Get to Heaven"**

Our music minister, Scott, moonlighted as a pizza delivery person when he needed money for a new transmission for his car. He even planned to work on his birthday. But the choir heard about it and made a deal with his boss. They arranged for Scott to deliver 20 pizzas to another church where they were hiding themselves. When Scott arrived, they yelled, "Surprise! Happy Birthday!" Scott's boss gave him time so he could enjoy the impromptu party. And the choir gave him a generous tip—equal to what he still needed for the transmission.

God enjoys throwing that kind of celebration for us. When a financial need is met unexpectedly, or a friend happens to call when we just need to talk, God has arranged that mini party.

Of course, we can't plan these things because, as Paul tells us, we can't even imagine how such blessings might unfold. And the ultimate party, Heaven itself—who knows what's in store for us there! Surely that eternal existence will more than pay for the sufferings of our brief time here on earth.

Lord, I can't conceive of Heaven's blessings, but I long to be with You there. In Jesus' name I pray. Amen.

Jesus Freak!

The man without the Spirit does not accept the things that come from the Spirit of God, for they are foolishness to him, and he cannot understand them, because they are spiritually discerned (1 Corinthians 2:14, *New International Version*).

Scripture: **1 Corinthians 2:11-16**
Song: **"Spirit of God, Descend Upon My Heart"**

In the 1970s, my car sported a popular bumper sticker in fluorescent orange: "Maranatha: What a Way to Go!" It expressed my exuberant but somewhat immature faith. As I pumped gasoline one day, the attendant asked me, "What does *Maranatha* mean?" I replied, "It's Greek for 'Our Lord, come.'" His face changed from idle curiosity to disgust. "Oh. You're one of *those* people, a Jesus freak." His reaction left me speechless.

I visited the station again, and the attendant responded with the same vehemence. I couldn't understand why a bumper sticker meant to cause a smile engendered such hostility. He gave me no opportunity to explain, and I felt too intimidated to pursue a conversation.

Today I realize that, no matter how persuasive I may be in my witness for Christ, the Holy Spirit must give people understanding of God's truths. This relieves me from the burden of converting the world. Yet it powerfully challenges me: am I relying on the Spirit to infuse my words with heavenly wisdom?

Father, only Your Spirit can change my weak words from foolish to profound. Today, may I speak the words You give me. In Jesus' name, amen.

Deeper Roots

When the sun came up, the plants were scorched and dried up, because they did not have enough roots (Matthew 13:6, *Contemporary English Version*).

Scripture: **Matthew 13:3-9**
Song: **"Come, All Christians, Be Committed"**

I placed a flowering plant on my patio. Protected by the shade of a huge tree, the plant thrived. Except during the hottest part of the summer, I could easily get by with watering it a few times a week. The plant gave me a sense of peace and satisfaction, even during days filled with endless tasks.

The tree was ailing, though, and a tree expert confirmed what we already knew: we'd need to remove it or face major damage to our porch.

With the tree gone, scorching sun replaced cool afternoon shade, and my once-vibrant patio plant couldn't survive my infrequent attention. Supple green leaves turned crispy brown; flowers faded and withered.

How many times have I confined myself to a small container and become scorched by the world around me? Why have I refused to dig deeper into God's Word or take the step of obedience?

Lord, today let me thrive in the shade of Your everlasting love. And sink the roots of my being deep into the good soil of Your Word. Through my Lord Jesus Christ I pray. Amen.

June 12–18. **Claudean Boatman** is a writer and teacher in Windsor, Colorado. She enjoys photographing nearby mountains during motorcycle trips.

Nurturing the Weeds

While everyone was sleeping, an enemy came and scattered weed seeds in the field and then left (Matthew 13:25, *Contemporary English Version*).

Scripture: **Matthew 13:24-30**
Song: **"In the Garden"**

I enthusiastically prepared the soil for my first real flower garden and gently planted the mixed flower seeds. Each day I visited my new garden spot until I saw the first shoots pop through the ground.

Weeks passed. Buds appeared and began to open. Violets, marigolds, and moss roses filled the yard with vivid colors. Daily I inspected the progress. I didn't recognize one particular plant, though. It grew taller than the others and had a single, long, narrow bud. Anticipating a grand flower, I waited and waited for a bloom.

Then I happened to walk by a friend's home while he was out taking care of his flower bed. He yanked a plant out of the ground and commented, "This weed had roots down to China!"

I looked closely. It was just like the plant I had been so lovingly nurturing to maturity. But then, what else am I nurturing in my life these days? What is growing tall and waiting to bloom—perhaps today or tomorrow? Will it blossom into something beautiful for the Lord? Or will it just provide more fuel for the fires of judgment?

God, You are the gardener of good works, the harvester of all deeds. I give my whole life into Your care. In Jesus' name, amen.

Beyond the Basics

By now you should have been teachers, but once again you need to be taught the simplest things about what God has said. You need milk instead of solid food (Hebrews 5:12, *Contemporary English Version*).

Scripture: **Hebrews 5:7-14**
Song: **"Teach Me, O Lord, I Pray"**

In my sixth-grade English class, I must constantly remind students to begin their sentences with capital letters and end them with punctuation marks. But at this point in their education, shouldn't it be second nature?

When we have to keep relearning the most basic skills, it's hard to advance. The writer of Hebrews must have known this as he addressed his readers' spiritual immaturity. I can picture him going over and over the basics of the faith: Christ is your eternal high priest. You are saved by His sacrificial death. As He loved you, love one another. Don't grumble. Bless those who persecute you. Call upon God, and He will answer you.

While a Christian may act like my sixth graders, the consequences of ignoring God's teachings are much more serious. Our neglect keeps us from learning what prayer can do. It prevents our telling others about Christ. It keeps us trapped in infancy. Perhaps by now we should be adults feasting on solid food. And shouldn't we even be feeding those who are still young in the faith?

Holy Teacher, *make me a willing student and an eager learner of those spiritual truths You have for me. In the name of Jesus I pray. Amen.*

Just Too Wonderful

I want you to know all about Christ's love, although it is too wonderful to be measured. Then your lives will be filled with all that God is (Ephesians 3:19, *Contemporary English Version*).

Scripture: **Ephesians 3:14-21**
Song: **"Share His Love"**

My husband and I stood on the world's largest suspension bridge overlooking the Royal Gorge near Cañon City, Colorado. A powerful wind swept our hair as we gazed at the roaring Arkansas River below us. The light played hide-and-seek on the canyon walls as the clouds passed before the sun. We stood transfixed, silently breathing in the beauty of a place too large to comprehend; nothing in our realm of experience could compare.

Christ's love is all that and more. From His birth in a lowly manger to His resurrection, He demonstrated love too expansive, too wonderful to explain, too majestic to touch. Recalling the biblical examples of Christ's love, I'm reminded of the unfathomable depth of His sacrifice. After all, He existed in all the royalty of Heaven before humbling himself to become incarnate as a mere human.

Being rescued from sin by His death gives us eternal life. Following His example of service gives us an earthly purpose. All of this flows from His love, a love too wonderful to be measured.

O Lord, our Lord, grant my prayer that I would know Your love and be filled with all that You are. Through Christ I pray. Amen.

Together in the Garden

What, after all, is Apollos? And what is Paul? Only servants, through whom you came to believe—as the Lord has assigned to each his task. I planted the seed, Apollos watered it, but God made it grow (1 Corinthians 3:5, 6, *New International Version*).

Scripture: **1 Corinthians 3:1-9**
Song: **"Go Out and Tell"**

Angelina first came to our church during Vacation Bible School. She felt so welcomed that she soon began attending tutoring sessions, Wednesday night suppers, missions classes, and Sunday school. For two years the teachers in those ministries taught Angelina Bible stories, taught her how to pray, and demonstrated ways to help others. They included her in parties and in service projects, such as feeding the hungry, and providing Christmas for other children. During worship services, adults helped her take sermon notes and made sure she never sat alone.

When Angelina was baptized, she thanked all those adults who had invested in her, and each of us celebrated her entrance into new life. We recognized how God used each of us in our own ways—yet still working together—to help her open her heart to God's love for her. Angelina continues her faith journey. She is reading her Bible and praying for others. She too is now a fellow laborer in God's garden.

Holy God, *thank You for allowing me to work with other believers in Your garden. Let me produce good fruit for Your glory, through Christ. Amen.*

Wood Will Burn

Whatever we build on that foundation will be tested by fire on the day of judgment. Then everyone will find out if we have used gold, silver, and precious stones, or wood, hay, and straw (1 Corinthians 3:12, 13, *Contemporary English Version*).

Scripture: **1 Corinthians 3:10-15**
Song: **"Christ Is Made the Sure Foundation"**

Late in the evening on February 3, 1916, a mysterious fire broke out in the Centre Block building on Parliament Hill in Ottawa, Ontario, Canada. The devastation was overwhelming, leaving only the parliamentary library intact. The heavy metal doors separating it from the rest of the building, along with the heroic efforts of firefighters, saved it from damage.

When the Royal Commission investigated the fire, it concluded that a cigar left unattended in a reading room was the cause. Three factors accelerated the fire: poor ventilation, extensive varnishing, and dry pine. The building materials of this beautiful building became its undoing!

The Canadian government learned from the experience. New parliament buildings, opened in 1920, were less elegant than their predecessors, but they were more fire-resistant. Similarly, we build our lives with materials of our choosing, day by day, knowing they'll be tested by fire in the end. A little dry wood and straw just won't hold up.

Thank You, God, *for giving me the opportunity to build on the foundation You have provided. Help me to use the materials of love, joy, peace, and all the other qualities of Your indwelling Spirit. In Jesus' name, amen.*

Scammed into Foolishness

Don't fool yourselves! If any of you think you are wise in the things of this world, you will have to become foolish before you can be truly wise (1 Corinthians 3:18, *Contemporary English Version*).

Scripture: **1 Corinthians 3:18-23**
Song: **"We Praise You with Our Minds, O Lord"**

A Nigerian wants help getting his fortune to the United States, thereby protecting it from illegal seizure by his government. Will you help him? If so, he'll share a large portion of his bank account with you!

This tempting e-mail scam continues to put the hard-earned savings of well-meaning people at risk. I know one of the victims. She consulted lawyers (recommended by her e-mailer!) who approved of the deal. So sure she would receive the promised reward, she talked family members into backing the venture.

After several trips overseas, she lost her home—and family members may lose theirs. She continues to believe, however, that if she waits long enough, the promised fortune will arrive, and all will be well.

Will she ever wise up? The defense against foolishness is recognizing that our human wisdom is weak and vulnerable. Our hope for wisdom lies in humbling ourselves before God, who offers wise guidance to all who ask.

Thank You, Father, for being willing to give us wisdom. Help me to remember that You are the source of sound decisions of all kinds. In the name of Jesus, Lord and Savior of all, I pray. Amen.

It's No Secret

He does not live the rest of his earthly life for evil human desires, but rather for the will of God (1 Peter 4:2, *New International Version*).

Scripture: **1 Peter 4:1-11**
Song: **"It Is No Secret (What God Can Do)"**

Kerri had grown up in church, committed her life to Christ at age 17, and was attending Bible college. All her life she'd heard how she needed to seek God's will. In fact, it was a constant mantra—pray for God's will, search for God's will, know God's will. She began to feel like a detective with a magnifying glass, searching for clues.

"I still don't know what God's will for my life is," she lamented as Steven listened. "Kerri, He isn't hiding it from you," Steven answered. The statement hung in the air while she considered it. "God has been specific in His Word about how He wants us to live our lives," Steven continued. "If we will just read the Scriptures, we will know how to resolve conflict, how to treat others, how to pray, how to worship. It's all there."

Could we simply say that God's will for us is to live by His Spirit each moment of every day? Then the big questions, like whom to marry or where to live, won't be so difficult to answer.

Lord, open my eyes to the practical application of Your holy Word. Align my will with Yours, starting with this moment. In Christ's name, amen.

June 19–25. **Guyla Greenly** lives with her two children in Casper, Wyoming. She is an avid scrapbooker and addicted to TV decorating shows.

Holy Pedicure

He poured water into a basin and began to wash his disciples' feet, drying them with the towel that was wrapped around him (John 13:5, *New International Version*).

Scripture: **John 13:2-9**
Song: **"Are You Washed in the Blood?"**

When my Aunt Judy was in the hospital after giving birth to twins, the nurse came into the room and said, "Oh, what pretty feet you have!" As soon as the nurse left, Aunt Judy burst into tears and asked my Uncle Glen, "Do I look so horrible that the only thing she could find to compliment were my feet?"

Aunt Judy thinks feet are the ugliest part of the body and is repulsed by them. Decades later, as my grandparents aged, Aunt Judy found herself having to clip Grandma's toenails and smooth out her calluses. How she dreaded the task!

Aunt Judy could have refused, could have pressed someone else into service, or paid to take Grandma to the salon for regular pedicures. But she knew Grandma felt more comfortable at home with people she knew. Even though it was difficult for Judy to groom someone else's feet, she followed the example of Christ and humbled herself to perform a selfless act of service.

Heavenly Father, help me today to see ways in which I can reach out to others. Help me to step out of my comfort zone to fulfill these needs with an attitude of humility. In the name of the one who cared even for the feet of His beloved followers, amen.

Where Do I Begin?

Now that you know these things, you will be blessed if you do them (John 13:17, *New International Version*).

Scripture: **John 13:12-17**
Song: **"There Shall Be Showers of Blessing"**

I'm a smart girl, but sometimes I become so overwhelmed with the size of my to-do list that I don't know where to begin. I've even been known to ask a friend to tell me where to start. Of course, he says, "I can't tell you what to do." (I don't see why not, but arguing it has never got me anywhere.)

Like me, have you ever wanted someone to tell you what to do, how to do it, when to do it—and then let you know how it will all turn out? No one can do that for us—except God. He has already written our to-do lists for us:

"Pray without ceasing."

"Hide my Word in your heart."

"Love your enemies."

"Do good to your neighbor."

"Walk humbly with your God."

The list continues, of course. But when I don't know where to start, it helps me to begin with prayer and the reading of Scriptures. Oddly enough, the "task" of greatest importance to the Lord is that I simply "be still, and know that [He is] God" (Psalm 46:10). How He values my sincere, attentive presence!

Lord, thank You for showing me how to act. But let all my deeds for You flow from my deep fellowship with You! Through Christ I pray. Amen.

Lead with Love

The Son of Man did not come to be served, but to serve, and to give his life as a ransom for many (Mark 10:45, *New International Version*).

Scripture: **Mark 10:41-45**
Song: **"He Leadeth Me"**

Who comes to mind when you think of great leaders? Along with all the well-intentioned men and women we could name, what about people like Saddam Hussein or Adolph Hitler? These men were great strategists, men of vision. But their plans were for evil. To promote their own ambitions, they led people to their deaths rather than doing things to improve the quality of their lives.

Dr. Richard Kriegbaum writes: "Leadership and followership are both about loving people, as they are and as they could be." Great leaders serve the needs of their followers. They love enough even to sacrifice their own interests for those they lead.

Jesus modeled this style of leadership throughout His ministry. He could have demanded respect and servitude and ruled like a tyrant. However, people have willingly loved and served Him for centuries because He first loved and served them. It's amazing to think that the king of the universe could humble himself. But that is exactly what God did, in the form of His only Son.

Dear God, examine my heart. Do I serve with humility? Do I lead by loving first? Inspire me to care and serve with a joyful heart today, that I might honor Your Son, in whom I pray. Amen.

Only One Body

Now it is required that those who have been given a trust must prove faithful (1 Corinthians 4:2, *New International Version*).

Scripture: **1 Corinthians 4:1-7**
Song: **"Healed"**

After my husband left me, I would avoid bedtime. I didn't want to lie there alone, thinking about him and his girlfriend. I watched TV, checked e-mail, scrapbooked—anything to avoid going to bed. Sleep deprivation, emotional fatigue, and "stress eating" were taking their toll. I lost 10 pounds because I couldn't eat, and then I gained 15 because I couldn't *stop* consuming soda and curly fries!

I was a mess, all right, but when God is trying to tell me something, I seem to hear it everywhere. For example, when I read Welby O'Brien's book *Formerly a Wife*, the first chapter discussed taking care of yourself so you have the energy to deal with everything required of you. O'Brien stated, "I have learned that if I don't take care of myself, I can't rely on any other human to do it." Then I attended a women's conference, and the speaker spoke on the importance of managing physical resources.

God has entrusted only one body to each of us. I've come to appreciate the need to faithfully care for it amid all our stresses. In this age of super-sized drive-thru meals and sedentary jobs, it's harder than ever.

Heavenly Father, help me to be a faithful steward of all You have given me, especially this physical body. And thank You for loving the whole me—in the best of times and the worst of times. In Jesus' name, amen.

Equally Blessed

Already you have all you want! Already you have become rich! You have become kings—and that without us! How I wish that you really had become kings so that we might be kings with you! (1 Corinthians 4:8, *New International Version*).

Scripture: **1 Corinthians 4:8-13**
Song: **"Count Your Blessings"**

When my sisters, cousins, and I would visit, Grandpa Walt always made perfectly round, fluffy pancakes for us. He served them with butter and homemade chokecherry syrup. In fact, he would make us whatever we ordered—and our order usually included those favored flapjacks. For supper, we might say: "Hamburgers and pancakes!" And that's exactly what we got.

We haven't outgrown our love for those golden pancakes. With families of our own, we can't always coordinate our visits. However, when one of us has been to see our grandparents, we call the others and with great maturity say in our best holier-than-thou voices, "I had Grandpa's pancakes—and *you* didn't! Ha-ha!"

But sometimes that attitude isn't very funny. The Corinthian Christians had decided they were pretty hot stuff. They separated themselves from others, even setting themselves above the apostles. They looked at others and seemed to be saying: "God blessed me more than you!"

Dear God, help me to remember that every believer receives all of You dwelling within. Keep me from any form of pride, for Your love knows no boundaries—for any of us. Praise to You, through Christ my Lord! Amen.

Walk the Talk

The kingdom of God is not a matter of talk but of power (1 Corinthians 4:20, *New International Version*).

Scripture: **1 Corinthians 4:14-21**
Song: **"Walking in the King's Highway"**

My 9-year-old son told me that a certain lady had said she was a Christian—but he was confused because of her questionable lifestyle and sarcastic attitude. I answered as any mother would: "I'm best friends with Mel Gibson."

"Uh-uh, Mom. You are *not!* I've never seen you with him. I've never heard you talk to him."

"So? Mel and I are tight."

"But you can't be best friends with somebody you don't hang out with," he concluded.

"You mean saying something doesn't make it true?"

Okay, you get my point: the truth is made clear by our actions. Now, I can't definitively know the heart of another person, but I wanted to teach my son how important it is to look for actions that back up words.

The tricky thing is that Christians are saved by the power of God alone. Their actions are being transformed by that power, day by day, and it is a slow process of growth. So when someone says he or she believes in Jesus, I pray that that person will rely on His power and become more like Him. (And that is how I want you to pray for me as well.)

Father, let my words and actions be powered by Your power today. I pray in the name of Christ the Lord. Amen.

What Is Real Love?

This is real love. It is not that we loved God, but that he loved us and sent his Son as a sacrifice to take away our sins (1 John 4:10, *New Living Translation*).

Scripture: **1 John 4:7-16**
Song: **"Tell Me the Story of Jesus"**

Week after week, reality TV informs us that love is a self-serving conquest, a game of manipulation, wooing the other through the trappings of pretense and performance. Tragically, this sad distortion has permeated every generation since time began.

The apostle John counters with the truth. Real love, he says, finds its beginning and ending in God. His initiative, not our effort. His self-sacrifice, not our performance. His mercy and grace (in full view of our sinfulness), not our pretense of worthiness. His redemption, not our righteousness.

Apart from Him, the love we offer others will always be tainted with self-interest. Only to the measure we have experienced His real love can we truly love one another selflessly. Only as dearly loved children, daily receiving and walking in the reality of His love, can His love be "brought to full expression through us"(v. 12, *NLT*).

Lord God, thank You for your extravagant, selfless love! May I daily bow at the foot of the cross and love others in the way You have loved me. This I pray in the name of the one who gave His life to give me Heaven. Amen.

June 26–30. **Carol Floch** is pursuing a master's degree in counseling. She lives in Dallas, Texas, with her three children.

Self-Satisfying or Self-Sacrificing?

Since there is so much immorality, each man should have his own wife, and each woman her own husband (1 Corinthians 7:2, *New International Version*).

Scripture: **1 Corinthians 7:1-5**
Song: **"O Perfect Love"**

Written around A.D. 56, less than 30 years after Christ's ascension, Paul's letter to the Corinthians addresses significant problems among these first-generation Christians. They had been raised in a culture saturated with promiscuity and immorality. The Corinthian worship of Aphrodite, goddess of love, even included temple prostitution. The culture promoted sex for recreation apart from relationship. How like our twenty-first-century world!

But Paul offered a different perspective to worshipers of the true God of love. The monogamous relationship between husband and wife pictures the relationship between Christ and His church. In humility and love, Christ surrendered His rights, giving of himself fully and sacrificially for the sake of His bride. Christ's followers respond to Him in kind, with humility and love, no longer living for themselves but for His sake.

So it is with the love between husband and wife. Sexual intimacy, reserved for marriage, celebrates this bond of covenant love. It is pure, self-sacrificing, nurturing, and life-giving. In this way, God is glorified.

Heavenly Father, renew us in Your love, that we might love one another purely and sacrificially. Through Christ I pray. Amen.

Chasing Contentment

God gives some the gift of marriage, and to others he gives the gift of singleness (1 Corinthians 7:7, *New Living Translation*).

Scripture: **1 Corinthians 7:6-11**
Song: **"Never Alone"**

The midday long-distance call was a pleasant surprise, but my delight quickly turned to concern. Julie's voice broke as she said, "I'm thinking about taking the kids to Mom's for a while. Steve and I have some things to sort out." I listened attentively as she told the story of Steve's recent choices—and her resulting hurt, disappointment, and disillusionment.

It was clear to me that Julie had called because she knew I would speak to her in truth and love. It was equally clear that there were no issues of abuse or marital unfaithfulness in her situation. "Julie, the reasons you leave now will be the reasons you won't want to go back to Steve later," I gently warned. "I think you need to stay there, face this together, and work it out."

Whether we're married or single, dissatisfaction tempts us to chase after an old illusion: that by changing or escaping our circumstances, we will finally find contentment. But could we see things a little differently? Suppose our painful circumstances create opportunities to grow in holiness and to glorify God in our responses?

Lord, I know You don't cause the troubles in my life. But let me see how my circumstances can be redeemed for the good through Your power at work within me. In Jesus' name, amen.

Faithful Devotion

The Christian wife brings holiness to her marriage, and the Christian husband brings holiness to his marriage. Otherwise, your children would not have a godly influence, but now they are set apart for him (1 Corinthians 7:14, *New Living Translation*).

Scripture: **1 Corinthians 7:12-16**
Song: **"Great Is Thy Faithfulness"**

When I was a child, Lynn's high energy, joyful countenance and encouraging smile set her apart from most of the other grown-ups I knew in our rather strict church. But Lynn was also different because she was "spiritually single." She brought her children to church with her, week after week, while her husband remained at home.

Did she grow weary of being the sole spiritual influence in her home? Did she walk a daily tightrope, balancing honoring her husband and honoring her Lord? Did she battle envy as other couples worshiped together?

I don't know the answers to these questions. I do know that her children "caught" what she taught through words and example. They grew to be intentional followers of Christ, eventually choosing Christian mates and raising Lynn's grandchildren to know the Lord. In later years, David left Lynn. But God never left; His holy purposes for Lynn and her children were accomplished through her faithful devotion—to God, her husband, and her family.

Dear Lord, may we, as the family of God, embrace and nurture the families You have placed among us, for the sake of Your kingdom. In Jesus' name, amen.

Stay There!

Dear brothers and sisters, whatever situation you were in when you became a believer, stay there in your new relationship with God (1 Corinthians 7:24, *New Living Translation*).

Scripture: **1 Corinthians 7:17-24**
Song: **"I Am His and He Is Mine"**

With marriage comes change. When Sarah and Mike got married, they left separate apartments to live in an adorable new home. Wedding gifts supplied them with an abundance of home furnishings, granting a fresh start to their new life together. However, their jobs remained the same, and they kept their old friends; much in their external lives stayed the same.

By far, the biggest change came to their sense of identity. Leaving behind their families of origin, they established themselves as a brand-new entity—a unique husband and wife, a new couple. "From this day forward," they have a new frame of reference for their sense of belonging, significance, and security.

So it is with us as Christ's beloved; we have a new identity. But our outward circumstances need not change. As the apostle Paul knew, God will grow us and use us right where we are. Apart from Christ, we long to "find ourselves" in myriad forms of status or ego-gratification. Paul's gracious words remind us that our truest source of significance and security remains solidly in Christ.

Lord, show me how to live from the inside out, letting my identity in You inform every word and action. In the name of Jesus I pray. Amen.

My Prayer Notes

DEVOTIONS®

Gary Allen, editor

***K**now ye not that they which run in a race run all, but one receiveth the prize? So run, that ye may obtain.*

—1 Corinthians 9:24

JULY

Photo © Comstock

Attachment Warning

Those in frequent contact with the things of the world should make good use of them without becoming attached to them, for this world and all it contains will pass away (1 Corinthians 7:31, *New Living Translation*).

Scripture: **1 Corinthians 7:25-31**
Song: **"Just a Closer Walk with Thee"**

My friend Cindy is the queen of e-mail. When she sends me an attachment, I know it's safe to open and that it comes with the promise of humor, insight, or relevant information. But this is not always the case with attachments from other sources; I've learned valuable lessons about this . . . the hard way.

Attachments with pictures take forever to download, impeding access to other messages and using up precious memory on my computer. Some attachments, masked with friendly or curious subject headings, carry viruses that may completely disable my computer! I delete those immediately.

Likewise, Paul warns that seemingly good earthly attachments can impede our ability to serve God, robbing us of valuable time and energy. Other attachments, packed with promises of significance, status, or security, carry temptations that can completely derail us from God's purposes.

Lord God, help me to hold earthly blessings loosely, with open hands, grateful to You the giver. And may I be ready to release them, lest they hold me instead. I pray in Jesus' holy name. Amen.

July 1, 2. **Carol Floch** is pursuing a master's degree in counseling. She lives in Dallas, Texas, with her three children.

Undivided Devotion

I am saying this for your own good, not to restrict you, but that you may live in a right way in undivided devotion to the Lord (1 Corinthians 7:35, *New International Version*).

Scripture: **1 Corinthians 7:32-40**
Song: **"Be Thou My Vision"**

The television cameras zeroed in on the young Rumanian gymnast's tear-stained face as her country's flag was hoisted, strains of her national anthem filling the Olympic stadium. This moment concluded a rigorous year. With undivided devotion the team of young girls had lived and trained together, forsaking families, friends, and all other pursuits to chase the coveted gold medal. What an unusual path this child had traveled—and what an extraordinary reward she received!

What kind of passion drives such commitment? And how do I nurture that kind of devotion to Christ—in myself, and in my children? Our culture, and often the subculture of the church, encourages seeking a "happily ever after" with a mate. But Paul pins true soul-satisfaction on the single-minded pursuit of serving the Lord with an undivided heart. Later in this same letter he reminds us: "They do it to get a crown that will not last; but we do it to get a crown that will last forever" (1 Corinthians 9:25, *NIV*).

Heavenly Father, show me in the most practical terms what it means to be undivided in my devotion to You. Empower me for the hard work and sacrifice You will call me to endure. And thank You for the gleaming reward You promise. In Christ's name, amen.

The Word

In the beginning was the Word, and the Word was with God, and the Word was God (John 1:1, *New International Version*).

Scripture: **John 1:1-5**
Song: **"He's Everything to Me"**

The young man painstakingly pecked out one letter at a time on the computer while his mother supported his arm. Then he pressed a button and the computer-generated voice repeated what he had typed, "I need you to know what it is like to have autism and to be able to talk after 20 years of silence."

The profound significance of words came across in Michael's message. Through the innovation of computer-aided communication, he could now convey his wants, needs, likes, dislikes, and opinions. In essence, he could finally communicate to the world who Michael is: "I need you to know. . . ."

In effect, God said, "I need you to know . . . me" through the Word, Jesus Christ. Every word Jesus spoke, every move Jesus made, and every touch Jesus gave communicated who God is to the world. Through the life of Christ and His sacrifice, God said, "I need you to know my love, my mercy, and my grace."

Father, what do You want me to know of Your nature, Your character, Your will today? Let me see Jesus more clearly, beginning in this very moment. Through Him I pray. Amen.

July 3–9. **Gayle Gresham** lives with her husband and two children in Colorado. She enjoys writing, camping with her family, and exploring mountain trails.

Cut Off My Hand?

If your hand causes you to sin, cut it off. It is better for you to enter life maimed than with two hands to go into hell, where the fire never goes out (Mark 9:43, 44, *New International Version*).

Scripture: **Mark 9:42-48**
Song: **"What Can Wash Away My Sin?"**

I have a Wild West outlaw rooted in my family tree. My great-great-uncle Ernest was a cattle rustler with a reputation for handling a running iron (used to change brands) and a gun with equal ease. Ernest was arrested in 1883 in a Colorado mountain town while selling 70 head of altered-brand cattle to the butcher.

What if Ernest had cut off his hand after he stole the first steer and changed its brand? A change of heart at that time may have prevented significant prison time and wrenching heartbreak for his wife and children. As a matter of fact, it appears Ernest did change after getting *out* of prison. Reading his 1939 obituary, one would never know about his wild days.

Even literally cutting off a limb to prevent sin wouldn't work without a change of heart. A heart turned away from sin is what God desires. As you consider sin in your life, what needs to be removed if your heart is to stay pure? Thankfully, we can open our hearts, deal with the sin, and stay away from it . . . while retaining our limbs.

Dear Lord, *give me the courage to face the things in my life that displease You. Help me to see that they hurt You in part because they are so self-destructive to me. In the name of Jesus I pray. Amen.*

Needed: Proportionate Passion

Love the Lord your God with all your heart and with all your soul and with all your mind and with all your strength (Mark 12:30, *New International Version*).

Scripture: **Mark 12:28-34**
Song: **"All I Want Is You"**

My daughter Kate decided to try out for the high-school softball team in a neighboring town. Although she played on the varsity baseball team at her own small high school, she had never touched a softball until she played in a charity tournament the weekend before tryouts.

During tryouts Kate excelled at fielding the ball, but she had difficulty adjusting her hitting. I thought she should tell the coaches she'd played baseball so they would understand her inconsistency, but Kate didn't think that was necessary. Before I knew it, I turned into a sports-crazed mom, obsessing all week about Kate's making the team. Each night she came home to a barrage of questions: "Did you hit the ball? Did you talk to the coach? Did you make any errors?"

Then I thought: "Suppose I were consumed with God like that—with all of my heart and soul?" At least I know what it feels like to be so passionate about one single thing! Now my prayer is: Let my passions be proportionate according to their kingdom importance.

__Lord,__ I can become overly obsessed about life. Forgive me when my heart, soul, and strength are inordinately consumed with any one thing. I want You to be my magnificent obsession amid all things. In Jesus' name, amen.

No Sheep Eyes

The kingdom of God is not a matter of eating and drinking, but of righteousness, peace and joy in the Holy Spirit (Romans 14:17, *New International Version*).

Scripture: **Romans 14:13-19**
Song: **"We Are One in the Spirit"**

My family enjoys watching the television show *Fear Factor.* We hold our breath through the thrilling stunts, waiting to see whether the contestants can crash a car, climb a rope up to a helicopter, or stay in a pit for three minutes with giant bugs crawling over their bodies. But when a segment about eating certain disgusting "foods" appears, my husband quickly grabs the remote control and changes the channel. You see, in order to win the prize money, contestants must eat and keep down unthinkable items. Sometimes these are foods that are considered delicacies in other cultures.

My point is: I'm thankful that eating sheep eyes is not a requirement for salvation. And I imagine my aversion to the *Fear Factor* "foods" rivals the Jews' aversion to pork.

In our Scripture passage, Paul said he was convinced that no food in itself was unclean. The kingdom of God is so much more than what our consciences allow us to eat or drink. Focusing on righteousness, peace, and joy in the Holy Spirit keeps everything in perspective.

Father, take my eyes off the nonessentials of the faith. In gray areas let me be tolerant. In the essential truths—Your death, resurrection, and promise to return—may I be absolutely unmoving. Through Christ, amen.

Hugging in Heart

We know that an idol is nothing at all in the world and that there is no God but one (1 Corinthians 8:4, *New International Version*).

Scripture: **1 Corinthians 8:1-6**
Song: **"God of Wonders"**

It's hard for me to imagine creating and bowing down to a golden calf as the Israelites did. Why worship a finite, man-made creation when the glory of the infinite creator is all around us?

While camping in the mountains of Colorado recently, I was overpowered with His glory on two special occasions. The first time, I had hiked to the top of a mountain with my daughter to watch a golden sunset. As I walked back down, enthralled by the beauty of God's glory reflected in shining aspen leaves, I just wanted to hug God. The second time, my family had got up at midnight and ridden four-wheelers to the top of another mountain. Stars shot across the sky all around us as we sat there in the cold night air. Then three stars streaked by at once, causing me to gasp in amazement.

Oh yes, there is no God but one. Only one God who creates aspen trees that quake and stars that scribble in the sky. And me to give Him hugs in my heart.

O God, thank You for the glimpses of Your glory in everything You have made. Let me see You not only in the sky and mountains but also in the smile of my child and the face of my neighbor. In the name of Jesus, by whom all things were created and in whom all things consist, amen.

Freedom—or Chains?

Be careful, however, that the exercise of your freedom does not become a stumbling block to the weak (1 Corinthians 8:9, *New International Version*).

Scripture: 1 Corinthians 8:7-13
Song: "It Is Well with My Soul"

While working on a magazine article, I struggled with writer's block and worried about my looming deadline (which happened to be the day before my in-laws' 50th wedding anniversary). When I mentioned my worries to my friend Pam, she said, "It sounds like you work best under pressure. I bet you won't write your article until that busy week." Pam's words proved prophetic when I ended up writing the article the day before my deadline in the middle of preparing for the anniversary party.

I no longer live in a state of panic weeks before a deadline because I know I will do my best work at the last minute. Because I love my new freedom so much, I could encourage my writer friend Dianne to work the same way. But it would be a stumbling block to her. She works steadily on an article until it's complete. Waiting to write an article two days before a deadline would throw her into a state of sheer terror. That's why Scripture reminds us to consider the believers around us. We can remember that what brings us freedom may feel like a set of heavy, enslaving chains to someone else.

Lord, make me aware of stumbling blocks I may place before other believers. Help me use liberty with responsibility. In Jesus' name, amen.

A Preschooler's Fight

Nobody should seek his own good, but the good of others (1 Corinthians 10:24, *New International Version*).

Scripture: **1 Corinthians 10:23–11:1**
Song: **"Blest Be the Tie That Binds"**

When my children were preschoolers, they had an odd fight one day.

"The horned cow is ours," Katie said.

"No, it isn't," 3-year-old Kenny replied. "It's Grandpa's!"

"It is *too* ours," big sister Katie stated calmly.

"No, it's Grandpa's cow!" Kenny yelled.

By this time Kenny was crying because he knew the cow with horns belonged to Grandpa. But Katie would not give up. Finally, I told her to go to her bedroom. After a few minutes, I asked her to tell me why she was in trouble. "I'm not supposed to say the horned cow is ours," she mumbled. I will never know why Katie chose that particular battle on that particular day, but I know she thought she she was right, and wasn't going to back down.

But I've been there too! And I certainly have to wonder how many of my self-generated battles look quite childish to God. They're always motivated by my desire to look out for Number One. Yet Paul admonishes me not to seek what's in my best interest only, but to look out for the good of others as well. Did the great apostle ever observe preschoolers at war? I wonder . . .

O Lord, so many times I just have to be right. Let me learn to live in love and peace, leaving my good in Your capable hands. In Jesus' name, amen.

A Balanced Life

Keep your mind on Jesus. . . . Then you won't get discouraged and give up (Hebrews 12:3, *Contemporary English Version*).

Scripture: **Hebrews 12:1-12**
Song: **"Turn Your Eyes Upon Jesus"**

Amber Trotter knows what it means to run the race and keep her eyes on the goal. She also knows how great it feels to win. At 17 years of age she won the Foot Locker® Cross Country Championships National Title in 2001, smashing the previous time record. She had tried soccer, basketball, and swimming, but nothing matched the joy she felt while running. "It doesn't matter if I win by 5 seconds or 40 seconds; it just feels great to win," she said.

The year before, however, an eating disorder had nearly ruined Amber's track career. She lost her enthusiasm for running and dropped out of competition. "I was pretty miserable," she said. Eventually she faced her problem and learned to balance running with the rest of her life. Her physical condition improved, and her career took an upward swing.

As Christians, we learn to keep our lives in balance by following Jesus' example. Although He suffered, He never gave up or lost sight of His goal. Let's focus on Christ who began—and finished—the race.

Without Your help, God, my life is unbalanced. Yet You've promised me a bright future as I choose to serve You. Thank You. In Jesus' name, amen.

July 10–16. **Wesley Sharpe** is a freelance writer and retired school psychologist living in Little River, California.

Life or Death Struggle

Let the mighty strength of the Lord make you strong (Ephesians 6:10, *Contemporary English Version*).

Scripture: **Ephesians 6:10-20**
Song: **"A Mighty Fortress"**

In today's Scripture, Paul speaks to the Ephesian church members. A minority group living in Ephesus, they were surrounded by non-Christian neighbors who worshiped the goddess Artemis. Paul was concerned: would the leaders of the Christian community have the courage to stand firm amid the city's paganism?

Small Christian groups still live and work within cultures of various religions. For instance, less than one percent of China's Pumi tribe is Christian. As one of China's officially recognized minority groups, most of the 38,000 Pumi practice a mix of polytheism, animism, ancestral worship, and Buddhism. To survive, Pumi Christians use every God-given piece of armor available to them as they seek to reach out to their neighbors with Christ's love. A significant breakthrough came in July, 2004, when six Pumi became Christians. "They're the firstfruits of a historic event," said Christians working with the tribe.

All of us believers walk a fine line in our witness. We must be strong *against* Satan but also courageously *for* the ones in his grasp. Only by God's mighty strength can we hope to move forward without stumbling.

Dear God, nothing is sure except Your eternal promises. Teach me to trust You as my fortress, my "bulwark never failing." In Christ's name, amen.

Healthy, Helping Religion

Religion that pleases God the Father must be pure and spotless. You must help needy orphans and widows and not let this world make you evil (James 1:27, *Contemporary English Version*).

Scripture: **James 1:19-27**
Song: **"Here I Am, Lord"**

Author Rick Warren tells us that in China new believers are joyfully welcomed into the church with these words: "Jesus now has a new pair of eyes to see with, new ears to listen with, new hands to help with, and a new heart to love others with." With this statement ringing in their ears, the new Christians eagerly begin serving others.

Closer to home, Julia needs someone to be her eyes, ears, and hands. She lives in an assisted-living home, and on Sundays she rides the church bus to our morning worship service. Her hearing is impaired, and her speech is raspy and difficult to understand. But if you listen carefully, you'll hear her say something like, "Another beautiful Sunday at church. I never want to miss."

Our world is full of fatherless children, collapsed families, men and women trying to regain hope. The question is, how much of our time are we willing to give them? I'm quite sure that if I ask Him today, God will show me how to be His eyes, ears, and hands for someone in need.

Lord, I simply can't respond to every need, but You can show me one way to help. Open my eyes to the possibilities! In Jesus' name, amen.

What's Your Goal?

I have not yet reached my goal, and I am not perfect. But Christ has taken hold of me. So I keep on running and struggling to take hold of the prize (Philippians 3:12, *Contemporary English Version*).

Scripture: **Philippians 3:12-16**
Song: **"Precious Lord, Take My Hand"**

Recently, a student from the University of California (Davis) claimed to have broken the world record for the longest paper clip chain. In 24 hours he linked 40,000 of the metal clips into a chain stretching 5,340 feet. "I've always wanted to break a world record," the student said. He failed once, ending with a chain so tangled he couldn't measure its length. This time, with the help of friends, he got it right. He broke the previous record in just 12 hours, but he decided to continue and accomplish his personal goal of hooking together a mile-long chain.

Paul the apostle had a goal too: winning the prize of eternal life. Instead of moping in a Roman prison, he wrote about the good news of salvation through Jesus. Paul wasn't sure whether he would be set free or whether he would be executed. But he was certain that he would live with Jesus in Heaven someday, no matter what.

Paul said he tried to forget the past and reach for a future with Christ. That was a good motto for first-century Christians, and it still works for us today.

Lord, You've taken hold of me! No matter the circumstances coming my way today, keep me moving forward in Your will. Through Christ, amen.

A Prize Worth Winning

You know that many runners enter a race, and only one of them wins the prize. So run to win! (1 Corinthians 9:24, *Contemporary English Version*).

Scripture: **1 Corinthians 9:22b-27**
Song: **"Crown Him with Many Crowns"**

In *Time* magazine's 2004 Olympic preview, a headline read "U.S. swimmer is hungry for gold. Will he make Olympic history?" Like many athletes around the world, Michael Phelps trained for the fierce competition, eager to win a gold medal.

The Olympic Games were held as early as 776 B.C., and until the fourth century A.D. spectators came to the Olympics to watch athletes compete. Victorious athletes won prizes that included statues, clothing, money, free meals for life, and a pension plan that could be sold.

Paul, a Roman citizen, may have witnessed the races at a first-century stadium; he was certainly familiar with the hard training necessary to win. His challenge to the Corinthians was, "Run to win. All good athletes train hard. They do it for a gold medal that tarnishes and fades. You're after one that's gold eternally" (1 Corinthians 9:24, 25, *The Message*). Paul wanted the Christians in Corinth to go for the gold, and to live lives that would win them an everlasting crown. That challenge still stands. And if we are faithful, our reward will be a crown that lasts forever.

Wonderful Lord, out of gratitude for Your work of salvation, I freely offer You my best in my kingdom work today. In Jesus' name I pray. Amen.

Warning: Deadly Virus

God was not pleased with most of them. . . . Do not be idol-aters, as some of them were (1 Corinthians 10:5, 7 *New International Version*).

Scripture: **1 Corinthians 10:1-7**
Song: **"Change My Heart, O God"**

Recently a computer virus named the Blaster Worm attacked my computer. I lost data, my e-mail service was interrupted, and the computer was barely functioning when I finally took it to the repair shop. I learned that several versions of the worm lurked in my computer's files, requiring major repairs. Although I'd read virus warnings posted on the Internet, I had failed to upgrade my protection software, which could have squished that worm.

Paul knew that idol worship, a deadly virus, had attacked the Israelites of old. Although God's people had once trekked under a guiding pillar-cloud, walked across a sea on dry land—and even received ethical direction written in stone—they continued to disobey God. Now the same virus was loose among the Corinthians, and Paul wanted to squelch it.

His warning applies to us too. We have our own idols, all the things that draw our affections away from the Lord Jesus. And like a computer virus, those things must be quarantined and eliminated. Otherwise, might our enthusiasm for God's work trickle to a halt?

God, I truly desire a changed heart. Show me my sin for what it is, and help me to erase the idols that control my life. Thank You in Jesus' name. Amen.

When Temptation Becomes Sin

You are tempted in the same way that everyone else is tempted. But God can be trusted not to let you be tempted too much, and he will show you how to escape from your temptations (1 Corinthians 10:13, *Contemporary English Version*).

Scripture: **1 Corinthians 10:8-13**
Song: **"Trust and Obey"**

Martin Luther said, "You cannot keep birds from flying over your head, but you can keep them from building a nest in your hair." In other words, you can choose not to dwell on the tempting thoughts that assault your mind.

And that's Paul's message to the Corinthians. He wanted them to understand that the Israelites were punished because they *acted* on their temptations, not just because they were tempted. He had outlined the sins committed by Israel, and now he hoped the Corinthians would pay attention to God's warning.

But Paul wasn't sure they could avoid making the same mistakes, so he even gave them a list of ways to defeat temptation: Don't do shameful things, don't stir up discontent, don't grumble, and don't try to reduce God to something you can control.

So next time you're in the clutches of temptation, ask yourself: "What do I *really* want?" Sit with the question. Open your heart. God will show you the way out.

Father, when I face temptation, give me the courage to pause and look up to You. Let me open my heart to the way out—and then rest in Your goodness. In Christ's name I pray. Amen.

Bringing Out the Best

So that you may be able to discern what is best and may be pure and blameless until the day of Christ (Philippians 1:10, *New International Version*).

Scripture: **1 Corinthians 14:6-12**
Song: **"I Love You with the Love of the Lord"**

The last coronation of an English monarch took place on June 2, 1953, at Westminster Abbey. A kneeling Elizabeth II received a sword taken from the altar and handed to her by bishops. Then she heard these words: "Receive this kingly Sword. . . . With it do justice, stop the growth of iniquity, protect the holy church of God, help and defend widows and orphans, restore the things that have gone to decay, maintain the things that are restored, punish and reform what is amiss, and confirm what is in good order; that doing these things you may be glorious in all virtue; and so faithfully serve our Lord Jesus Christ in this life, that you may reign forever with Him in the life which is to come." Imagine if every Christian had a coronation service—a marker experience conveying the sword of truth.

It's already happened. The day you were born again you received the best gift of all—Jesus inside. Now you can be the best. You have Jesus and the sword of truth.

Thank You, Lord, for being so generous with us. And help me never to love the gifts more than the giver. Through Christ I pray. Amen.

July 17–23. **Ron Rose,** a recognized storyteller, writes two subscription-based (free) weekly e-mail newsletters: "FaithMail" and "Out of the Box."

Living So God Looks Good

So whether you eat or drink or whatever you do, do it all for the glory of God (1 Corinthians 10:31, *New International Version*).

Scripture: **1 Timothy 6:13-19**
Song: **"Glorify Thy Name"**

Cerebral palsy had ravaged Robert's body and left him spastic and wheelchair bound, but his heart overflowed with an infectious zest for life. He had severe limitations; he couldn't run and pass a football, he couldn't drive a car, he couldn't even feed himself. But Robert could touch your heart and make you smile.

I met him in college, and he changed my life. It took Robert a little longer to graduate than most of us, but he finally got his diploma. After college this wheel-chaired preacher moved to Lisbon, Portugal. He filled his days rolling around the streets of the city, putting in a good word for Jesus and handing tracts to strangers on the street corners. This man, who found it difficult to talk, knew how to tell people about Jesus. Before long he began teaching college-level classes and eventually was responsible for bringing more than 70 people to the Lord during his six-year stay in Lisbon. He married one of his converts and fathered faithful children.

Robert made God look good. With limited resources, he fought the good fight and lived to glorify God. Along the way, he showed me how to do the same.

Lord, keep me from being so distracted by daily concerns that I forget my primary purpose: to glorify You. In Jesus' name, amen.

Give Those Gifts!

We love because he first loved us (1 John 4:19, *New International Version*).

Scripture: **1 Corinthians 12:1-6**
Song: "Freely, Freely"

The celebrated musical *Les Miserables* tells the story of Jean Valjean. Jean spent 19 years in prison, a slave to the law, condemned for . . . stealing a loaf of bread. Resentment and bitterness made a permanent home in his heart. His life had been reduced to disgrace, and his name replaced with a number—prisoner 24601. Even after his parole, he felt rejected by a graceless society. He wandered the streets, lonely and lost.

Then he came to the bishop of Digne for help. The man of God provided food, shelter, and compassion; but once the bishop was asleep, Jean stole all the silver he could find, and then he ran. Only two silver candlesticks remained in the house.

Jean was quickly captured and, without hope, was headed back to prison. But the bishop changed everything. When the police returned the silver, he claimed that the silver had been a gift to Jean and asked Jean why he had forgotten the candlesticks. Prisoner 24601 was "claimed for God." He was given grace, and the rest of the story is about Jean Valjean *living* that grace, giving what he could, when he could. All God's gifts are meant to be given.

God, sometimes we try to keep Your gifts to ourselves. Forgive me for hoarding what You provide so freely. In Your holy name I pray. Amen.

God Packs the Backpack

We are God's workmanship, created in Christ Jesus to do good works, which God prepared in advance for us to do (Ephesians 2:10, *New International Version*).

Scripture: **1 Corinthians 12:7-11**
Song: **"God Will Make a Way"**

My grandson, Grant, takes his backpack everywhere. He's only 4, but on the way to the car he automatically picks up the backpack and drags it straight to its place, beside his car seat. He's prepared for anything because it seems as if everything is in the backpack.

His mom makes sure he has the right stuff inside. She packs in snacks, toys, books, a change of clothes, games, batteries, stuffed animals, his Bible, a few surprises, shoes, medicine, paper, crayons—and whatever else she believes he may need for the day.

No, he doesn't have to carry it on his back; he just drags it along wherever he goes. He likes it that way. When he walks in our front door, he says, "Hi, Granddad! Wanna see what's in my backpack?" He drags his backpack into the playroom, and we get on the floor to explore.

Here's the thing: God packs our backpacks. The Spirit of God puts in them whatever we need in order to do what He wants done. He uses it to shape us and make us more like Jesus. It's all been prepared in advance.

Lord, any work I do for You can come only from using the tools You've graciously provided. We ourselves are Your work! Help me trust Your Spirit to produce the fruit of good works through me. In Christ's name, amen.

This Is Where I Belong

You are no longer foreigners and aliens, but fellow citizens with God's people and members of God's household (Ephesians 2:19, *New International Version*).

Scripture: **1 Corinthians 12:12-20**
Song: **"Something Beautiful"**

A few years ago at the Seattle Special Olympics, nine contestants, all physically or mentally challenged, assembled at the starting line for the 100-yard dash. The stands were filled with family, friends, and a few news reporters looking for a story.

At the gun the contestants all started out, not exactly in a dash, but with determination. A little more than halfway down the track, one of the young runners stumbled, lost control, and rolled over a couple times. When he came to a stop, he curled up into a ball and began crying. The other eight runners, all of whom were ahead of the boy, heard him crying, stopped, and looked back at him. Then, to the amazement of the crowd, they all turned around and went back—every one of them.

One girl with Down's syndrome bent down and kissed the fallen runner, saying, "This will make it better." When the young man got up, all nine contestants linked arms and walked to the finish line. One of the kids later said, "He's our friend; you always help your friends."

Those kids found the secret to belonging!

Lord, it feels so good to know that I belong to You. Help us learn how to belong to each other as well. I pray in Christ's name. Amen.

We Really Need Each Other

If one part suffers, every part suffers with it; if one part is honored, every part rejoices with it (1 Corinthians 12:26, *New International Version*).

Scripture: **1 Corinthians 12:21-26**
Song: **"Getting Used to the Family of God"**

As the thunder and lightning crashed all around him, the boy ran to his dad crying, "Daddy, Daddy, I'm afraid!" Together they walked back into the bedroom and sat down on the bed. The little boy sobbed as he told his dad about the terrible thunder and lightning.

Dad said, "Now, son, remember: any time you're afraid, it's time to talk to God. Tell him about your fear and about how tough it is, and He will help you with it. Can you do that, son?"

"I think so," the little boy replied. So, together they prayed that God would help him with his fear. And after a bit, everything seemed fine. The little boy cuddled back into bed, Dad kissed him goodnight, and then headed back to the living room. But without warning, lightning and thunder struck again, and the youngster made a bee-line straight for Dad. He jumped up into Dad's lap without saying a word. "I thought we talked to God about this," said Dad.

"I know, Dad, but I just want somebody with skin on!"

Lord, we really need each other. Thank You for sending me people who become Your skin for me at just the right time. I am so thankful. In Jesus' name, amen.

One of a Kind, with Purpose

Let the peace of Christ rule in your hearts, since as members of one body you were called to peace. And be thankful (Colossians 3:15, *New International Version*).

Scripture: **1 Corinthians 12:27-31**
Song: **"Thank You, Lord"**

I remember experiencing my first West Texas thunderstorm. The lightning strikes and thunder rolls were spectacular. Everything else in my life seemed to stand still until the storm passed.

While we were living in Lubbock, Texas, I heard of a young girl who also was captivated by thunderstorms. Once the thunder and lightning got close enough to fill the sky, she ran to the living room and pulled back the drapes. She stood there frozen in time, smiling at the sky. When her mother walked past the doorway, she saw her little girl standing in front of the big picture window, staring into the heavens.

"Honey," she cried, "get away from the window. Aren't you afraid?" Just at that moment a thunderous flash of lightning filled the sky and rattled the walls. "No, I'm not afraid. God's taking my picture!"

God is still taking pictures, and when He does, He gets all of us together so we can say "cheese." We may be different, but when we are together, it's worth a picture.

God, why are we so forgetful? We know we are different, with various gifts and personalities, but we forget how special it is when we all get together. Do whatever is necessary to make us one! In Christ I pray. Amen.

A Better Purpose

God did not send his Son into the world to condemn the world, but to save the world through him (John 3:17, *New International Version*).

Scripture: **John 3:16-21**
Song: **"Bind Our Hearts with One Great Purpose"**

Our meeting with the new store manager for W. T. Grant concerned all of us—especially me. I had been the first employee hired when Grants decided to build this newest store in Reedley, California—as a test case; we were an experiment.

Apprehension filled the room as Mr. Akins walked in. Business was slow, and our jobs were on the line. Did Grants plan to cut their losses, lay off half the employees, or simply close the store? None of us knew what to expect.

The new manager looked around the room, smiled, and then told us his plan. He had come to save our jobs and the company, but he needed our help, our sacrificial help. With a show of hands, we gladly pledged our support.

Jesus also came to save lives, not condemn them to a horrible fate. Salvation is God's divine plan for the world, but He calls for our help in sharing the good news. When we work together as believers, we show others that God's true purpose is salvation, not condemnation.

Most precious God, fill me with Your love that I might tell my friends why Jesus was sent into the world. In His name, amen.

July 24–30. **Charles Harrel** has been a minister for more than 30 years. He currently directs His Place Outreach in Portland, Oregon.

Inseparable Love

Who shall separate us from the love of Christ? Shall trouble or hardship or persecution or famine or nakedness or danger or sword? (Romans 8:35, *New International Version*).

Scripture: **Romans 8:31-39**
Song: **"O Love That Will Not Let Me Go"**

Heather's stomach twisted in knots as she punched numbers into the phone. The news she bore unsettled her, and being unmarried only made it harder. *How will I explain this to my parents?*

Maybe it was too early to call; she could hang up now. No, she needed to tell them this morning. They had to know the truth: she was pregnant.

Tears were running down her cheeks by the time the phone was answered. "Hi Dad, can I come over and talk? It's kind of important. There's this problem. . . . I hope that you and Mom will still love me."

Her father's reply filled her with hope: "Heather, nothing you've done will ever stop us from loving you."

Children often wonder whether parents will quit loving them because of their troubles. In fact, we love them more. God feels the same about His children—and how hard it must be for Him to watch us in our self-destructive ways! Romans mentions many things that might be deemed powerful enough to separate us from God's love, but Christ allows none of them. His love remains.

Lord, You came not for the righteous, but for sinners. Here I am, a prime candidate. I rest confidently in Your love. Through Christ, amen.

One of *Them?*

By this all men will know that you are my disciples, if you love one another (John 13:35, *New International Version*).

Scripture: **John 13:31-35**
Song: **"Lord, Lay Some Soul upon My Heart"**

It was after midnight when I slipped out the side door of my apartment. I could hear someone crying. As assistant manager of the Lassam Terrace, it was my duty to check out disturbances on the premises. I soon discovered the reason for all the noise: a man stumbling across the street. He stopped for a moment and leaned against the mailboxes, using them for support. He looked sick and lost, another patron from the tavern up the road.

The man never asked for a handout. He only wanted to get home and needed directions to the nearest tram station. But that was miles away, and he'd never reach it on foot—not with the temperatures near freezing.

As I drove Mike home, we talked. He was shocked that I wanted to help him. Most people just gave him a few bucks and told him to move along. So he asked me, "Are you one of them—you know—them Christians?" I nodded. "I knew it," he said. "You people are different."

That made me think. People who attend my church know I am a follower of Jesus. But I wish my neighbors knew it too. When we love others, we demonstrate to the world that we are—you know—one of *them.*

Lord, today let me show, with acts of love, who owns my heart. Please guide me in this endeavor. In Christ's name I pray. Amen.

Outshine the Darkness

The night is nearly over; the day is almost here. So let us put aside the deeds of darkness and put on the armor of light (Romans 13:12, *New International Version*).

Scripture: **Romans 13:8-14**
Song: **"Soldiers of Christ, Arise"**

"You lose again, General!" My cousin's choice of words annoyed me. He knew how to rub it in. John and I were playing a strategy game with military figures, known as war gaming. It's a popular hobby—educational and entertaining. After painting tiny lead soldiers for months, we brought them together to show our handiwork and fight a battle. We used historical settings for our armies and preferred the ancient days of swords and armor.

My army had suffered a horrible defeat that day. I felt I was a good strategist, so I asked John why I kept losing. He told me I had used the wrong armor: "The right armor protects the warrior while equipping him for victory."

As Christians, we need the right armor as well. Since we face an enemy who uses the deeds of darkness, we should put on the armor of light—Jesus Christ. We arm ourselves for battle by praying, knowing the truth of God's Word, and bearing our faith as a mighty shield. Armored in this fashion, we outshine the darkness.

Dear Father, dress me each morning with the right armor. Remind me that the battle is not won by my own efforts or strategies, but by using the unseen armor of light. May it give light to my path and victory to my day. I pray through my mighty deliverer, Jesus. Amen.

Actions Speak Louder

Dear children, let us not love with words or tongue but with actions and in truth (1 John 3:18, *New International Version*).

Scripture: **1 John 3:11-18**
Song: "Love Found a Way"

I forget how it all started. It may have begun as a misunderstanding, a disagreement, or an unresolved problem. One thing seemed certain, though: I'd allowed an emotional hurt to fester in our marriage, and now it had surfaced.

My wife and I loved each other, yet neither of us knew how to end this upsetting conflict. Although I cared and tried to help, nothing I said improved the situation. We were both worn out and frustrated. I left the room to offer a silent prayer and reflect for a moment when a thought came to mind. Maybe I could *show* her how I felt.

Throwing a bath towel over my shoulders, I returned to our bedroom carrying a bowl of water. She looked bewildered and a bit annoyed. Nevertheless, I told her one more time that I was sorry and that I truly loved her. Then, kneeling in front of her chair, I asked, "Laura, may I wash your feet?"

When our actions speak louder than our words, so will our love. Truthful actions add clarity to love and the freedom to express it.

Dearest Lord, when words are not enough, show me how to communicate my love with actions that bring healing. May these actions always reveal my true feelings and intentions. In the name of Jesus I pray. Amen.

Whole Bunch of Nothing

If I have the gift of prophecy and can fathom all mysteries and all knowledge, and if I have a faith that can move mountains, but have not love, I am nothing (1 Corinthians 13:2, *New International Version*).

Scripture: **1 Corinthians 13:1-7**
Song: **"Love, Wonderful Love"**

A colorful brochure in the mail drew my attention. The cover page promised to turn everyone who took the three-day seminar on ministry gifts into supernatural believers. When the seminar ended, we'd have the power to heal the sick, speak as prophets, perform miracles, understand all the mysteries of God, and . . . (it was a long list).

The last benefit, outlined in bold print, included "inheriting the wealth of the nations." People would give us their money because we had such great faith. Awesome! But something was missing—not one word about love. I tossed the brochure in my "circular file."

Without love, we have nothing. All of our faith and abilities count as nothing when love is missing. Even our greatest sacrifices or acts of benevolence mean nothing without love. Nor can any of our spiritual gifts redeem such a sad situation. However, when love becomes our motivation, even the slightest effort in Christ can make an eternal difference.

Loving Lord, I realize a day will come when You examine everything I've said or done in this life. That day will reveal my greatest efforts, and I hope love will have motivated them. In Jesus name I pray. Amen.

Legacy of Love

Love never fails. But where there are prophecies, they will cease; where there are tongues, they will be stilled; where there is knowledge, it will pass away (1 Corinthians 13:8, *New International Version*).

Scripture: **1 Corinthians 13:8-13**
Song: **"Unfailing Love"**

Mom died a few years ago. On that day, the hardest morning of my life, I not only lost my last surviving parent, I lost my best friend. The sorrow still overwhelms me.

I had watched helplessly as her health declined. After she fell and shattered her leg and hip, she needed to use a walker for support. A pinched nerve in her back complicated matters and limited her to short trips. Next, the veins in her retinas ruptured, and she became legally blind. Then came heart failure.

Mom always had such energy as she tirelessly took care of her family; nothing seemed to slow her down. So it broke my heart to see her slip away, month after month. One thing in her life, however, never failed: her love.

The Bible tells us that most things in life will cease, be stilled, or simply pass away. That is not so with love. Love never weakens, nor does it ever fail. It continues forever. Just as Jesus did at the cross, my mom gave the greatest and most precious thing of all: a legacy of love.

Dear God, one day I hope to leave the same unfailing legacy of love to my own children. Prepare me in the present day for that day. In the name of the Father, the Son, and the Holy Spirit, I pray. Amen.

Don't Wait to Forgive

Forgive us our sins, just as we have forgiven those who have sinned against us (Matthew 6:12, *The Living Bible*).

Scripture: **Matthew 6:9-15**
Song: **"Whiter Than Snow"**

As a child living in the North, I loved the new-fallen snow: white, fresh, clean, and beautiful. But after a short time it collected dirt and was no longer white and beautiful. We called it slush, a dirty brown mess.

Our lives, just like the snow, collect a dirt we call sin. We do things we know we shouldn't do, and we need to ask forgiveness and make a fresh start. God gave us the Lord's Prayer to help us prepare for that fresh start. (For example, try praying verse 12 at the beginning of each new morning. What a great way to head into the day!)

Perhaps you know God well enough to know that He forgives your sins, freely, through the work of Christ. But do you tie that blessed forgiveness to your willingness to forgive others? Whether or not there is a direct cause-and-effect relationship—we can leave that to the theologians—there is obviously some kind of tie-in between forgiving and being forgiven. So why take a chance on holding a grudge? Why wait around while keeping your neighbor on the hook? Do the right thing. Forgive!

Heavenly Father, please give me the grace to forgive others as You have forgiven my own faults and failures. Thank You in Christ's name. Amen.

July 31. **Mary Shaw** is an Army veteran of World War II now living in Orlando, Florida. She has three great-granddaughters.

DEVOTIONS®

***B*e sober, be vigilant; because your adversary the devil, as a roaring lion, walketh about, seeking whom he may devour.**

—1 Peter 5:8

AUGUST

Photo © Digital Vision

Gary Allen, editor

Mercy for Every Slave

Should you not also have had mercy on your fellow-slave, even as I had mercy on you? (Matthew 18:33, *New American Standard Bible*).

Scripture: **Matthew 18:21-35**
Song: **"Amazing Grace"**

The mother of a little boy named John taught him to pray and filled his mind with Scripture. But when John was about 7, his mother died, and John's life became a disaster. At age 11 he joined his evil sea captain father and got involved with the African slave trade.

Eventually, a close brush with death brought John the remembrance of his mother's teachings. He repented, felt called to preach, and began writing hymns. In fact, John Newton wrote the beloved hymn "Amazing Grace," which is his life's testimony.

John never forgot God's goodness to him. Shortly before his death, he said, "My memory is nearly gone, but I remember two things: I am a great sinner, and God is a great Savior." Knowing the boundless, infinite grace of God makes forgiving others 490 times seem much less daunting, doesn't it? We can do it. We *must* do it.

Dear Heavenly Father, when I think of all You have forgiven in my life, my heart reaches out to those who seek my mercy. In light of Your love, how could I refuse them? I pray this prayer in the name of Jesus, my merciful Savior and Lord. Amen.

August 1–6. **Mary Shaw** is an Army veteran of World War II now living in Orlando, Florida. She has three great-granddaughters.

There You Have It!

I tell you, whatever you ask for in prayer, believe that you have received it, and it will be yours (Mark 11:24, *New International Version*).

Scripture: **Mark 11:20-25**
Song: **"Teach Me to Pray"**

What is your definition of *prayer?* Is it simply talking to God? I've found it to be much more: it means learning to listen, too, and developing a love relationship with one who will become your best friend.

The disciples asked Jesus to teach them to pray. They wanted to know how to pray with power, how to pray so that they would be ushered into the throne room of God. When Jesus went back to Heaven, He gave us a teacher to help us to pray in the same way—God the Holy Spirit.

What a privilege! I spent 26 years in a ministry founded on prayer. Everything in the day's activities was surrounded with prayer; however, as I continue studying the Bible, I discover I still have much to learn. I am thankful the Spirit is a good teacher and always there to nudge me and teach me, for He knows God's will and wants me to know it as well.

When I am walking close to the Lord, talking and listening, developing the relationship, then my askings grow closer and closer to what God has always wanted for me. Of course, then, whatever I ask is already mine.

Almighty God, keep me close to Your will by keeping me ever close to Your heart. Through Christ I pray. Amen.

Perfect Peace

Let the peace of God rule in your hearts, to the which also ye are called in one body; and be thankful (Colossians 3:15).

Scripture: **Colossians 3:12-17**
Song: **"Sweet Peace, the Gift of God's Love"**

Our family consisted of Mother and Dad, plus seven boys and two girls. This meant many school and work lunch pails to pack each day. One of my responsibilities was to bake a cake for those lunch pails. I loved reading the cookbooks to see if I had all the necessary ingredients. It always amazed me to see that I could follow the instructions and end up with a beautiful, tasty dessert.

Now that I'm older, I think life is like finding a recipe and making a wonderful cake. It takes a lot of different ingredients, but when Bible instructions are followed, a beautiful life comes to pass. These are some of the necessary ingredients: a tender heart, mercy and kindness, a forgiving spirit, acts of love, and a thankful heart.

Today peace is the heart cry heard around the world. Somehow, the necessary ingredients have been forgotten, misplaced, hidden from view. Yet Christ is our prince of peace. And while we may or may not see that translated into peace among the nations on earth, we ought to see it in His body, the church. That will happen when each of us invites Him to rule in our hearts. That is the recipe for unity and fruitfulness among us in the body of Christ.

Dear God, thank You for the peace that rules in my heart. I pray for peace in the body of Christ and in a troubled world as well. In Jesus' name, amen.

Not So Easy: Reconciling

A further reason for forgiveness is to keep from being outsmarted by Satan; for we know what he is trying to do (2 Corinthians 2:11, *The Living Bible*).

Scripture: **2 Corinthians 2:5-11**
Song: **"O, for a Thousand Tongues to Sing"**

How would you describe the tongue? I would say it is a fleshy muscle in the mouth that helps you form words. It is little, boneless and weak, but it can crush and kill the spirit. It can be slow to speak or swift as a deer. It is small but powerful and can sing praises to God or utter all forms of profanity. The Bible compares the tongue to a raging forest fire.

The mouth and that little tongue can cause a lot of trouble—trouble that can quickly spread to many people before it gets stopped. Perhaps that's the reason the tongue is one of Satan's favorite tools. He can use it to cause misunderstandings and quarrels, spreading guilt and blame on the winds. Then he stands in the way of true forgiveness and the freedom it brings.

Most scholars identify the situation Paul addresses in this text with the issue in 1 Corinthians 5. Still, Paul could say of the offender: "Forgive him, comfort him, and . . . confirm your love towards him." If Paul could offer reconciliation in Corinth, then surely I can seek forgiveness and reconciliation for those who have offended me with thoughtless or unkind remarks.

Holy Father, help me to remember Your example of forgiving and forgetting. Fill my heart with love, I pray, in Jesus' name. Amen.

Letters of Encouragement

I have great confidence in you; I take great pride in you. I am greatly encouraged; in all our troubles my joy knows no bounds (2 Corinthians 7:4, *New International Version*).

Scripture: **2 Corinthians 7:2-7**
Song: **"Rejoice, Ye Pure in Heart"**

I met Pat on one of my many trips from Missouri to New Jersey. Pat became my mentor and later my prayer partner even though we lived miles apart and had only recently met. We agreed we would pray for each other every evening at 7 o'clock, which established a special bond between us. We also corresponded regularly, and she always wrote about someone we both knew, the Lord Jesus Christ.

Pat had a physical disability: she had only one lung. Every breath and every step she took were painful. Yet she never complained. She lived by herself, took care of her everyday needs, and spent much time in prayer along with writing letters of encouragement.

Her letters were a great inspiration—and challenge—to me, just as Paul's letter to his friends at Corinth must have been. Most Bible students believe Paul had some kind of disability too. This, coupled with my experience of Pat, tells me that God will use anyone who is open to spreading His love, joy, and encouragement.

I'd like to be one of those persons.

Father, thanks for Your gift of joy. And may my joy be contagious, spreading encouragement to each person I meet today. In Jesus' name, amen.

God Used Sorrow

Your sorrow led you to repentance. For you became sorrowful as God intended and so were not harmed in any way by us. Godly sorrow brings repentance that leads to salvation and leaves no regret, but worldly sorrow brings death (2 Corinthians 7:9, 10, *New International Version*).

Scripture: **2 Corinthians 7:8-16**
Song: **"Thank You, Lord"**

After 12 years of marriage and two children, my husband asked for a divorce. Having been raised as a churchgoer, I'd thought I was a Christian. But now when I truly needed God, where was He?

I looked in all the wrong places, attempting to recover some happiness, when a friend asked if I'd like to read the book *Beyond Our Selves* by Catherine Marshall. One night home alone in bed, reading that book, I discovered I had never really opened my heart to Christ. I slipped out of bed and unto my knees, where I prayed, confessed my sin, and invited Jesus to come into my life.

The very next morning the desire for my old lifestyle was gone; my greatest sorrow had led to my greatest joy. Forty years later, joy is still with me as I look forward to the day when God will call me home.

The apostle Paul showed the Corinthian believers how their sorrows could lead to salvation. I know it's true; it happened to me.

Precious God, thank You for leading me, even by the pathway of sorrow, to the waters of baptism. Praise You for eternal life! In Jesus' name, amen.

The Change Purse

He also saw a poor widow put in two very small copper coins (Luke 21:2, *New International Version*).

Scripture: **Luke 20:45–21:4**
Song: **"Give of Your Best to the Master"**

We never had a lot of money while I was growing up, but my mom was always faithful about giving at church. Yet when I was a teenager, I was embarrassed when she'd empty the contents of her change purse into the plate.

Now I can see Mom in light of the widow in Luke. They both gave, believing that God would take care of them. Even though I grew up observing Mom's faithfulness and experiencing God's care of our family, I still had to learn these things for myself as an adult.

One thing I do know: how else can we learn to depend on God unless we offer all that we have? Clearly, this requires more than giving money. My oldest daughter told me she wanted to be a missionary. As hard as it was for me to accept this, knowing the difficulties and hardships she'd likely face, I had to give her up to God so that His will could be done. We haven't crossed that bridge yet, but I am trying to prepare myself, so that if God wants, I will be able to give up even my children.

Lord, help me give whatever You want of me, whether money, time, or family members for difficult service. And remind me of the heavenly reward— a treasure far outweighing earthly sacrifices. In Christ's name, amen.

August 7, 8, 10–13. **Ruth O'Neil** is a wife and the mother of three children. She lives in Lynchburg, Virginia, staying busy with freelance writing and homeschooling.

What Are *You* Doing?

The Grecian Jews among them complained against the Hebraic Jews because their widows were being overlooked in the daily distribution of food (Acts 6:1, *New International Version*).

Scripture: **Acts 6:1-6**
Song: **"Be Glorified"**

Ever complain about the people in your church who "never do anything around here"? I confess. While my plate is full trying to keep up with five or six different duties, I see others who I think could pick up some of the slack. Yet warming the pew seems to be their sole function! Of course, it's not for me to determine who is being fruitful in the kingdom and who isn't. Outward appearances can be quite deceiving.

Anyway, I was fussing to one of my friends about some of the women who could surely take a turn in the nursery with me. My friend pointed out that these ladies did participate in the work of the church, but they worked in ways that weren't necessarily visible. Of all people, I should have recognized that because it's the way I myself like to work: behind the scenes, with no one knowing.

I had to ask forgiveness, not only for gossiping about ladies in my church family but also for not taking care of my own responsibilities in the meantime. Instead of complaining, I could have been working.

Father, help me keep my eyes on the tasks You've set before me rather than looking to see how You're working with others. I pray through Christ, amen.

August 9

Different Gifts for Different Service

But each man has his own gift from God; one has this gift, another has that (1 Corinthians 7:7, *New International Version*).

Scripture: **Romans 12:3-8**
Song: **"The Family of God"**

My husband's computer desktop is covered with various software applications. I asked him why it was necessary to have such a variety of programs. He replied, "Well, dear, each of these is used for a different purpose. A word processing program is useful to writers. Those interested in visual results use graphics. Businesses take advantage of spreadsheets."

The Lord created us and equips us with spiritual gifts that He thinks are best. He gave the Holy Spirit to lead us in service and sends us the opportunities in order to use our special gifts for Him.

Paul wrote in Ephesians 1:7 *(NIV)* that God gave "according to the riches of His grace." He did not say "out of his riches," which would be like a millionaire putting a dollar in the offering plate. *According to* means in proportion to, and God's proportionate provisions and gifts come without measure.

I want to use to the fullest the gifts God has given me!

Dear heavenly Father, thank you for the talents and abilities You have given me. I pray that I will recognize and use each one in the way that You have determined I should. In Jesus' name, amen.

August 9. **Jean Sours Kindegran** lives in Polk City, Florida. She has been published in numerous Christian publications.

Working Hard

Therefore, my dear brothers, stand firm. Let nothing move you. Always give yourselves fully to the work of the Lord, because you know that your labor in the Lord is not in vain (1 Corinthians 15:58, *New International Version*).

Scripture: **1 Corinthians 15:58–16:4**
Song: **"Take My Life, and Let It Be"**

My husband has the difficult task of teaching children of various ages at church. In different classes he has age 3 right up through high school youth. On Sunday evenings, often a bit discouraged, he'll ask me, "Do you think they were listening?"

"Of course they were," I say. "Sometimes you don't think kids are listening at all, but they still pick up what you're saying—and what you're modeling for them."

The principle holds for virtually any ministry. Yes, it can be difficult to keep working when we don't see tangible fruits of our labor after long periods of time. But the Scripture tells us: "Stand firm."

It simply means that, whatever you do as a ministry, *don't stop!* Pray for yourself and your friends in every work they are doing in the kingdom. God is the one who empowers You, and He is the one who guarantees results, whether seen and rewarded here . . . or *there.*

Dear God, some days I feel as if I can't go any farther in this ministry. But help me recognize that the work is the "work of the Lord." Assure me, deep in my heart, that no effort carried out through Your Spirit is ever in vain. Through my Lord Jesus Christ I pray. Amen.

Obviously?

The acts of the sinful nature are obvious: sexual immorality, impurity and debauchery (Galatians 5:19, *New International Version*).

Scripture: **Galatians 5:16-26**
Song: **"O Be Careful Little Eyes"**

One day I happened to watch some cartoons with my daughter. I was shocked. The values coming through were hardly what I wanted for my little girl. Right then and there I prayed that God would open my eyes and ears and help me see when something on TV wasn't appropriate for my children to watch.

And were my eyes ever opened! It came to a point where I hardly wanted to turn on the TV at all.

Television producers have always tested society's tolerance, venturing little by little beyond accepted norms to redraw the lines of acceptability. But sometimes they go way over the line. By now, worldly values—and "the acts of the sinful nature"—pervade so much of what our kids see and hear. And we adults so often remain blissfully unaware. But this is not the day of *Leave It to Beaver* and *Ozzie and Harriet* anymore. Impurity, immorality, and debauchery—have you noticed that these are the standard lifestyles coming through in most sitcoms?

God has given us clear instructions on what is good and what isn't. Let's make sure this remains obvious.

Father, make me so sensitive to the acts of the sinful nature that I can't ignore their subtle workings in my culture. Help me to stand and protect myself and my family. In the name of our pure and holy Savior, amen.

Whole-Life Giving

I testify that they gave as much as they were able, and even beyond their ability. Entirely on their own . . . (2 Corinthians 8:3, *New International Version*).

Scripture: **2 Corinthians 8:1-7**
Song: **"His Eye Is on the Sparrow"**

Friends of ours were starting a church. They had little money, though, and Shelly was trying to save by gardening. That year the weather was horrible, and most gardens were producing next to nothing. Except for Shelly's garden. It was beautiful, filled with luscious veggies. As little food as they had, she shared her vegetables—and was happy to do so.

We hear much about giving our money, but I believe God calls us to give of our whole lives. For example, when God calls us to pray, we need to stop what we're doing and lift our hearts to the Lord. Sometimes God calls us to give our time, our talents, or our service in a special way to someone in need. At other times we help by just being there for a person.

You may not have any idea what people around you are going through, but God does. Giving even the smallest offerings of help and kindness can mean so much. But it is actually beyond our ability to keep doing so with a cheerful heart. That can only be the work of the Spirit within us.

Lord, help me see the needy around me and offer my whole self to You, in service to them. In the name of Christ, the Lord and servant of all, amen.

Complete This: *Be* There!

Now finish the work, so that your eager willingness to do it may be matched by your completion of it, according to your means (2 Corinthians 8:11, *New International Version*).

Scripture: **2 Corinthians 8:8-15**
Song: **"Give Them All to Jesus"**

I am definitely a starter of projects, not a finisher. I have more dresses lying almost-completed in a basket in my sewing room than my girls actually have hanging in their closets. Even if I did finish the dresses, it has been so long since I cut them out that they wouldn't fit anybody now!

Sadly, I seem to be this way about everything, even projects I begin for God. I like to think it's just a sign of the times: Our society is so busy today that it's hard for any of us to avoid the constant distractions—coming from the cell phone, TV, Internet, radio—that keep us from completing even the smallest of tasks.

But who said it would be easy to follow the Lord? And how "eager" am I for the work of God? Busyness is, indeed, a sign of our times. But then I consider the words of Martin Luther: "Work, work, from morning until late at night. In fact, I have so much to do that I shall have to spend the first three hours in prayer." Perhaps the first unfinished project for any Christian to tackle is to pick up the stillness once again and just *be* in God's presence.

Lord, You know we all are busy; let me never get so busy that I neglect the sweet fellowship with You. Remind me that in Your strength all things necessary will be completed. In Christ's precious name I pray, amen.

See . . . and *Do?*

Temptation is the pull of man's own evil thoughts and wishes (James 1:14, *The Living Bible*).

Scripture: **James 1:12-17**
Song: **"Dare to Be a Daniel"**

It's a familiar game and can be great fun—the tug-of-war contest. No company picnic or church outing seems to be complete without it.

Playing tug-of-war can start at a very early age. Try taking a favorite toy from a toddler and see what a struggle you'll have on your hands. This is especially so if the toy has fallen on the ground and you know it should be cleaned before being played with again. And what if the child has hold of an object he or she definitely shouldn't have? Naturally, this makes the tugging even more enthusiastic because the thing desired is so enticingly naughty.

But don't we adults react similarly? We're free to choose what is right and good. But the questionable things, just beyond our moral boundaries, seem to beckon, and we grab ahold tightly. A popular TV character from the 1970s used to say: "The devil made me do it." Perhaps it would be more accurate to say, "The devil let me *see* it." I chose, though, what to do next.

Precious Lord, *sometimes I really do want what I shouldn't have. So help me today to relax my grip on the things that can only lead to my unhappiness. In Jesus' name I pray, amen.*

August 14–20. **Jimmie Oliver Fleming** of Chester, Virginia, regularly contributes devotionals to various periodicals. She also enjoys playing the piano at church.

Repayment? Impossible!

If you lend to those from whom you expect repayment, what credit is that to you? (Luke 6:34, *New International Version*).

Scripture: **Luke 6:32-38**
Song: **"Jesus Paid It All"**

Have you ever been summoned for jury duty? If so, you're familiar with the steps involved in a jury selection process. After hearing information about a particular case scheduled for trial, you're asked certain questions that will reveal the real you. Whether you are chosen will depend on your answers.

How often Jesus asked questions in order to reveal hearts! In today's verse, the basic question is whether you can love your enemies. For example, does anyone owe you money? What if that individual refuses to pay you back?

As the lender, I may write it off in my mind as a bad debt and vow never to be duped by that person again. But I'd better look out! What does the Scripture say? If we are to be true children of God, we must be willing to take an extra step: lend without expecting to get anything back.

Yes, that's radical. But it seems less so when I ask myself one more important question: can I ever repay the debt Jesus paid for me?

Dear Lord and Master, please help me follow Your ways in all areas of my life. Let me hear the questions You ask as the wisdom I need. Take control of all I am and have, for I owe You everything. In the name of Jesus, Lord and Savior of all, I pray. Amen.

Reigning at the Center

Take care! Don't do your good deeds publicly, to be admired, for then you will lose the reward from your Father in heaven (Matthew 6:1, *The Living Bible*).

Scripture: **Matthew 6:1-6**
Song: **"To God Be the Glory"**

Think about the phone calls you've received in the previous 24 hours. At least one of them likely asked for your financial support. You've probably also received various mailings asking for money. Tomorrow, similar opportunities will come again.

Giving is the one thing you'll always have a second chance to do. In fact, through your will, you can give even in death. However, God is concerned with our giving while we're here on earth. Notice the similarity in the spelling of the two words—*giving* and *living*. Be aware also that you make a profound statement about your character in the way you give. Today's verse draws a distinction between those who give in order to be admired and those who give because it's the right thing to do. Notice who receives a lasting reward.

Is this the reason some people choose to make anonymous donations to particular charities and organizations? Perhaps they don't want to be guilty of starting an admiration society with themselves at the center—the place where God alone must reign.

Father, what good can I do, really, without Your power providing the means? Praise to You, in Jesus' name! Amen.

By Way of the Giver

I am sure that when I come the Lord will give me a great blessing for you (Romans 15:29, *The Living Bible*).

Scripture: **Romans 15:25-29**
Song: **"It Pays to Serve Jesus"**

Have you ever forgotten to say a blessing before a meal? In some circles you might be accused of spiritual amnesia. In other circles (which perhaps include Mother and Father and a host of visiting relatives), this would be "guaranteed" to never happen again.

You may have made guarantees of your own, such as the apostle Paul did when he told the church members that the Lord would surely provide them with a blessing. Of course, God is the source of all blessings. Even when we say a blessing before a meal, we are only giving back, with our thankfulness, what God has already given.

Christians in Macedonia and Achaia had received a blessing from the Jewish Christians in Jerusalem because the news about Christ came to these Gentiles from the church of Jerusalem. After hearing that some of the people in the Jerusalem church were going through hard times, those at Macedonia and Achaia were happy to give financial aid to them. Here again, as in every circumstance, giving proceeds ultimately only from the hand of the great giver.

Father, I love You because You first loved us. And I can give only because You first gave. Thank You especially for the gift of Your Son, Jesus, in whose name I pray. Amen.

Encouraging Reminders

I realize that I really don't even need to mention this to you, about helping God's people. For I know how eager you are to do it (2 Corinthians 9:1, 2, *The Living Bible*).

Scripture: **2 Corinthians 9:1-5**
Song: **"Count on Me"**

Fall is approaching. Perhaps it's that time of year for you to complete certain home projects you've delayed. What has held you back so far? Do you remember? Was it the hot summer weather? Your financial situation? Or were you simply not motivated enough to follow through on your plans? Well, consider this an encouraging reminder. Hopefully, it will give you the motivation to spring into action.

Our lack of action, of course, can affect others. Paul pointed this out in his letter to the Corinthian church. He reminded the Christians there to prepare for his visit by completing the offering they had started during the previous year. Paul also reminded those believers of how their enthusiasm in giving had influenced other churches.

In light of all the good that can come from being a worthy example, we might assume we never need a reminder to keep our excellent behaviors flowing. But we're human. As Paul encouraged his friends to keep keeping on, let's do the same for our brothers and sisters in Christ today.

O God, help me follow through on my commitments, knowing the good that comes from doing what I have said I would do—and from letting others observe my commitment. In Jesus' name, amen.

August 19

Planting, Reaping, and Giving

Whoever sows generously will also reap generously. Each man should give what he has decided in his heart to give, not reluctantly or under compulsion, for God loves a cheerful giver (2 Corinthians 9:6, 7, *New International Version*).

Scripture: **2 Corinthians 9:6-10**
Song: **"Pass It On"**

"I guess at his age he should be slowing down, but he's not going to do it. And to tell the truth, I should be slowing down, too, but I'm not."

I'd heard these words from my friend Barbara before, and I also knew that they were true. She and her husband Jerry weren't slowing down at all. Even though they were in their 70s, no one could guess it from their active lifestyles.

One thing that kept them so active was the large vegetable garden they planted each year. It wasn't just for themselves; they thoroughly enjoyed sharing its fruits with others. One day when Barbara brought me some fresh green beans, she also brought me a vegetable I didn't recognize. "These are leeks," she said. "Jerry decided to plant them just to see what would happen." What happened was a great blessing for me because I created a new recipe just so I could use those leeks.

Our recipe for giving can be a blessing to others as well, with cheerfulness being the main ingredient.

Thank You, Father, for so richly blessing us to share with others. Let me cheerfully pass along all that You give me. In Jesus' name, amen.

Deeds As Doctrine

Those you help will . . . praise God for this proof that your deeds are as good as your doctrine (2 Corinthians 9:13, *The Living Bible*).

Scripture: **2 Corinthians 9:11-15**
Song: **"Make Me a Blessing"**

The young man could have been the same age as one of my own three sons. Noticing the sad look on his face as he sat on the bench in front of our motel, I felt moved to stop and speak to him. "Hi. How are you today?" I also decided to give him one of the little booklets about prayer that I had in my handbag. "I have something for you," I said. "I think it will help you."

"Not interested," he said. "All I need is help with my car. If you can't help me with some gasoline, you can keep that stuff about God to yourself."

I almost walked away. Then I remembered the ten dollars I had in my wallet. I didn't want to part with all of my cash, so I decided to give the young man half of it. I placed a five-dollar bill inside the tract and handed it to him. "Here you are," I said. "I hope this helps."

"Thank you," he said. "It will."

I too was thankful, thankful that my Christian doctrine left me no choice but to help in some practical way. I know it is blessed to do so. As John Bunyan once put it: "The more he cast away, the more he had."

Thank You, Lord, for placing it on my heart to help others. I pray they will see Jesus in me. In His precious and holy name, amen.

Compare and Contrast

Just as the result of one trespass was condemnation for all men, so also the result of one act of righteousness was justification that brings life for all men (Romans 5:18, *New International Version*).

Scripture: **Romans 5:12-21**
Song: **"No One Ever Cared for Me Like Jesus"**

Teachers regularly call upon their students to make comparisons and contrasts. And why not, since doing so is an excellent way to study and learn a subject? The teaching method is not something new to our age. It was well known and frequently used in the Bible, and our text is a classic example. Here, Paul shows similarities and differences between the two Adams—the one associated with the Garden of Eden and the other one with the garden of the resurrection.

On a personal level, can we can profit by comparing and contrasting ourselves with other Christians? Yes, but we must not choose as our object the most spiritually anemic brother or sister in the congregation. To benefit, we should select the most devout, most dedicated, most faithful Christian we know. The apostle Paul recommended this when he said: "Follow my example, as I follow the example of Christ" (1 Corinthians 11:1, *NIV*).

Father, I am grateful that the kind act of one man, Jesus, in dying on the cross, made redemption possible for all. Praise to His name! Amen.

August 21–27. **Thomas D. Thurman** is retired after a varied career in ministry. He has been married for 54 years and has three children and seven grandchildren.

How to Be Strife Free

What causes fights and quarrels among you? Don't they come from your desires that battle within you? (James 4:1, *New International Version*).

Scripture: **James 4:1-10**
Song: **"Where the Spirit of the Lord Is"**

As a boy preacher, I had a brief relationship with a little church that could well have been called a war zone. As always, a number of issues were involved in the bickering, but the chief one concerned how to keep children off a newly constructed platform, a spot where traditionally they had held their youth meetings.

Whether it's a church squabble, a family feud, a neighborhood brawl, or an all out, full-fledged nation-against-nation war, the ultimate origins of human conflict can be traced to the same sources. James mentions three: wrong desires, wrong motives, and the wrong kind of prayer life. So if we want to be a strife-free church, a happy family, a cheerful neighborhood, and a conflagration-free world, we need to do as James commands. Let us submit to God, resist the devil, wash our hands, purify our hearts, grieve, mourn, and wail. And, as his capstone, James says we need to master a particularly difficult art: humility. What would it take for you to start practicing that peace-producing virtue this very day?

Dear God, I want very much to see peace in our world. Most of all, I want to have peace within my heart. Help me in my quest, and begin with a challenge to my pride. In Jesus' name, amen.

The Roaring Lion

Be self-controlled and alert. Your enemy the devil prowls around like a roaring lion looking for someone to devour (1 Peter 5:8, *New International Version*).

Scripture: 1 Peter 5:5-10
Song: "Yield Not to Temptation"

During my years as a missionary in Africa, I saw all kinds of exotic wildlife—elephants, rhinos, hippos, giraffes, baboons, monkeys, crocodiles, deer, snakes, and the list goes on. I earnestly wanted to see a lion strolling menacingly across the veld or lying lazily under an acacia tree, but it never happened.

I actually did see a lion on one occasion, but it was not out in the bush. It was an old lion in captivity that, I was told, had been used in movies. I remember its distinctive feature: a black mane. It owners had dyed it black to make the lion look more frightful. In reality, though, I don't believe the old cat was ferocious any longer. Age had reduced its roar to a mere squawk, its teeth were worn smooth, and it seemed to prefer napping to any other activity.

This is *not* the animal Peter had in mind when he compared the devil to such a beast. The devil is still as active and mean as ever, so we must be alert, lest our ancient enemy devour us with the most subtle of tactics.

Dear Lord, help me to realize that the most effective way to avoid being eaten by a lion is to stay out of its territory. May I escape "the roaring lion" by distancing myself from the places of my special temptations. I pray in the name of our great deliverer, Jesus. Amen.

All by Grace

By the grace of God I am what I am, and his grace to me was not without effect. No, I worked harder than all of them—yet not I, but the grace of God that was with me (1 Corinthians 15:10, *New International Version*).

Scripture: **1 Corinthians 15:3-10**
Song: **"Work, for the Night Is Coming"**

A small, reserved boy named Roy applied for admission at our secondary school in Rhodesia. The young man had exceptional academic records and a pleasant personality. However, he had one deficiency: he'd been educated at a farm school. From past experience, we knew that students taught in such simple schools often received inferior teaching. Still, after much thought, we decided to accept Roy, and our decision proved to be a good one.

Like Paul, who called himself "the least of the apostles," Roy could have proclaimed his inferiority to the other students. I don't know that he ever did, but I do know that like the apostle he "worked harder" than many of the other children. I trust that he also put great reliance upon the grace of God. When he left our high school, he was given a government grant at the University of Rhodesia, where he again excelled. The last I heard of Roy, he was a member of his country's parliament.

I would like to think that, if Roy were asked about his success, he would say: "It's all by the grace of God."

God, who of us can claim our works as our own? All I am and do flow from Your grace, which always comes first. Through Christ I pray. Amen.

Awesome Examples

Are they servants of Christ? (I am out of my mind to talk like this.) I am more. I have worked much harder, been in prison more frequently, been flogged more severely, and been exposed to death again and again (2 Corinthians 11:23, *New International Version*).

Scripture: **2 Corinthians 11:23-29**
Song: **"Faith Is the Victory"**

Few Christians have suffered more hardships and deprivations than the apostle Paul. He was imprisoned, flogged, beaten with rods, stoned, shipwrecked, and starved. Yet his attitude was like that of the other apostles who rejoiced "because they had been counted worthy of suffering disgrace for the Name" (Acts 5:41, *NIV).*

The pattern has been emulated time and again. When the Japanese took possession of the Philippines during World War II, they interred many missionaries, two of whom were Leslie and Carrie Wolfe. The Wolfes suffered greatly at the hands of their captors until MacArthur liberated the islands. Leslie lived to enjoy that glorious day but died shortly thereafter of malnutrition and exposure.

We can thank God for Christians like the Wolfes—and the apostle Paul—who have been willing to endure every form of hardship in order to extend the borders of God's kingdom. What awesome examples they are!

Dear God, I take great comfort in knowing, as Paul said, that to be absent from the body is to be present with the Lord. May this hope ever enable me to endure whatever hardships come my way. In Jesus' name, amen.

The Need for Humility

I will boast about a man like that, but I will not boast about myself, except about my weaknesses (2 Corinthians 12:5, *New International Version*).

Scripture: **2 Corinthians 12:1-6**
Song: **"More Like the Master"**

Alvin C. York was a typical Tennessee boy who, as a young man, "got religion." As should always be true, his conversion to Christ had a profound influence upon the rest of his life. When the U.S. government was drafting an army to fight against the Germans in World War I, York got his draft notice. Initially he was hesitant. His "religion and . . . experience" he wrote in his diary, told him not to go to war, but "the memory of my ancestors" told him to go.

Eventually, York became convinced that some wars are just, and he believed the current war was such a one. From then he never wavered. In an action in the Argonne Forest on October 8, 1918, he almost single-handedly defeated a German machine-gun battalion. In doing so he killed a number of the enemy and took captive 132 prisoners. Yet the trait that has forever endeared York to Americans was his humble spirit about his heroism.

York, like Paul, was reluctant to brag about his accomplishments, but maintained a humble, Christlike spirit. Both men, the soldier of the cross and the soldier of liberty, have set us remarkable examples.

Lord, let me be honest about my weaknesses—and seek prayer for them—rather than bragging about my accomplishments. In Jesus' name, amen.

Pray Sincerely

There was given me a thorn in the flesh, a messenger of Satan, to torment me. Three times I pleaded with the Lord to take it away from me (2 Corinthians 12:7, 8, *New International Version*).

Scripture: **2 Corinthians 12:7-13**
Song: **"As We Come to Thee in Prayer"**

God's Word condemns meaningless repetitions but commends sincere pleadings. Three times Jesus prayed to be spared His cup of suffering, and although His prayer received only a negative response, still He was not condemned for the asking. The reason, of course, is that the Father knew the sincerity of His prayer.

Three times Paul asked to have his thorn in the flesh removed, and although it remained, there's no indication he was chastened because of the number of times he asked. In fact, God comforted him by assuring him of the power of His grace.

Surely there are causes in your life about which you have prayed not once, twice, or thrice, but innumerable times. Be assured that God isn't unhappy with you for requesting the same thing a hundred times—if each time you have made the request with genuine sincerity. Remember that Elijah had to pray and send his servant to look out to the sea seven times before the rain he prayed for finally came. Your blessing may be a single prayer away, so . . . ask again.

Dear God in Heaven, may this and every other prayer that I offer to You be lifted up in complete sincerity. I pray in Jesus' name. Amen.

Making Metaphors

Your righteousness is like the mighty mountains, your justice is like the great deep. O Lord, you preserve both man and beast (Psalm 36:6, *New International Version*).

Scripture: **Psalm 36:5-9**
Song: **"Jesus Never Fails"**

We humans like to make likenesses. That is, we like to liken one item to another. It adds luster to our lives. These likable likenings may take the form of similes (using the word *like*) or metaphors (with the *like* omitted). Sara Paretsky used a similar technique when she talked about toughness being "like rowing a boat through molasses."

Psalm 36:5-9 is full of similes and metaphors about God. How many can you find?

In verse 6 the writer spoke of God's righteousness being "like the mighty mountains"—or rock solid, staggeringly vertical, and something to look up to. Furthermore, God's justice is likened to "the great deep." It has depth to it, for God knows all the ins and outs and complex motives of our situations. Therefore, I hope you'll take heart in knowing the heights and depths of God's awesome greatness as you meet all your many challenges today.

God, help me remember the depth of Your goodness today as I face problems that sometimes seem insurmountable. In Christ's name, amen.

August 28–31. **Jim Townsend** was formerly the Bible editor at David C. Cook Publishing. He now spends his time teaching college classes, preaching on Sundays, and writing for Christian publications. He lives in Elgin, Illinois.

What's in Your Cargo Hold?

Take with you seven of every kind of clean animal, a male and its mate, and two of every kind of unclean animal, a male and its mate (Genesis 7:2, *New International Version*).

Scripture: **Genesis 7:1-12**
Song: **"Near to the Heart of God"**

Annie Dillard won a Pulitzer Prize for her book *Pilgrim at Tinker Creek* in 1974. The book offers an ideal way to learn about nature, for she teaches the reader to see so much more than most of us would superficially observe. In order to write the book, she camped out during winter in an unheated cabin in Virginia. Obviously, a strategic question to ask when preparing for such an adventure is: What do I need to take with me in order to make it through such a grueling enterprise?

Noah probably thought of that same question. In his case, God informed him in Genesis 7:2, 3 what some of his ship's cargo was to be—including something extra for devotional purposes.

Aren't our homes usually swamped with a lot of extra and unnecessary baggage—in closets, garages, attics, etc.? Also, don't we sometimes fill our mental cargo hold with much frivolous and even detrimental baggage? Like Noah, are we allowing room for that extra (yet oh-so-essential) space for the Lord?

Lord, help me be sensitized to the overwhelming needs elsewhere on this planet, and also to leave plenty of space for You in the cargo hold of my mind. I pray this in the name of Jesus my Lord. Amen.

Survivors

Only Noah was left, and those with him in the ark (Genesis 7:23, *New International Version*).

Scripture: **Genesis 7:13-24**
Song: "We Have an Anchor"

In Daniel DeFoe's *Robinson Crusoe*, only one survivor is left from a shipwreck off a deserted island. In *Swiss Family Robinson*, the survivors prove to be a family in a similar situation. In William Golding's *Lord of the Flies*, a group of boys manages to survive the modern equivalent of the other two—a plane crash. And a popular TV show in recent years is called *Survivor*.

Genesis 7:23 leaves us with the super-solemn line: "Only Noah was left, and those with him in the ark." Those eight were the original "survivors."

Second Peter 3:6, 7 forecasts a future flood of fire to come. The holocaust of World War II was not the final holocaust (or consuming catastrophe). However, thankfully, God has not said, "Leave no survivors." He has made a way to survive as surely as He gave Noah directions to build the ark.

All survivors are going to need the right fire insurance though. Only those in the ark (who is Christ) will be able to survive the future fiery holocaust. I wonder, who of my friends and acquaintances needs to hear of Christ today?

Lord, I pray for those I know who seem oblivious to the future holocaust. May they soon take refuge in Your true ark, who is Christ—and so become eternal survivors. In Jesus' name, amen.

A Tale of Two Birds

[Noah] sent out a raven, and it kept flying back and forth until the water had dried up from the earth (Genesis 8:7, *New International Version*).

Scripture: **Genesis 8:1-12**
Song: **"May the Mind of Christ My Savior"**

The raven and the dove are birds of a different feather. Evidently they are earmarked by their eating habits. The raven (in Genesis 8:7)—apparently by feeding on the floating filth of a devastated civilization—could keep on flying over the flood until it subsided. The dove (of Genesis 8:11) had a different diet. It couldn't be content with vulturely victuals!

I knew one friend my age (60) who was regularly in church, but he had an avid appetite for cigarettes and potato chips. He's now deceased. I have another friend who knows a lot of Bible verses, but the type of music he likes is full of messages about rape and suicide. He himself has tried to commit suicide. Hmm. Maybe his head-food needs a change. Maybe he is too much raven, not enough dove.

I have a relative who is a single person. She is also a Christian. Into her head she pipes Christian videos of music and sermons. She almost always wakes up to the sound of "Because He lives, I can face tomorrow."

Am I a raven or a dove? What kind of brain-food am I feeding myself? Is it perhaps time for some changes?

Dear Lord, may my spiritual input be of the type that will produce an attitude and actions that please You. I pray in Jesus' name. Amen.

DEVOTIONS

As for me and my household, we will serve the Lord.

—Joshua 24:15

SEPTEMBER

Photo © Comstock

Gary Allen, Editor

September 1

Everything in Order

As long as the earth endures, seedtime and harvest, cold and heat, summer and winter, day and night will never cease (Genesis 8:22).

Scripture: **Genesis 8:13-22**
Song: **"He Has Never Failed Me Yet"**

What if you looked out at the nighttime sky and saw about 20 comets and meteors hurtling through the velvety darkness, headed your way? Of course, once in a great while a meteor does thud onto our planet. However, by and large, we don't face such chaotic randomness. Our universe runs pretty fixedly.

God has signified that fixity as we see it in the four seasons. True, during my five years of living in southern California, we may have had about one rain for perhaps three days straight. But even there we still had the regular rhythm of predictable seasons. So Genesis 8:22 is a handle to hold onto; we have a God of order.

An excellent application for us comes through in 1 Corinthians 14:40, which advocates doing everything in an orderly way. Do I show up on time for my appointments? Can people bank on my word? These are some of the questions I ask myself as I ponder God's trustworthiness in my life and in His running of the entire universe.

Lord, enable me to mirror Your orderly faithfulness. Through Christ, my Lord and Savior, I pray. Amen.

September 1–3. **Jim Townsend** of Elgin, Illinois, spends his time teaching college classes, preaching on Sundays, and writing all manner of Christian literature.

Enjoy It All!

Everything that lives and moves will be food for you. Just as I gave you the green plants, I now give you everything (Genesis 9:3).

Scripture: **Genesis 9:1-7**
Song: **"Break Thou the Bread of Life"**

Funny what we remember. I can still recall a particular hamburger I ate years ago in a little out-of-the-way restaurant in San Diego's Old Town. And in a German restaurant in San Francisco, I consumed the most wonderful sauerbraten. And there was the sliced roast beef cooked outdoors in Memphis, Tennessee, at a church picnic (remembered from my childhood). No wonder I relish the words of 1 Timothy 6:17—that God has lavishly supplied us with "everything for our enjoyment." G. K. Chesterton said that he even "enjoyed his enjoyment."

In Genesis 9:3 God permitted humanity to enjoy a vegetable-plus diet. Of course, the medical profession may need to warn us that a heavy diet of bacon, sausage, and other red meat is not so hot for our hearts. Still, I'm glad that Genesis 9:3 is in the Bible. It tells me that God has made our palates for the pleasurable.

We also need to remember the palates of the needy. Meanwhile, thank God for roast beef and charbroiled lamb chops (don't forget to add the mint jelly).

Thank You, Lord, that so many of us don't have to go hungry. You've even given us variety. And help us to remember the Golden Rule when it comes to food. In the name of Christ I pray. Amen.

No Arrow Here

I have set my rainbow in the clouds, and it will be the sign of the covenant between me and the earth (Genesis 9:13).

Scripture: **Genesis 9:8-17**
Song: **"There's a Light upon the Mountains"**

Lucy and I were sitting on Lake Avenue (on restaurant row) in Pasadena, California, when we happened to have one of our rare California rains. Since the sun was shining brightly, you know what we could see in the sky.

Believe it or not, if I had had a camera then, I could have raked in big bucks with a unique shot. Why? The rainbow we saw in the sky ended not in a pot of gold, but in the bucket of that famous fast-food chicken place right across the street!

God is pro-rainbows. But have you noticed that a rainbow *is* a bow—but without any arrow in it? God has set this weapon of warfare up in the sky, but He has signaled us that all that might be menacing is missing. There is no arrow of anger aimed at us.

God has made His armistice and peace treaty at Christ's cross. The cross is almost a plus sign; it's positive. God is *for us* (Romans 8:31).

A little rainbow never hurt anybody. As God washed Noah's world clean, so He can wash our hearts clean with His forgiving love.

Bless You, Lord, for Your full and free forgiveness. Help me to laugh in belief the next time I spot a rainbow. I pray this prayer in the name of Jesus, my merciful Savior and Lord. Amen.

Sources of Encouragement

We who have fled to take hold of the hope offered to us may be greatly encouraged (Hebrews 6:18).

Scripture: **Hebrews 6:13-20**
Song: **"Trusting Jesus"**

David Brainerd, an eighteenth-century missionary to the American Indians, died of tuberculosis at age 29. Jonathan Edwards later published Brainerd's diary, which spoke of spiritual struggles, weakness from his disease, frequent fastings, and his burden for lost souls. Missionary William Carey took a copy of the book with him to India. Though Brainerd was no longer alive, his steadfast faith in the midst of trials served to encourage Carey.

In an effort to encourage Jewish Christians, the writer of the book of Hebrews used the example of Abraham's faith. Though Abraham and Sarah had no children, God told Abraham he would have many descendants. For 25 years Abraham waited for his first child.

Had God forgotten? No, Abraham could hold tight to God's promise. In the same way, the discouraged Hebrews could count on God's unchanging nature; He cannot lie. When we struggle to believe, observing the lives of other faithful believers can make all the difference.

Dear God, *I thank You for the testimonies of believers who kept the faith amid severe circumstances. In Jesus' name, amen.*

September 4–10. **Jewell Johnson** writes from Arizona where she enjoys walking, reading, and quilting. She and her husband, LeRoy, have seven grandchildren.

Pilgrim Attitude

They were longing for a better country—a heavenly one (Hebrews 11:16).

Scripture: **Hebrews 11:8-16**
Song: **"What a Day That Will Be"**

"There it is! I see the big wheel!" I yelled from the back seat of the car when I saw the Ferris wheel in the distance. The county fair was the biggest event of the summer for my brothers and me when we were kids. We talked about it for months, saved our money for the concessions, and wore new outfits for the occasion.

Anticipation comprises much of the pleasure of any enjoyable event. At the beginning of his journey, Abraham didn't fully comprehend his destination. He lived in tents among strange peoples, often his enemies. He believed God for a son even when Sarah was old and barren. He obeyed God even when the instructions he received did not seem to make sense, because he looked beyond his situation to Heaven, to a better place.

No one is sick in Heaven. No one dies. There are no prisons or crime. Rather, that better country has mansions, rivers, fruit trees, the saints of all ages, and Jesus our Savior. Think about it, read about it, dream about that place as Abraham did. What will it be like to live forever with your Lord?

Heavenly Father, as a pilgrim on this earth, I shade my eyes and look toward Heaven's horizon. Thank You for this hope of a better world to come. Let its vision strengthen my courage today. In the name of Jesus, amen.

The Heavens Speak

Look up at the heavens and count the stars—if indeed you can count them (Genesis 15:5).

Scripture: **Genesis 15:1-6**
Song: **"Look, Ye Saints! The Sight Is Glorious"**

As a child I lived in an area where, on cold winter nights, the flickering, shifting northern lights put on a display comparable to fireworks. In summer, the Milky Way galaxy, with its billions of stars, caused me to ooh and aah.

God often gets our attention through nature. When He wanted to assure Abram that He would make of him a great nation, He took him outside on a clear night for a lesson from the heavens. Although Abram and Sarai had no children, God told Abram that his descendants would someday be as numerous as the stars. Abram reasoned that his heir would be his trusted servant Eliezer. No, God said. The heir would come from Abram's own body.

I wonder what it was like to hear God's voice while gazing at the myriad shining lights overhead. In the future, when I can't figure out how God will fulfill my heart's deepest desire, I'm going to try counting stars. I can remember that my awesome creator merely spoke, and galaxies appeared. Surely He will give good things to all who place their trust in Him.

Lord, assure me today that I am constantly in Your mind. Your love for me is greater than the galaxies, and Your blessings as numberless as the stars. I place my whole life in Your hands! In Jesus' name, amen.

Inner-Circle Friendship

You, however, will go to your fathers in peace and be buried at a good old age (Genesis 15:15).

Scripture: **Genesis 15:12-21**
Song: **"What a Friend We Have in Jesus"**

Joanne and I became acquainted through work, but we didn't have an in-depth conversation until the day she shared with me about her family's problems: a daughter suffering an abusive marriage, a son threatening suicide. In turn, I told Joanne about our daughter's struggle with an eating disorder. As we wept together and comforted one another, we became good friends, bonded by common difficulties.

Abram (Abraham) was called the friend of God (2 Chronicles 20:7). He asked God questions, and God told him of things to come. His descendants, God said, would be in slavery for 400 years, but the nation that enslaved them would be punished. As a true friend, God comforted Abram, assuring him that he wouldn't live to see the impending sorrow. And after four generations, his nation would return to their land.

Often deep friendships develop from shared problems. While it may be difficult to find someone we can trust with our deepest cares, Jesus is such a person. As we regularly share our concerns with Him, He becomes our most trusted inner circle friend.

Dear Lord, thank You for listening intently to my cares and concerns today. You are my Savior and friend. I love You! In Christ I pray. Amen.

He Sees

She gave this name to the LORD who spoke to her: "You are the God who sees me," for she said, "I have now seen the One who sees me" (Genesis 16:13).

Scripture: **Genesis 16:1-15**
Song: **"'Tis So Sweet to Trust in Jesus"**

Fifteen-year-old Lori, distraught because her mother had remarried, left home and headed for Mexico. In a small town on the border, she became afraid and called a minister who eventually reunited Lori with her mother, thus sparing the family further suffering.

Family conflicts also caused Hagar to flee from home. Her mistress, Sarai, frustrated because she had no children, suggested to Abram that he have a child by the slave girl. He agreed. But when Hagar became pregnant, she began to despise her mistress. In turn, Sarai treated her servant shamefully. Overwhelmed and hurt, Hagar fled the impossible situation.

I've felt like running a few times. Have you? But I know God sees what's happening in my life. I also know that if I'll stop and listen with an open heart, I will see His way to proceed. The Lord, who parted seas and rained down manna in the desert, is never without guidance for us. And even our mistakes—when placed in divine hands—can work for good.

God who sees, remind me today that when You look into my life, You see with compassion. You offer answers for my dilemmas, courage for my fears, and peace in my times of turmoil. Thank You, in Jesus' name. Amen.

Godly Influence

I will establish my covenant as an everlasting covenant between me and you and your descendants after you for the generations to come (Genesis 17:7).

Scripture: **Genesis 17:1-8**
Song: **"Just a Closer Walk with Thee"**

At a family reunion we listened to a reading of Grandma Johnson's testimony, written 150 years earlier. We, her descendants, were deeply moved as we heard of her decision to follow Christ, her anguish over the loss of a child, her husband's year-long illness, and the agonizing decision over whether to stay in Norway or move to America.

Each generation affects the next. When Abram entered into a covenant with God, promising to obey Him, he could hardly comprehend the scope of that decision. God planned to give him countless offspring. Nations would descend from him, and the covenant would endure for all time.

Abram's steady faith-walk, in spite of delays and adversities, stands as a solid example for his offspring. By his resolve to covenant with God, we too—his descendants by faith—will forever reap God's blessings: "If you belong to Christ, then you are Abraham's seed, and heirs according to the promise" (Galatians 3:29).

Remind me, Lord: the decisions I make today will have lasting consequences. As I choose to follow You, my influence is not lost to future generations. Let those who follow me feel the impact of Your blessing in my family. Through the holy name of Jesus, my Lord and Savior, I pray. Amen.

Ready with Blessings

As for Ishmael, I have heard you: I will surely bless him; I will make him fruitful and will greatly increase his numbers (Genesis 17:20).

Scripture: **Genesis 17:15-22**
Song: **"Child of Blessing, Child of Promise"**

Our daughter's wedding was a happy occasion, yet I felt a twinge of sadness that day. Our relationship would forever be changed. Now her life would revolve around her husband. She would visit us, but our home was no longer hers. She would establish her own new household.

Abraham must have had mixed emotions when God announced that, in one year, Sarah would bear the covenant child. On one hand, surely Abraham was glad that he'd finally see God's promise fulfilled. On the other hand, he voiced concerns for Ishmael, his beloved 13-year-old by Hagar. No doubt this father and son had developed a strong bond.

So what would become of Ishmael? God would bless him too. And that was all Abraham needed to know. He accepted God's plan and moved on.

No person is insignificant to God; no detail escapes His attention. Let us talk to Him about all those we love, those who may be close at hand or far away. Commit them to His love, for God is ready with His blessings.

Dear Lord, You care so deeply for me and mine! Continue to shower blessings on those I love and on those I miss today. And thank You for the Scripture that says: "I have heard you." In Christ's name, amen.

A Heart of Delight

Direct me in the path of your commands, for there I find delight (Psalm 119:35).

Scripture: **Psalm 119:33-40**
Song: **"Joyful, Joyful, We Adore Thee"**

My 5-year-old granddaughter is a wellspring of joy. Her infectious laughter surrounds any activity she enters, whether she's playing house with her dolls or taking on a new role as a bride or special princess. From the minute she enters my door, she flits around the room giggling and dancing, asking the rest of us to join in.

To me, this is the picture of delight. No restraint—only boundless enchantment. When I watch her, I am reminded that God is watching me to see if I am filled with delight in reading His Word, in serving Him, in praising Him. And do others see the wonder in my eyes, my words, and my actions because of God's awesome grace?

These days, my body often wants to take its ease and refresh itself. But even though I am not dancing on the outside, I can still be filled with fascination for God's ways, ever so delighted to be His child.

Lord, I delight in Your Word. It gives me the strength to face each day and provides the guidance I need to make good decisions. Fill me with immeasurable joy as I hold tightly to Your hand, and create in me an ever-deepening hunger for Your Word. I pray this prayer in the name of Jesus, my marvelous Savior and Lord. Amen.

September 11–17. **Jeanne Harmon** of Colorado Springs, is a mentor for the Christian Writers Guild. She and her husband, Pat, have two children.

Choosing the Capable

He chose capable men from all Israel and made them leaders of the people (Exodus 18:25).

Scripture: **Exodus 18:13-27**
Song: **"Learning to Lean"**

As an American, I have the distinct privilege of voting for the men and women of my choice to act as public servants. This right was given to me by the Constitution of the United States, and as a resident of a democratic country, I play a part in choosing who will govern me. This is a daunting responsibility for us citizens.

Since every candidate claims to be the best person for the job, how can we decide? After all, in our day of modern technology, we receive news reports claiming to have the truth about the candidates, but it seems that so little remains completely unbiased. Ultimately, we must rely on our own resources to check a candidate's voting record on the issues and learn all we can about his or her character.

The responsibility of choosing is left to us, just as Moses was allowed to choose the leaders he deemed capable. As we pray and seek God's guidance *about* our leaders, let's remember that He also asks us to pray *for* our leaders, whoever is chosen.

Dear Lord, often I take for granted the rights and privileges given to me as a citizen. Never let me forget the sacrifices that have been made on my behalf. Remind me to seek after You as my guide and to vote for capable people to govern me. I pray in Jesus' holy name. Amen.

The Blessing of Obedience

If you obey me fully and keep my covenant, then out of all nations you will be my treasured possession (Exodus 19:5).

Scripture: **Exodus 19:1-9a**
Song: **"I Have Decided to Follow Jesus"**

Dan found that raising a teenager in today's world was harder than he'd once assumed. Efforts to reach out to his son Josh met with resistance. Arguments over clothes, music, curfew, and friends seemed unending. Dan's overtures only made his son run in the other direction. "I make my own choices," Josh said, "so leave me alone."

How Dan longed for a loving relationship with his son! He dreamed of sharing all the good things a father has to give. He wanted to shower Josh with rewards for respect and obedience. This was not to be. Even though Dan loved him, Josh's continual disobedience drove a wedge into their relationship.

Regretfully, we are sometimes like this with our heavenly Father. We pray for guidance, feel the tug in our hearts, and then fail to act. What blessings we give up!

Perhaps it is our fear, our need for security that keeps us in such a state of struggle. Yet God treasures us and our fellowship. And when it comes to security, I am reminded of some good words a missionary once spoke to me: "The hand that *points* the way is the same hand that *provides* the way." What greater safety than that?

Lord, help me remember today that obeying You leads to blessing and peace. Guide me, and I will follow. Through Christ I pray. Amen.

ig
);
ng
%;
hydrate

629)
er

More
+)

% Daily Value*:
;

Protein
6g
6%

Vitamin A
6%;
Vitamin C
4%;
Calcium
15%;
Iron
4%;

Exchanges:

1 1/2 Starch; 0 Fruit; 1 1/2 Other Carbohydrate; 0 Skim Milk; 0 Low-Fat Milk; 0 Milk; 0 Vegetable; 0 Very Lean Meat; 0 Lean Meat; 0

Carbohydrate Choices:

3

*Percent Daily Values are based on a 2,000 calorie diet.

REVIEWS & COMMENTS–

Be the first to review this recipe!

Discern and Follow

Direct my footsteps according to your word; let no sin rule over me (Psalm 119:133).

Scripture: **Exodus 19:9b-15**
Song: **"Footprints of Jesus"**

Moses received specific directions from the Lord about how to approach God. He followed, and he serves as a good example for us. In contrast, King Saul, failed to follow.

Before Saul went to battle the Philistines, he took things into his own hands and offered a sacrifice to the Lord without waiting for Samuel to do it. So God took the kingdom from Saul and gave it to David. For Saul, how to respond to following directions was the key to a smashing success . . . or total failure. Psalm-writer David must have known this, for he called out to God: "Direct my footsteps."

Thankfully, God is willing to show us His ways and guide us into His plan. This doesn't mean we will see the future, of course. It simply means determining something crucial in advance: that when we have a choice to make, we will make it according to every bit of heavenly guidance discernible. As Christian apologist C. S. Lewis put it: "Total renunciation can only mean a total readiness for every *particular* renunciation that may be demanded." Your very next decision, then, is quite important.

Father, my will is to do Your will. But I know I can't follow "in general." I will face specific choices at particular times and places. May I be ready! Through Christ, my sovereign Lord, I pray. Amen.

Commandments of Protection

Great peace have they who love your law, and nothing can make them stumble (Psalm 119:165).

Scripture: **Exodus 20:1-17**
Song: **"Thy Word"**

My husband and I were casually chatting as we forged through the late afternoon traffic. After stopping at an intersection, the car in front of us proceeded forward. Suddenly, from out of nowhere, another car sped into the intersection without slowing. We witnessed screeching tires, flying glass, and spinning automobiles. Confusion erupted, and soon ambulances rushed to the scene.

Whenever someone breaks the law, it affects more than just that individual. In this case, a man suffered a severe back injury because of another's irresponsibility. In fact, the accident affected everyone involved—families, friends, even the witnesses.

God gave Moses the Commandments so that people could live in right relationship with their creator and with their fellow human beings. That's why the psalmist could speak of *loving* God's law. Those rules—and all their societal derivatives—are clearly for our own good. They protect us against sin and destruction. And the rewards of keeping them are simply out of this world.

Dear Heavenly Father, I know that keeping Your laws can't save me. But because of Your great and gracious salvation, I can strive to obey You out of love and gratitude. Thank You for giving me peace as I give up sin. In the name of Your Son, my Savior, I pray. Amen.

Keep Pedaling

We will do everything the Lord has said; we will obey (Exodus 24:7).

Scripture: **Exodus 24:3-8**
Song: **"Be Glorified"**

This guy can ride a bicycle! As the most celebrated contributor to the sport of cycling, Lance Armstrong is a two-time Olympian and a five-time winner of the Tour de France. None of these honors came without significant sacrifice and some cruel setbacks.

In 1996, Lance experienced excruciating pain, and tests revealed cancer that had spread to his brain and lungs. The news stunned the world. Doctors said his chances of survival were less than 50-50. Frightened but determined, Lance took aggressive measures to fight his cancer. Two years later, he had achieved a remarkable recovery and once again challenged the world's bicyclists in competition. As of this writing, he says his cancer experience was a wake-up call that led him to be a spokesman for cancer research.

At times in this race of life I want to give up. In my pain I wonder, "How can I persevere?" At those times I'm reminded of my deep-down commitment to the Lord. In happier times I have often echoed the words of the ancient Israelites: I will obey. Now I recall the motto of Lance Armstrong: Despite the odds, don't quit.

Dear Father, help me face today's circumstances with confidence, knowing that You are in control. In the name of Jesus I pray. Amen.

Savor the Solitude

Moses entered the cloud as he went on up the mountain. And he stayed on the mountain forty days and forty nights (Exodus 24:18).

Scripture: **Exodus 24:12-18**
Song: **"Go Tell It on the Mountain"**

Sarah looked forward to the women's retreat every fall. Ladies from several churches would gather at a campground to worship and hear from God. Silent moments alone with the Lord refreshed Sarah every morning, and she loved singing praises in the solitude of the forest.

She relished escaping her world of e-mailing, car pooling, grocery shopping, and cell-phoning as she spent time in prayer and the Word. Then, leaving the retreat, she was ready to face another year with a renewed spirit.

When she reached home, Sarah nearly burst with joy upon sharing every moment with her husband. He listened patiently, but something was lost in the retelling. Later, in prayer, Sarah sensed the Lord's whisper: "Some things are meant for the secret places You and I share."

I think Moses must have reveled in his 40-day mountain getaway with the Lord, just as Sarah so enjoyed her own retreat. Both were involved in serious business with God, and both would extend their blessings to others. Yet when God meets us, He meets each of us as an individual, beloved child. Do savor that one-to-one relationship.

Father, help me find time today to go to the mountain and commune with You. Thank You for wanting me. In Jesus' name, amen.

Zapping the Joy Killers

Restore to me the joy of your salvation and grant me a willing spirit, to sustain me (Psalm 51:12).

Scripture: **Psalm 51:1-12**
Song: **"Joy to the World"**

Have you noticed that to-do lists can be joy killers? I looked at my list one Saturday morning and wanted to crawl back into bed rather than face the day ahead. I had committed to hosting a dinner at my house that evening. But after an exhausting week, the last thing I wanted to do was to clean house, shop for groceries, and prepare a meal for 12 adults I barely knew.

Tasks on a list aren't the only thieves of joy in life. Boredom, worry, anger, hurt, regret, and exhaustion move us into gloom and even take our eyes away from God. For the psalmist, sin sat at the top of the joy-killer list. Only confession would restore David's zest for life.

Are there joy killers in your life these days? When we ask God to restore our joy, He often takes us to the source of our joy killer. As difficult as it may be, when we face that thing squarely, we've taken the first step toward spiritual renewal. The Lord restored my joy on that Saturday by reminding me of the purpose of my to-do list: to minister to potential new friends through heartfelt hospitality.

Father, zap any joy killers in my life by helping me confront their source. In the name of Your Son, my Savior, I pray. Amen.

September 18–24. **Jane Hampton Cook,** author and speaker, is the former White House Deputy Director of Internet News Services for President George W. Bush.

Oldies but Goodies

Write down for yourselves this song and teach it to the Israelites and have them sing it, so that it may be a witness for me against them (Deuteronomy 31:19).

Scripture: **Deuteronomy 31:14-23**
Song: **"There's a Glad New Song"**

"Was that song before your time?" my older husband often asks me when we hear an oldie-but-goodie on the radio or in a restaurant. He enjoys being reminded of an earlier time as the tune conjures good memories of the past. A simple tune can place us in a time warp, taking us back to a more sentimental season in our lives.

God commanded a dying Moses to teach the Israelites a song about His covenant with them. The emotional power of music would help keep His promise alive among the Israelites in the years to come after Moses was gone. It's as if the Lord was the author of the very first oldie-but-goodie.

How has God used music in your life? Does a favorite hymn or praise song draw you to Him as soon as you hear it or sing it? God created music to connect us to Him quickly and emotionally. As He did in the lives of the Israelites, He still uses hymns and spiritual songs to speak to the deepest places of our souls.

Heavenly Father, thank You for the gift of music. I lift my voice to You in praise and worship. Send me a new song today or use an oldie to remind me of Your love for me through Your covenant in Christ. For it's in His matchless name that I pray. Amen.

My Hero!

Have I not commanded you? Be strong and courageous. Do not be terrified; do not be discouraged, for the Lord your God will be with you wherever you go (Joshua 1:9).

Scripture: **Joshua 1:1-9**
Song: **"Surely the Presence of the Lord Is in This Place"**

Five years ago today President George W. Bush spoke to the American people and the world by addressing a joint session of Congress following the September 11 terrorism attacks. He uttered six simple words that described my heart at the time: "Freedom and fear are at war." Like many Americans, I found myself afraid to go to work after the attacks. I was also a bit jumpy in other circumstances, such as when the lights suddenly went out during a church service, or whenever I stepped into a subway car.

The Israelites faced a war of freedom versus fear as well. They longed for freedom, but they feared the dangers keeping them from the promised land. So the Lord asked them to be strong and courageous. He didn't guarantee a safe journey, but He promised to be with them amid any dangers they encountered.

You and I hear of tragedies every day. We cannot watch the news on television without observing another incarnation of violence. Yet God calls us to approach life with courage and rest on His promised presence. He is our warrior hero when freedom and fear fight within us.

Dear Lord, may I rest in Your freedom instead of living in my fear. Thank You for Your promise to be with me always. In Jesus' name, amen.

Living in the Desert?

Then you lived in the desert for a long time (Joshua 24:7).

Scripture: **Joshua 24:1-7**
Song: **"Shall We Gather at the River?"**

Deserts are sandy, desolate, and wild. They are dry and waterless, burning hot during the day and bone-chilling at night. We may not live there geographically, but sometimes we find ourselves in a desert of spirit. Jobs become stale, finances evaporate, friends disappoint us, and marriages lose their intimacy.

My desert place? Graduate school. I knew God had clearly placed me there—but the dryness I encountered! My finances dipped lower than ever, and my hope for a prosperous career dissolved as I encountered hostility toward my faith from professors and fellow students.

My desert lasted less than four years, but the Israelites lived in the wild for much longer. After experiencing God's miracles and escaping from Egypt, they lived in a barren land that forced them to cry out to God frequently. He heard them and supplied their needs.

The beauty of landing in any desert is God's provision, His ability to sparkle above the sand and grit. Although they lived in the desert for 40 years, the Israelites didn't live there forever. Just as the Lord delivered them, so He will deliver us from our times of desolation.

O Lord, thank You for the desert, for its rugged beauty, and for Your sustenance when I enter it. And thank You for Your eternal river of life that cleanses me and refreshes my spirit. In the name of Christ I pray. Amen.

Inherited Blessing

I gave you a land on which you did not toil and cities you did not build; and you live in them and eat from vineyards and olive groves that you did not plant (Joshua 24:13).

Scripture: **Joshua 24:8-13**
Song: **"Faith of Our Fathers"**

When did you last buy something new? There is something special about the smell of a brand-new car, the crispness of a new shirt, or the clarity of a new cell phone. A feeling of excitement and enthusiasm sweeps over us when something in our life is "the latest thing."

We often measure an item's worth based on its newness. But Joshua 24:13 reveals that God also values what already exists. He reminded the Israelites that their blessings resided in what they had inherited. They lived in cities they did not build and ate from vineyards they did not plant. The old was just as much a blessing as the new.

We have received a rich inheritance. So many of our blessings flow from the work of those who have gone before us. Colonists established townships that are now thriving cities. Inventions, such as Henry Ford's automobile and Thomas Edison's lightbulb, transformed society into the mobile world of communication we enjoy today. Our lifestyle—our inheritance—is as much a blessing as the new things in life. Let us appreciate the past and those who walked before us.

Lord, today may I value the old along with the new. And help me leave a legacy of faith to those who will come after me. In Jesus' name, amen.

Leading by Example

As for me and my household, we will serve the Lord (Joshua 24:15).

Scripture: **Joshua 24:14-18**
Song: **"The Family of God"**

Children are great imitators, often learning by watching adult behavior. When I spent several days with a friend and her six-month-old son, I could easily get Jackson to smile at me just by looking into his eyes and curling up the corners of my mouth. Within seconds his cheeks dimpled into the cutest grin.

As children grow, they continue to imitate their parents in many ways. Even as young adults they often make choices based on parental modeling through the years.

Joshua's words about serving the Lord were credible because he lived them before his followers. When he called on the Israelites to choose whether or not to serve the Lord, he didn't coerce them into it. Instead, he provided a practical model of obedience for them to imitate.

Whether we realize it or not, we serve as models for those around us, especially the youth who are looking on. We have a great opportunity to lead by example. Our words and actions, if compatible, will powerfully influence the coming generation. What a privilege is ours!

Heavenly Father, show me how to lead by example today. Reveal where I need to change so others may follow not just my words, but my behavior. Thank You that You sent Your Son, Jesus, as the great model, whom I can imitate. I pray in His precious name. Amen.

Serving, Step by Step

Joshua said, "You are witnesses against yourselves that you have chosen to serve the Lord." "Yes, we are witnesses," they replied (Joshua 24:22).

Scripture: **Joshua 24:19-24**
Song: **"I Would Be True"**

Witnesses are a crucial component of our legal system. They provide accountability in transactions. Attorneys call witnesses to the stand to testify about a case. Marriage licenses, wills, and mortgage contracts require witnesses. But to be credible and effective, they must be truthful.

The Israelites sealed with the oath of witnesses their commitment to serve the Lord. As Joshua banged the gavel, the people agreed to serve the Lord. They also agreed to serve as their neighbors' witnesses.

God didn't need witnesses to know the true intention of their hearts, of course. But they themselves needed the accountability. By public declaration, the Israelites made themselves answerable to their families and communities.

I'm thankful that my service to the Lord is a commitment sealed by the deposition of my own heart. And God serves as both my witness and judge. He knows when my testimony is reliable and honest. He also offers forgiveness when I fail. That is such a good thing because so often my journey down the path of service proceeds with two steps forward and one step back. How is it with you?

Father, may I be a reliable servant and witness for You. Search my heart and show me where I need to change or improve. Through Christ, amen.

Son, It's the Law!

Talk about them when you sit at home and when you walk along the road, when you lie down and when you get up (Deuteronomy 6:7).

Scripture: **Deuteronomy 6:4-9**
Song: **"The Law of God Is Good and Wise"**

As a former state trooper, my father wanted to make sure that I knew all the rules of the road as I prepared to take my driver's license exam. He would drill me at night. He would quiz me in the car. He would create scenarios and have me explain what I should do. Road signs, speed limits, safety rules—he covered them all. Eventually I knew I could handle any question on that test.

Many people find it hard to observe laws and rules. Too restrictive! Thus our prisons teem with people who are paying for their limitless "freedom."

Shall we take God's commandments less seriously than we take our society's laws? Hardly! Just as Moses urged the Israelites to continually observe God's laws and to make sure their families knew them well, our families need to know and follow God's commandments. Thankfully, the one who kept all the commandments perfectly tells us: "My yoke is easy and my burden is light" (Matthew 11:30).

God, may I see Your commandments not as shackles but as opportunities to show my gratitude for Your salvation. Through Christ my Savior, amen.

September 25–30. **Jeff Friend** is a speaker and freelance writer living in Largo, Florida, with his wife, Nancy. He is a big fan of the Baltimore Orioles.

Stories for the Ages

We will tell the next generation the praiseworthy deeds of the Lord, his power, and the wonders he has done (Psalm 78:4).

Scripture: **Psalm 78:1-8**
Song: **"Life in the Loon"**

As we walked through the Baseball Hall of Fame in Cooperstown, New York, my father pointed out various bats, uniforms, gloves, and other items on display. He told my brothers and me little stories about some of the great players who had used that equipment in earlier years. Though the names were unfamiliar to me at the time, my father had vivid memories of many of those men, and he enjoyed retelling their historic accomplishments. Other players he knew about from accounts he'd read or heard from others as he was growing up.

Countless museums around the world preserve memories and mementos. By understanding the past—in cultures, sports, art, and myriad other areas—we can relate it to our own lives (and better prepare for the future).

How much more important to tell our children and grandchildren how God has protected and provided for His people down through the generations! We need to share with them His faithfulness, love, and mercy toward us. Then they will know God can be trusted to lead them through whatever they may face.

Heavenly Father, may I joyfully share the stories of Your faithfulness to me so I can encourage others to follow You. I pray this prayer in the name of Jesus, my praiseworthy Savior and Lord. Amen.

Slow Down and Listen

I am listening carefully to all the Lord is saying—for he speaks peace to his people, his saints, if they will only stop their sinning (Psalm 85:8, *The Living Bible*).

Scripture: **Psalm 85:4-13**
Song: **"Softly and Tenderly"**

The irate customer ranted at the man behind the counter. She opened the box, yanked out the small appliance, and began waving it in the clerk's face. He tried to interrupt her, but she refused to give him an opening. She just continued to voice her displeasure with the product—and the store in general.

Again the man tried to ask a question, but he was rudely cut off. Then, as another outburst finally subsided, the employee saw his opportunity. "Ma'am, I understand that you are very upset," he said. "But I'm still not sure what is wrong with the product. All I want to do is help you get satisfaction, so please just calm down so we can resolve this." Having been disarmed by the employee's quiet demeanor, the woman apologized and explained the problem. If she'd been willing to listen to him earlier, she could have avoided such an embarrassing confrontation.

When God talks to us, let us listen carefully instead of plunging ahead with any self-centered plans. Hearing Him speak will bring peace to our lives as no other voice can.

Lord, in my busy world it's easy to let Your voice be overwhelmed by all the noise around me. Help me slow down and listen. In Christ's name, amen.

Legitimate Shame

Yet you have disobeyed me. Why have you done this? (Judges 2:2).

Scripture: **Judges 2:1-5**
Song: **"O How Happy Are They Who the Savior Obey"**

Why? The question expresses our desire to understand, often when we seem confused and overwhelmed. The dying patient asks, *"Why* did I get this disease?" The laid-off worker asks, *"Why* did I lose my job?" The rejected spouse asks, *"Why* did she walk out on me?" All of us know the feeling of despair that so often accompanies a "why?" But does God know too?

I remember when my parents had warned me, over and over again, not to do something—but I did it anyway through sheer teenage rebellion. I can still recall that look of frustration and disappointment on their faces as they asked, *"Why* did you disobey us?" Then, even though they loved me, they needed to show me that disobedience carries a price to pay.

God also knows about children who disobey. He had instructed the Israelites to tear down the altars of false gods, but they didn't do it. Since they had broken the covenant, they faced God's judgment. But they also had to hear those anguished, pleading words that bring legitimate—and potentially healing—shame to a child: "Why have you done this?"

God, *I know that obeying You is the way to glorify Your name. May I do Your will with gladness and singleness of heart today. In Jesus' name, amen.*

Keep Telling It

After that whole generation had been gathered to their fathers, another generation grew up, who knew neither the Lord nor what he had done for Israel (Judges 2:10).

Scripture: **Judges 2:6-10**
Song: **"Someone Must Tell the Glad Story"**

When my brother decided to research our family tree, he spent hours scanning genealogy books. He mailed several letters to various agencies, requesting copies of birth and death certificates, marriage licenses, land records, and anything else he thought might help him piece together our family's past. He also interviewed relatives near and far to dig up anecdotes about our ancestors.

I thought his project was a big waste of time. Why should I care about somebody who lived decades before I was born? But then I began wondering whether there might be some things from my forefathers' lives that could instruct me. Were there perhaps certain traditions or beliefs that should not be discarded so lightly?

The Israelites suffered the consequences of ignorance about their ancestors. An entire generation grew up without knowing the Lord or His great works among earlier generations. How sad that they would end up repeating many of their fathers' mistakes, simply because they didn't know how to follow and trust God.

God, help me commit to telling the next generation about Your faithfulness and all the great things You have done for me. Our young people need to know that You are able to do the same for them today. In Jesus' name, amen.

Avoid the Miserable Misery

The Lord had warned Israel he would do this, and now the Israelites were miserable (Judges 2:15, *Contemporary English Version*).

Scripture: **Judges 2:11-15**
Song: **"Draw Me Closer, Lord"**

Stop signs. Medicine labels. Flashing lights. Every day we see warnings of various kinds. Some are obvious and shout at us: Caution! Danger! Do Not Enter! Others may be more subtle, like Fasten Your Seatbelt. But all warnings have one thing in common: they try to keep us safe from some form of danger. If we don't do what the warning says, we may have to deal with some unpleasant consequences.

Disregarding a policeman's warning may get us arrested. Ignoring a medication label may lead to painful side-effects. Laughing off our employer's caution may end in unemployment. But it is always up to us to choose whether to heed a warning.

God's warnings intend to keep us from making decisions that may damage our souls or displease Him. He knows of the dangers that lie ahead in our paths. By reading His Word and listening when He speaks to our hearts, we can count on our Father to guide us into lives of integrity. We won't avoid all danger, of course. But we will no doubt save ourselves significant misery.

Dear Father, because of Your great love for me, You warn of dangers ahead. How can I ever thank You enough? Through Christ I pray. Amen.

My Prayer Notes

DEVOTIONS®

*I*n the morning, O Lord, you hear my voice; in the morning I lay my requests before you and wait in expectation.

—Psalm 5:3

OCTOBER

Photo © Artville

Gary Allen, Editor

Can You Hold, Sir?

I will use [the nations] to test Israel and see whether they will keep the way of the LORD and walk in it as their forefathers did (Judges 2:22).

Scripture: **Judges 2:16-23**
Song: **"Wait, O My Soul, Thy Maker's Will"**

"Thank you for calling. Please wait for the next available representative." As the soft music began playing in my ear, I felt like slamming the telephone down in protest. They want me to wait? *I'm busy!* But this company was the only one that had the data I needed. If I hung up now, I would just have to call back some other time. So I decided to wait it out. . . .

I often find it difficult to wait. It's hard not to have any control over a situation, to want something right away but, for reasons I may not know, to have it withheld.

In the days of the judges, the Lord did not drive out some nations from Israel because He wanted to test His peoples' devotion to Him. Surely the people pleaded for deliverance . . . but the Lord let them wait.

When God doesn't act on our prayers right away, we must believe that He has a reason. Are we willing to trust His wisdom? He does hear, and He *always* answers: sometimes "Yes," sometimes "No," and sometimes "Wait."

Dear God in Heaven, help me remember that Your timing and Your ways are far wiser than mine. All praise to You, through Jesus Christ, amen.

October 1. **Jeff Friend** is a speaker and freelance writer living in Largo, Florida, with his wife, Nancy. He is a big fan of the Baltimore Orioles.

Our True Shelter

He that dwelleth in the secret place of the Most High shall abide under the shadow of the Almighty (Psalm 91:1, *King James Version*).

Scripture: **Psalm 91**
Song: **"Hiding in Thee"**

Four cottonwood trees continue to cast their shadows over the South Dakota prairie as they have for more than 100 years. Author Laura Ingalls Wilder's father, Charles Ingalls, planted one for each of his daughters, marking off his homestead claim. The trees provided shady protection in the summer and shelter from pelting snow in the winter. Any home tucked beneath a tree's shadows is safer than one more exposed to the elements.

Yet life itself exposes us to many elements we'd rather not face. A row of trees can't protect us from job layoffs, sicknesses, broken relationships, and other problems.

But God promises to be with us in trouble. Living under His shadow, we are held secure in His love. When we feel we are under attack, God's protective presence is there.

The Ingalls' homestead is long gone, but Pa's cottonwoods remain. Our problems come and go, but God, our loving protector, remains with us forever.

Great Protector, help me turn to You with full confidence that You are more powerful than any of my problems. Thank You, in Jesus' name. Amen.

October 2–8. **Jane Heitman** is a library technician living in Grand Junction, Colorado. Among other works, she has authored two books for school librarians.

Spiritual Muscles: Toned Up?

The LORD is my light and my salvation; whom shall I fear? The Lord is the strength of my life; of whom shall I be afraid? (Psalm 27:1, *King James Version*).

Scripture: **Psalm 27:1-6**
Song: **"Shouting His Praise"**

A young couple relaxes under an umbrella at the beach. Just as they get comfortable, a bully appears and kicks sand in the young man's face. The humiliated youth is too weak to defend himself.

This 1930s advertisement promoted an exercise system designed to strengthen a man's muscles so he'd never need to fear bullies. But we believers have something much more potent than any exercise system. The Lord himself gives us strength and salvation. He has already conquered sin and death through Jesus' death and resurrection. So no matter what battles we face, or who our enemies are, the almighty Lord is with us. Yes, we will have trouble in this sinful world, but God is stronger than any trouble. We can face our enemies confidently, knowing that God fights with us and for us.

An exercise system can build strong muscles for a fight with bullies. But exercising spiritual disciplines, such as prayer and Bible study, prepares us for a daily battle of cosmic proportions (see Ephesians 6:12). How is your muscle tone at the moment?

Lord, my light and salvation, thank You for fighting my enemies through the victory of the cross. In the name of my victorious Savior, amen.

Special Delivery

When the children of Israel cried unto the Lord, the Lord raised up a deliverer to the children of Israel, who delivered them, even Othniel the son of Kenaz, Caleb's younger brother (Judges 3:9, *King James Version*).

Scripture: **Judges 3:7-11**
Song: **"Come, Thou Long-Expected Jesus"**

If you must send a package to arrive across the country within two days, you compare shipping companies serving both your area and the destination. You consider which one will get the package where it needs to go, guaranteed on time, for the lowest cost. After you make your choice, you complete the paperwork, and send the package. Then you trust that the company will deliver as promised.

Long ago, the people of Israel trusted God to provide a deliverer. He gave them Othniel, who delivered them from Mesopotamia into a peaceful 40 years. Still, Israel continued to sin. God knew that they—and we—needed more than an earthly deliverer, so when the time was right He sent His Son, Jesus, to offer the perfect, eternal sacrifice for our sins. Jesus' death and resurrection conquered sin forever and delivered forgiveness. And Jesus promises to return to deliver all believers into eternity.

Dear Heavenly Father, we long for our deliverer as the ancient Israelites did. Unlike them, we know our deliverer is Jesus. Thank You that He will deliver us as promised—on time, guaranteed, with no paperwork, at His cost. Come, Lord Jesus, the one in whom we pray. Amen.

The Hall of Faith

By [faith] the elders obtained a good report (Hebrews 11:2, *King James Version*).

Scripture: **Hebrews 11:1, 2, 32-34**
Song: **"Faith of Our Brothers"**

Family manors frequently have halls lined with portraits of ancestors. A tour through such a home reveals not only the home's current residents but also the generations who built and owned the place down through the years. Though each ancestor is painted to his or her best advantage, his or her *accomplishments* tell the real story. How did each one help build up or tear down the family?

The "hall of faith" described in Hebrews 11 paints pictures of many brave men and women devoted to God. While faith is a gift from God and isn't transmitted genetically or culturally, we can admire these resolute ones as our faith ancestors. When our own faith is flagging, we can be inspired by their perseverance.

Thankfully, we can add to Hebrews' portrait hall of the faithful by naming people in our own lives today who have helped our faith grow. (Whose picture comes to mind right now?) And with God's help, we can live a faithful life so that we too may obtain a good report. Then, next to our portraits in the hall of faith will appear the portraits of those we have encouraged in Christ.

O Lord, may I be remembered as a builder of Your family through those I've won to You and encouraged in spiritual growth. Thank You for the biblical accounts of the faithful who inspire me. Through Christ I pray. Amen.

Can You Go Alone?

Barak said unto her, If thou wilt go with me, then I will go: but if thou wilt not go with me, then I will not go (Judges 4:8, *King James Version*).

Scripture: **Judges 4:1-10**
Song: **"Alone with God"**

Two high school students trying to decide their futures consulted with a U.S. Marine recruiter. Fearful of leaving their small town alone, they enlisted under the buddy program, which guaranteed they would be together at least through basic training. They were proud of their decision and exemplified the Marines' motto, *Semper Fidelis*, which is Latin for "always faithful."

In the Bible, Deborah told Barak that God commanded him to enter battle—with a guarantee of victory. God did not command Deborah to go along, but Barak refused to go without her. We don't know why he didn't trust and obey God, but we might guess he was simply afraid. Deborah went along, but told Barak that he would not receive honor for the victory.

Sometimes God gives us buddies to help us face our trials. At other times He wants us to walk forward without human escorts. Either way, God is always faithful; He fulfills His promises. And no matter the earthly outcome, He remains in charge.

God, I know You want what's best for me, so give me the courage to face daily battles in fellowship with others—or even alone. And thank You so much for always keeping Your promises. I pray in Jesus' holy name. Amen.

All in Good Time

Deborah said unto Barak, Up; for this is the day in which the Lord hath delivered Sisera into thine hand: is not the Lord gone out before thee? So Barak went down from mount Tabor, [with] ten thousand men (Judges 4:14, *King James Version*).

Scripture: **Judges 4:12-16**
Song: **"Guide Me Ever, Great Redeemer"**

Timing is everything. Tenths of seconds make an Olympic athlete a winner. Seconds taken to administer emergency medical treatment can determine life or death. In minutes, flames can turn buildings to ashes. Timing was everything for Barak too. God told Deborah, His judge over Israel, the right time for Barak to fight Sisera. Barak acted then, and God gave him success.

I've noticed that God's idea of perfect timing rarely matches my own. I often want to charge ahead with an imperfect plan, eager to see results. I may procrastinate to avoid an unpleasant task, making it even more burdensome later. Or I shun service out of sheer laziness, and a wonderful opportunity slips by. Because I cannot see God's *entire* plan, I act blindly unless I allow God to guide me. Deborah recognized the right time because the Lord was with her.

God is also with us! He loves us and wants what is best for us. What would happen if we turned all our impatience, fear, and lethargy over to Him right now?

Eternal God, *today make Your plans my plans. Replace my impatience and apathy with courage and energy. Thank You, in Jesus' name. Amen.*

A Magnifying Melody

Hear, O ye kings; give ear, O ye princes; I, even I, will sing unto the Lord; I will sing praise to the Lord God of Israel (Judges 5:3, *King James Version*).

Scripture: **Judges 5:1-12**
Song: **"Sing, My Tongue, the Glorious Battle"**

Early in the morning, while New Yorkers scurry to work, a garbage collector goes about his job. He heaves smelly, dirty trash into his truck, singing as he goes. Show tunes, pop tunes, standards, arias—he sings whatever strikes him at the moment. Passersby smile and wave. Some call out requests or shout, "Good morning!"

A song can powerfully affect both singer and hearer. Deborah's song sprang from her heart, a hymn full of thanks that magnified the Lord. He had dramatically freed Israel from an oppressive king, and Deborah just had to burst forth in melody. Her song recounts Israel's history in the events leading up to, and including, the enemy's defeat. Anyone listening would know the whole story and join in praising God for deliverance.

Our songs and hymns of praise move our focus from the "trash" in our lives and remind us of the greatness of the king we serve. What hymn can we sing in praise to God today? What song do those around us need to hear?

Dear Lord, You delivered Your people from enemies time and again. Thank You for delivering us from the ultimate enemy, death, through Your Son, Jesus. Let our songs humble us and glorify You. Help us sing loudly and clearly so that others may come to know You too. In Christ's name, amen.

Watch for the Goodness

Devote yourselves to prayer, being watchful and thankful (Colossians 4:2).

Scripture: **Colossians 4:2-6**
Song: **"Prayer Is the Soul's Sincere Desire"**

Jim and Kathy have been married for 20 years. They are devoted to each other. Tom is devoted to football. Every season he's glued to his television set from the pre-season until the final playoff game.

Devotion is a good thing, as long as it is well placed. There is certainly nothing wrong with being devoted to our spouses or to a relaxing hobby, as long as it does not replace our primary commitment to God Almighty. In Colossians 4:2, Paul calls the church members to devote themselves to prayer. When we take the time to talk to God—and to listen for Him—things change, doors open, chains fall off.

Like breathing, our prayer life can be a rhythmic "in and out, in and out" as we pour out our hearts to God—confessing, adoring, thanking, and asking Him for what we need . . . and then receiving what He has to tell us. In our devotion to knowing God in this way, we can be on the lookout, watchful and thankful, for His goodness in our lives and in the lives of those for whom we pray.

O Lord, deepen my commitment to You, and increase my devotion to communicating with You through prayer. In Jesus' name, amen.

October 9–15. **Jackie M. Johnson** is a freelance marketing writer and creative writer. She has written articles, poetry, and hundreds of devotionals.

Honoring the Hours?

My times are in your hands; deliver me from my enemies and from those who pursue me (Psalm 31:15).

Scripture: **Psalm 31:14-24**
Song: **"Time, by Moments, Steals Away"**

How much is a basketball worth? A basketball in my hands—or yours—is worth about $20. In the hands of NBA superstar Shaquille O'Neal, it's worth quite a few million. Why? Because he is one of the best players in NBA history, and I am . . . *not.*

Psalm 31 tells us that our times are in God's hands. When God is the center of our lives, we can give Him our cares and concerns and trust that He will take care of them, time after time. In His hands, my time is absolutely precious. In my hands, time can be wasted and become virtually valueless.

The challenge, then, is to place ourselves in God's hands at all times—the good and bad times, the exciting and boring times. As novelist Susan Ertz once said: "Millions long for immortality who do not know what to do with themselves on a rainy Sunday afternoon." God knows what to do with our times. He has plans for us, work for us to do in His kingdom. If we will lift up our hearts to Him for direction and protection from enemies, He will surely guide us safely into service.

O Lord, how wasteful of precious time I can be! You have given me a limited number of days upon this earth, so let me use them wisely and productively in Your service. In the name of Your Son, my Savior, I pray. Amen.

Power of Promises Kept

I prayed for this child, and the Lord has granted me what I asked of him. So now I give him to the Lord (1 Samuel 1:27, 28).

Scripture: **1 Samuel 1:21-28**
Song: **"Precious Promise"**

"I promise to love, honor, and obey," said the woman to her groom, and they divorced five years later. "I promise to cut taxes and grow the economy, "said the politician to his supporters, and he didn't do either. Sometimes even our friends and neighbors disappoint us. "Sure, I'll come to your party," someone may say, and then never show up. Why is it so hard for some people to keep their promises?

Hannah wasn't one of those people. She had prayed fervently for a child, vowing that if God would give her a son, then she would give the boy back to Him for full-time service in the temple. When her prayer was finally answered, she kept her promise and took young Samuel to worship and serve God all of his life. God kept His promise to Hannah, and she kept her promise to God.

We serve a promise-keeping God. Therefore, it is a joyful thing to be familiar with all the things He has vowed to do in and among His people. Being aware of His promises, we can depend on them with our whole lives.

Father, never once have You failed to carry through on Your Word. Today may I depend on You without hesitation. Through Your faithful Son I pray. Amen.

Rejoice in Your Lord!

Then Hannah prayed and said: "My heart rejoices in the Lord" (1 Samuel 2:1).

Scripture: **1 Samuel 2:1-10**
Song: **"Worship the Lord in the Beauty of Holiness"**

When God answers prayer, the most appropriate response is to worship Him. Hannah did this with emphatic passion. She prayed with fervency and tears for a child of her own, and God granted the request of this barren wife. In return, Hannah poured out her soul in a joy-filled prayer of thankfulness for her miracle.

But how do we know when we are truly worshiping in a way that pleases God? True worship is our sincere, grateful response to God for who He is and what He has done. It is more than singing songs on Sunday morning. It is ascribing worth (adoration, reverence, and respect) to the only one who is truly worthy of our praise. In worship, we acknowledge God's awesome attributes: His character, beauty, majesty, and power. The focus is on God; it's all about Him.

Individuals and nations must carry on the worship of God. Sadly, a 2004 YouGov survey provided overwhelming evidence that the British are now a largely irreligious people, with only 44 percent even believing in God's existence. A tiny minority still attend worship services regularly. Will America soon emulate this once godly people?

Lord, *I adore You. Help me to focus on You and may others see the beauty of your holiness. In Jesus' name, amen.*

Invited to Hear

Eli told Samuel, "Go and lie down, and if he calls you, say, 'Speak, Lord, for your servant is listening'" (1 Samuel 3:9).

Scripture: **1 Samuel 3:1-10**
Song: **"Listen to the Blessed Invitation"**

What if you heard God calling your name, audibly, in the middle of the night? "Mary, Mary!" or "Bob, Bob!" What would you do? That very thing happened to young Samuel in the Old Testament. The boy was sleeping, and the Lord called out his name three different times. When Samuel ran to Eli, his teacher in the temple, with the same "Here I am" reply, Eli realized that it was the Lord calling the boy.

The Lord speaks to us in many ways since Jesus came —through our prayer times, through worship in a song or hymn, through the beauty of creation, and through our intuition. Because of the unfolding progress of revelation, the Old Testament believers literally heard and saw more of God in explicit action. In our day we live by faith, relying on all the wonderful resources God has provided—the Bible, centuries of church history, and His Spirit dwelling within us. Nevertheless, God still longs to reveal His character, His purposes, and His ways; therefore, He still speaks to our hearts in many ways. Whether in ancient or modern days, the key for believers is the same: to listen, to *really* listen—and then respond.

Lord, *I hear You through the Bible, through preaching, through Your Spirit. Help me to listen! In Christ's name, amen.*

Sheer Bliss (from God)

**Samuel said to the whole house of Israel, "If you are return-
ing to the Lord with all your hearts, then rid yourselves of the
foreign gods and the Ashtoreths and commit yourselves to the
Lord and serve him only, and he will deliver you out of the
hand of the Philistines"** (1 Samuel 7:3).

Scripture: **1 Samuel 7:2-6**
Song: **"Father, Whate'er of Earthly Bliss"**

Marcy enjoyed running, and she was good at it. Every
Saturday she would compete in local and regional races
and usually bring home a first-place trophy. Soon running
became a great love of her life; it was sheer bliss.

No doubt Marcy would second what Eric Liddell (the
great 1924 Olympic runner) once said: "I believe God
made me for a purpose, but He also made me fast. And
when I run, I feel His pleasure."

How wonderful to know deep joy in any pursuit—and
to recognize it as a gift from God! Perhaps that is the
essence of the difference between praising the creator and
somehow idolizing an aspect of His creation. Surely it's
what the ancient Israelites often failed to recognize. If only
they would take their deep desire to worship—a good
thing—and turn it toward the only one who deserved it.
Then they would feel His pleasure as well.

*Dear Heavenly Father, I'm thrilled with everything I'm involved in today
by Your grace. All good things come from You, and I can only return my
thankfulness. Please help me never to forget the source of my joy—You
alone! Through Jesus, my deliverer, I pray. Amen.*

Creative Heavenly Aid

While Samuel was sacrificing the burnt offering, the Philistines drew near to engage Israel in battle. But that day the Lord thundered with loud thunder against the Philistines and threw them into such a panic that they were routed before the Israelites (1 Samuel 7:10).

Scripture: **1 Samuel 7:7-13**
Song: **"Spirit of God, That Moved of Old"**

The man was trapped on the roof of his house in a flood, waiting to be rescued while the water overwhelmed the streets below—and kept on rising. A neighbor rowed by in a small boat and offered to rescue him, but the man replied, "I am waiting for God to help me." Next, a helicopter flew overhead, and the pilot asked whether he needed help. Again, same reply.

A silly story, yes. But it makes an important point: when the helping hand of God comes to us, we need to recognize it.

God is surely our helper, but He is also pure spirit (see John 4:24). So He often uses human beings and every form of material, or aspects of nature, to accomplish His purposes. While Samuel was doing the spiritual thing, a thunderstorm routed his enemies. The gracious hand of God alone can save us. But how creative He is in coming to our aid!

O Lord, my finite mind just can't comprehend the infinite choices available to You in dealing with Your universe. Open my mind to see Your hand at work. Through Your precious Son I pray. Amen.

Polish Those Nails?

The Lord does not look at the things man looks at. Man looks at the outward appearance, but the Lord looks at the heart (1 Samuel 16:7).

Scripture: **1 Samuel 16:1-13**
Song: **"So Let Our Lips and Lives Express"**

"I always judge a woman by her fingernails," Rick said. I quickly plunged my hands into my pockets. Rick's wife, Sara, has nails that are meticulously manicured, perfectly shaped. My nails are soft, and they chip easily. Obviously.

Sara is slimmer and more outgoing than I am. She is a better cook, a more excellent seamstress, a more prolific writer. Though I had many reasons to compare myself negatively to Sara, I knew I was better at one thing—keeping score: Jean—1, Sara—487.

Sometimes I'm quite thankful that God looks far beneath the surface. But at other times I wish I could touch up the ragged edges of my life with something as simple as a few swipes of an emery board.

"Search me, O God, and know my heart," pleaded the psalmist (139:23). So lately I've given up comparing myself to others. As I stand before my all-knowing God, I want my heart to be free of envy and pride.

Father, Your Word says I am fearfully and wonderfully made. Help me believe it, no matter whom I meet today. Through Christ, amen.

October 16–22. **Jean Davis** is a freelance writer who lives in Clarksville, Delaware, with her husband.

Atmosphere of Indwelling

One of the servants answered, "I have seen a son of Jesse of Bethlehem who knows how to play the harp. He is a brave man and a warrior. He speaks well and is a fine-looking man. And the Lord is with him" (1 Samuel 16:18).

Scripture: **1 Samuel 16:14-23**
Song: **"May the Mind of Christ My Savior"**

As a young adult, I couldn't talk about the inner turmoil I felt. I just didn't have the vocabulary to describe my feelings. But every time I visited one family in our church, I left their home feeling better. In their presence, my spirit quieted down. The atmosphere created by their presence—more than their spoken words—gave me peace. I knew the Lord was with them, and I found the comfort of the comforter simply by sitting on their sofa. In time, I found emotional healing as well.

Whatever spirit dwells in us seems to create an atmosphere. So do our words and attitudes. So does music. Though David's music soothed Saul's troubled spirit, surely David's presence did, too, because the Lord was with that young man.

When others come to me, I want God's presence in my life to create an environment that conveys openness, honesty, and love. When others speak of my character or accomplishments, may they say: "The Lord is with her."

Lord God, when others look at me, I want them to see Your Son, Jesus. May I bring comfort to the hurting by allowing Your comfort to dwell in me. All praise to You, in Christ's name. Amen.

Credentials, Please!

You are not able to go out against this Philistine and fight him; you are only a boy, and he has been a fighting man from his youth (1 Samuel 17:33).

Scripture: **1 Samuel 17:32-37**
Song: **"Victory All the Time"**

Last week my friend, a high school graduate, met a man who works in the same type of job she has, but for a competitor. After Dr. Somebody introduced himself, he raised one bushy eyebrow and asked, "So, what are your credentials?" Though the invitation to compare her background to his would have rattled her a few years back, my friend now had a ready answer: "Experience."

David knew what he was up against, and he also knew his experience. Was a giant target of a man a more dangerous foe than a bear or a lion—he'd been victorious over them? David was confident that the Lord who had delivered him before would deliver him again.

When we see a door of opportunity open, someone might say we're too young—or too old, too dull, too timid—for the challenge. We may be told we don't have the right education, we're not the right gender or race to get the job done. But if God has prepared us, we'll know we're ready.

Mighty Lord, when voices of doubt come, bring to my memory Your work in my life so far. And help me remember how You've prepared me for the task at hand. Let me move forward with confidence, boldly proclaiming, "The Lord is with me." I pray through my deliverer, Jesus. Amen.

Request and Expect

In the morning, O Lord, you hear my voice; in the morning I lay my requests before you and wait in expectation (Psalm 5:3).

Scripture: **Psalm 5**
Song: **"Jesus, Thine All-Victorious Love"**

I know a woman who daily fights the battle of the bulge as she maintains a weight loss of over a hundred pounds. Though she now eats nutritionally and exercises, part of her battle plan is to roll out of bed every morning . . . onto her knees. Each day she humbly asks God for His help with her food choices, emotions, appetites, family, job, and relationships.

Psalm 60:12 says, "With God we will gain the victory." David found the key to victory—praying, then waiting in expectation for the Lord.

I believe we can fight our battles as David fought his. In the morning—every morning—we can lay our requests before God. Yes, the enemies of fear and doubt will press to whisper lies like, "You can't do it; you'll never succeed, so why try?" Even after a colossal failure, we can wait in expectation for Him to do for us what we can't do for ourselves. We don't have to fight our battles alone. We can open our lives to God and let His victory become ours.

Dear Father, thank You for victory in Jesus. May I daily approach Your throne boldly, ever aware of Your great faithfulness as I wait in expectation for You and Your work in my life. In the name of the Father, the Son, and the Holy Spirit, I pray. Amen.

That's God

David asked, "Where shall I go?" "To Hebron," the Lord answered (2 Samuel 2:1).

Scripture: **2 Samuel 2:1-7**
Song: **"Shepherd, Show Me How to Go"**

My friend Barbara called to say she had several errands to run before we met for lunch. Since she couldn't tell me exactly what time she'd be through, I suggested we meet at one of her stops, the Division of Motor Vehicles.

A strange place to meet, but we soon saw God's hand in our decision. When Barbara asked to change the address on her license, a clerk told her that their records showed she had no insurance coverage. Though Barbara knew there must be a mistake, the clerk kept her license, and Barbara was stranded—or would have been if God hadn't provided transportation: my car.

OK, it's a small thing. But I believe God cares about each moment of our lives and delights in blessing us with His big and small gifts. With the bigger things—when we need direction in life, as David did—we can ask, and God will answer. At other times, our steps are being ordered by the Lord without our awareness.

While we waited for the return of her license, Barbara said, "Isn't it amazing we chose to meet at the DMV?"

"That's God," I said. "You always say that," she answered. Yes, and there's reason.

God, how can I thank You for the care You show me each day? I'm so grateful You enjoy surprising me with Your goodness! Through Christ, amen.

Humble Beginnings, God's Plan

Now then, tell my servant David, "This is what the Lord Almighty says: I took you from the pasture and from following the flock to be ruler over my people Israel. I have been with you wherever you have gone" (2 Samuel 7:8, 9).

Scripture: **2 Samuel 7:8-17**
Song: **"Little Is Much When God Is in It"**

When Ben Carson was in fifth grade, other students called him Dummy. There were reasons for the taunt. The African-American youngster missed most words on spelling tests and got every math problem wrong. But it didn't matter because God had a plan for Ben. For one thing, his mother saw the potential in all her children. After asking God for direction, she required both her sons to read two books per week and give her written book reports (though Mom couldn't read!). By the middle of sixth grade, Ben moved to the top of his class.

He is now Dr. Ben Carson, director of the Division of Pediatric Neurosurgery at Johns Hopkins, with three best-selling books to his credit. His brother, Curtis, is a successful engineer.

Who would have thought the fifth-grade "dummy" would one day perform brain surgery? Well, who would have thought a boy tending sheep would be king? Yet no matter where we've come from, God has been with us wherever we've gone. He also has our future in view.

Heavenly Father, You see the beginning and the ending, and with You all things are possible. I praise You through Christ my Lord. Amen.

Because We Needed It

King David went in and sat before the Lord, and he said: "Who am I, O Sovereign LORD, and what is my family, that you have brought me this far?" (2 Samuel 7:18).

Scripture: **2 Samuel 7:18-29**
Song: **"I Can Only Imagine"**

Ever get discouraged by the little irritations of life? A stubborn hangnail—or an ornery pup that just won't house-train—can certainly get on my nerves. But when I think about Jesus, about God's mercy, grace, and love, about where I am now and where I've come from . . . I find that my mood changes.

Oswald Chambers's March 27 devotional from *My Utmost for His Highest* offers this encouragement: "Compare this week in your spiritual history with the same week last year and see how God has called you up higher." I may look at my performance today and be discouraged, but when I consider how far God has brought me, I am filled with gratitude.

Who are we that God has chosen us? What manner of love is this to be given the privilege of living as children of the most high God? We have done nothing to deserve such mercy and grace. We've *received* it simply because we *needed* it.

Almighty God, when I think of Your faithfulness over the years, my heart rejoices. How can I be discouraged when I consider Your great love? You are so good! I praise You today through the wonderful name of Your Son, Jesus Christ my Lord. Amen.

Act, Don't React

He wrote [the proverbs] to teach his people how to live—how to act in every circumstance, for he wanted them to be understanding, just and fair (Proverbs 1:2, 3, *The Living Bible*).

Scripture: **Proverbs 1:1-7**
Song: **"Only a Sinner"**

My 10-year-old daughter's face was ashen. "The substitute teacher thought I took Lindsey's green pencil sharpener," she said, dropping her red book bag to the floor. "She asked me to confess, Mommy," she continued before bursting into tears. "But I *didn't* take it!"

"I'm sure it wasn't you, honey," I said, drawing her close to me. "I feel like calling the principal right now."

"No, it's OK, Mom. You don't have to do anything. We worked it out already," she continued. "After Lindsey cooled down, I told her why I had a green sharpener—that I'd traded my special pencil for Emily's green sharpener over the weekend."

"Well, I'm glad you two worked it out, but I don't like it when my sweet, well-behaved little girl is falsely accused by some uppity stranger who knows nothing about her good character!"

What about your character? my conscience prodded, just after I'd pounded my fist on the kitchen table. . . .

My Lord and King, *when anyone in my family is falsely accused, please help me respond calmly and wisely. In Christ's precious name I pray. Amen.*

October 23–29. **Linda Eckman,** a newspaper reporter and songwriter living in Kennett Square, Pennsylvania, began writing for Christian publications in 1990.

Wisdom: a Treasure Hunt

"It's not here," the oceans say; and the seas reply, "Nor is it here" (Job 28:14, *The Living Bible*).

Scripture: **Job 28:12-28**
Song: **"Teach Me Thy Way, O Lord"**

One of my daughter's favorite pastimes when she was little was to make me a treasure map and have me go scampering throughout the house to find a hidden surprise. "You're not warm at all, Mommy," she beamed on Mother's Day. "Over there, try over there!" she said, pointing behind the couch where a yellow tag was noticeably sticking out.

"Don't give it away yet, silly," I said. "Let me look just a little longer. I like this game, so don't make it so easy!" But finally, after she could contain herself no longer, she proudly handed me a handmade clay jar. "It's a special place to put your rings, Mommy. It's just like your growned-up glass one."

Chrissy had shown me what it meant to search for wisdom. On my own I sometimes find a tiny nugget of truth or just a glimpse of what seems to be wisdom. But if I want to be truly wise, I'll go to where it's "hidden": God's Word. To love and reverence the Lord is to be truly wise. However, we must be as little children to enter in and partake of wisdom's heavenly sweetness.

Father, I need wise guidance and encouragement daily. Thank You for providing the teaching and fellowship of the church to help meet this need. But most of all, thank You for Your written Word. In Jesus' name, amen.

Sweet, or Just Poison?

No, I haven't turned away from what you taught me; your words are sweeter than honey (Psalm 119:102, 103, *The Living Bible*).

Scripture: **Psalm 119:97-104**
Song: **"Sweet, Sweet Spirit"**

I'm a recovering sugar-holic and still crave my daily dose of chocolate. But I've found that honey can be a good alternative for soothing my sweet tooth. On the one hand, sugar is known to pervert our appetites and increase our chances for dental visits, diabetes, and pancreatitis. On the other hand, honey—in moderation—offers the body 15 nutrients and is an excellent food.

Sugar also causes fermentation in the stomach, leading to bacterial growth. But honey, in its raw state, tends to aid digestion. It even acts as a natural antibiotic as it satisfies the appetite and enters the bloodstream slowly.

I'm glad the psalmist likened God's words to honey. The Word brings a sweetness to life that satisfies our longing for rich intimacy. Nothing in our lives is so perfect as God's counsel.

I think it's safe to say that when the psalmist speaks of false teaching, he alludes to words that are nutrient-free. Like sugar, they are empty, non-sustaining, and can even be considered poison to our inner being.

Dear God, thank You for the gifts You've given me. Keep Your Word flowing in my soul and increase my love for Your Son, Jesus, in whom I pray. Amen.

This Seat: Reserved!

Then King David said, "Call in Bathsheba." So she came into the king's presence and stood before him" (1 Kings 1:28).

Scripture: **1 Kings 1:28-40**
Song: **"Face to Face"**

No doubt Bathsheba was shaking in her boots when she heard the ominous command, "Come, Bathsheba." This appointment with King David was no small thing. David was now very old, and one of his sons, Adonijah, had suddenly declared himself the next king. However, David had long ago promised Bathsheba that her son, Solomon, would be the next king.

When Bathsheba complained about Adonijah's actions, she simply had to hold her breath and await David's response. Would he remember and fulfill his promise to make Solomon the king after him? Or would David be angry with Bathsheba's nagging?

Yes, if I were Bathsheba, I might be quite nervous. However, David decreed that Solomon would indeed sit upon the kingly throne, just as promised. (Sigh of relief!)

Like Solomon, we've been promised a kingly inheritance: "Those who receive God's abundant provision of grace and of the gift of righteousness [will] reign in life through the one man, Jesus Christ" (Romans 5:17). You see, there is a place of honor already reserved for us.

O God, in my times of doubt or fear, help me recall Your precious promises to me. They are are so encouraging and uplifting. Thank You! In the name of the Father, the Son, and the Holy Spirit, I pray. Amen.

Imperfect? Still Ask!

The Lord appeared to him in a dream that night and told him to ask for anything he wanted, and it would be given to him! (1 Kings 3:5, *The Living Bible*).

Scripture: **1 Kings 3:3-9**
Song: **"Yesterday, Today, and Forever"**

Put yourself in Solomon's shoes for a moment and imagine that you're a young adult and almighty God appears to you in a dream. The Lord tells you to ask for anything you want; it will be given to you.

What's amazing to me is that Solomon's wish would be granted, regardless of whether or not he was perfectly following God. First Kings 3:3 reads, "Solomon loved the Lord and followed all of his father David's instructions except that he continued to sacrifice in the hills and to offer incense there"*(TLB).* The altar at Gibeon is where God appeared to Solomon in the dream—but Gibeon was apparently one of those "hills," a high place of disobedience.

Isn't it interesting that God looked beyond Solomon's imperfections and, with great grace, extended toward him the gift he sought? This problem of weakness and disobedience is something I have in common with Solomon. While I desire to please God in all ways, I fall short of the goal. Yet God—the same yesterday, today, and forever—still provides the gift of His forgiveness and blessing.

Lord of All, thank You that we can come boldly to Your throne of grace, not because we're good and deserving, but because we're sinners. Praise to You, in the name of Jesus, my merciful Savior and Lord. Amen.

A Double Dip for Me Too

I will also give you what you didn't ask for—riches and honor! (1 Kings 3:13, *The Living Bible*).

Scripture: **1 Kings 3:10-15**
Song: **"You Can Have a Song in Your Heart"**

I think I've caught King Solomon double dipping. This is one instance that I know of when a Bible character was actually awarded his cake and given permission to eat it too. Not only did God provide Solomon what he asked for (a wiser mind than anyone else's), but He awarded the young king with riches and honor too—things he *didn't* request.

Something like this happened to me recently. You see, four times a year I self-publish a free newspaper and hand-deliver all 7,500 copies throughout my county. My intent is simply to reach people with the good news of Jesus Christ. For the latest issue, God had apparently given me a retired newspaper editor to help me typeset the paper. But when that didn't work out, the paper came to a grinding halt.

Now I needed a particular publishing software, but I just couldn't afford it. So I petitioned God to intervene. He answered—sent me another newspaper lady . . . and . . . brought a computer-whiz stranger to my office. This man handed me (free of charge) exactly—to the T—the publishing software I needed. Talk about a double dip!

Heavenly Father, *thank You for answering my requests, spoken and unspoken. Through Christ, I praise Your holy name! Amen.*

Sands of the Seashore

God gave Solomon wisdom and very great insight, and a breadth of understanding as measureless as the sand on the seashore (1 Kings 4:29).

Scripture: **1 Kings 4:29-34**
Song: **"All Creatures of Our God and King"**

I head to Cape Henlopen in Delaware on a beautiful winter morning. Upon arriving at the eastern shore, my breath is taken away. I am captivated by the beauty of the endless coast, and that first glimpse of God's magnificent ocean always causes my heart to leap for joy.

At the height of the tourist season, I like to watch the children run and play in ankle-deep surf, while others tenaciously build castles in the sand, and numerous adults forget their problems and stress.

I find it amazing that God promised Abraham that his descendants would eventually number more than the sand on the seashore.

The metaphor of sand comes forth in our Scripture passage: Solomon's insight, wisdom, and understanding will be as measureless as the seashore's grains of sand. After reading this passage about Solomon's wisdom, I don't think I will ever be able to look at the millions of particles of loose, opaque grains in the same way. But what analogy could even begin to convey the measureless wisdom of God himself?

O Majestic Father, thank You for leaving us a visual reminder that Your wisdom is far beyond our comprehension. Through Christ I pray. Amen.

God, the Under-Appreciated

Great is the LORD and most worthy of praise; his greatness no one can fathom (Psalm 145:3).

Scripture: **Psalm 145:1-7**
Song: **"No Other Name"**

I'd spent over five months preparing an outreach event for some young people so they could minister in schools where I live in France. I poured myself completely into the project, and by the final presentation, I was exhausted in every sense of the term. I was shocked, therefore, when the leader of the speaking groups publicly thanked someone else profusely for . . . hardly doing anything at all.

Later, I thought about how often it must happen to God. He created a paradise for us, complete with beautiful oceans, majestic mountains, countless varieties of wildlife, and a perfect ratio of gases in the air for us to breathe. He even sent His own Son to pay for our sins.

Yet whom do we praise in our upside-down culture today? A movie star who plays wonderful roles but may lack everyday integrity? A billionaire who has stepped on countless people all the way up the ladder? A guy who can jump and put a ball in a basket? Even a minister who preaches powerful sermons? But guess who goes unnoticed, unrecognized, and thoroughly under-appreciated.

God, I have no excuse for ignoring Your greatness and worthiness of all praise today. I pause right now and say thanks! Through Christ, amen.

October 30, 31. **Tim Bennett** is a missionary to France involved in church planting. He has written two books: *With a Grain of Salt* and *Salt for the Supper Table.*

October 31

No Grave, Not Yet!

Great is your love toward me; you have delivered me from the depths of the grave (Psalm 86:13).

Scripture: **Psalm 86:8-13**
Song: **"Hear My Cry"**

It's easy to complain when we find ourselves in diffi-culties. Yet it's in difficulties that we can see the *depths* of God's love (you can't get much lower than a grave).

Have you ever wondered why David was so exuberant in his praise to God? It's easy. He knew that without God's intervention he'd be dead. The problem today is that we don't always see God's protective hand upon us; we fail to recall what He has saved us from (an eternal grave).

There was one time, though, when I saw it very clearly. I was peacefully driving a tiny rental car on wet pavement when it hydroplaned into a guardrail. A van then hit me from behind, and my dented car stopped cold.

I ran to see whether the other driver was OK. He was. I needed my suitcase, so I rushed back to my car . . . just before a semi truck ran over it. Then I heard these lyrics sounding from the still-playing radio: "He didn't bring us this far to leave us." The timing was too perfect. I sang the song for weeks around the house. The kids complained, of course, because of the repetition. But I had a joy that couldn't be quenched. I ignored them and kept singing. Hey, I'd been delivered from the cold earth!

Ever-caring Lord, I know You've protected me so many times, often with-out my knowledge. I praise and thank You in Jesus' name. Amen.

DEVOTIONS®

*I*n you my soul
takes refuge. I
will take refuge
in the shadow
of your wings.

—Psalm 57:1

NOVEMBER

Photo © Eyewire

Gary Allen, Editor

Reigning in My Life?

The Lord reigns, he is robed in majesty (Psalm 93:1).

Scripture: **Psalm 93**
Song: **"Awesome God"**

Sixteen-year-old Sarah Huoy crouched under a table in the library at Columbine High School in Littleton, Colorado, on April 20, 1999, as two fully armed teenagers taunted and killed 10 classmates all around her. Not knowing what else to do, she began to pray, "God, send down your angels and make us invisible."

Immediately she felt a peace beyond her understanding. Minutes later she could see the shoes of the killers directly in front of her desk. One of them bumped a chair that hit her. Then, for some reason, the killers hesitated and left the room. This gave Sarah and others precious time to run for safety.

It's unlikely that many of us reading this account will experience such a dramatic confrontation with death as Sarah did. Often we may get the idea, however, that we ought to be able to control our lives quite well; when things aren't going according to our plans, we become anxious. Yet, if we trust that God is truly reigning in our lives, and that He is ultimately in charge, we can be at peace, regardless of the circumstances.

__Lord,__ You are a God of peace. If I give You all my anxieties, You will take care of all the things troubling me. Thank You, in Jesus' name. Amen.

November 1–5. **Tim Bennett** is a missionary to France involved in church planting. He has written two books: *With a Grain of Salt* and *Salt for the Supper Table.*

No Satisfaction?

Elijah went before the people and said, "How long will you waver between two opinions? If the Lord is God, follow him; but if Baal is God, follow him" (1 Kings 18:21).

Scripture: **1 Kings 18:17-24**
Song: **"I Belong to Jesus"**

Today, in western countries, worshiping literal idols is a little out of fashion. We do, however, battle the world's way of doing things as opposed to God's way.

As a teenager I had rejected God and tried living virtually without a spiritual life. The world said, "You need a girlfriend to be happy." So I found one. The world said, "Love means you don't need to get married." So we lived together. The world said, "Do your own thing." So I just stopped working, read books, and went to therapy.

My psychologist told me that my problems were actually my parents' fault. Great! But why wasn't I *satisfied* with my life?

Finally, someone challenged me to accept what the Bible had to say about my root problems—pride and rebellion against God. Simply put, that meant I faced a choice: God or the world. No more wavering!

I chose the Lord, and when I entered the waters of baptism—that's when my life started to turn around. That's when the satisfaction started kicking in.

Lord, so often I seem to be of two minds. Forgive me for sometimes placing the world's standards above Yours. Empower me by Your Spirit today to live only for Your glory. In Jesus' name I pray. Amen.

Grateful Doing

Midday passed, and they continued their frantic prophesying until the time for the evening sacrifice. But there was no response, no one answered, no one paid attention (1 Kings 18:29).

Scripture: **1 Kings 18:25-29**
Song: **"All-Consuming Fire"**

How ridiculous those prophets of Baal! They tried everything to please their god but couldn't even attract his attention. It reminds me of a woman whose husband was quite demanding. Every day he would give her a long to-do list. Wanting to please him, she worked as hard as she could to finish all the tasks. But she was never sure whether she did the jobs well enough; she never knew if her work had gained the longed-for acceptance.

One day the husband died. The woman later married a man with whom she was very much in love. He was a different kind of husband and treated her kindly. She was delighted, therefore, to do all she could to return his love. Coming across one of the old to-do lists, she was amazed. She had done all those things that very day, but with a light heart of love rather than fear.

Clearly, the *reason* we serve God makes all the difference. Religion says we *must* do in order to earn God's favor. Christianity says we gratefully *can* do because we already have His full acceptance.

Father, You love me while I'm a sinner—and You can't possibly love me more than You already do. All praise to You, through Christ Jesus! Amen.

Keeping the Best?

Elijah said to all the people, "Come here to me." They came to him, and he repaired the altar of the Lord, which was in ruins (1 Kings 18:30).

Scripture: **1 Kings 18:30-35**
Song: **"On Bended Knee"**

At the altar of the Lord, the people of Israel were supposed to sacrifice their best animals and so obtain forgiveness of their sins. But Elijah found this altar in ruins; its function was no longer in vogue. Had the people simply decided to keep "the best" to themselves?

As a believer, I've found one of the hardest things for me to do is to lay my deepest desires and best dreams before God. For some reason I get the idea that I actually know better than God what is best for me. So I hesitate to offer my whole self—all I am and all I have. Yet I know God is waiting for me to lay it all down. That way, He can resurrect it, if it is of Him. Or He can let it die . . . so He can give me something better.

Years ago I sensed God leading me to buy a house. I found the perfect place, made an offer, and then watched it go to someone else. Feeling I'd misread God, I wanted to chuck the whole idea. Instead, God encouraged me (through Hebrews 10:39) not to "shrink back" into unbelief but to continue in faith. He ended up providing a much better house than the one I had set my heart on.

Lord, You know best what is best for me. Show me the relationship, the dream, the desire that I need to lay before You now. In Jesus' name, amen.

Time to Pray Aloud?

Answer me, O Lord, answer me, so these people will know that you, O Lord, are God, and that you are turning their hearts back again (1 Kings 18:37).

Scripture: **1 Kings 18:36-39**
Song: **"The Battle Belongs to the Lord"**

As Elijah's battle with the false prophets demonstrates, answered prayer has an amazing way of getting the attention of unbelievers. It can make a real splash!

Notice Elijah's heart in this passage. His motivation was the welfare of the onlookers. He wanted a manifestation of God's power, not so he could be a big shot in town, but so the people would know that God wanted their hearts back. In other words, Elijah already knew how awesome God was. He wanted the people to know too.

Sometimes, however, people are like the prophets of Baal—they aren't ready to be prayed for until they have exhausted all other possibilities. They are convinced they can solve their problems without God. This leaves them in control, and often they have to try everything before becoming desperate enough to let us pray for them.

Are there people in your life who have already tried everything to make life worth living—but still long for more? Perhaps now is the time to pray for them aloud, on purpose, in their presence.

Lord, show me if there are people in my life right now who are ready for me to offer prayer on their behalf. Give me the boldness to ask them, and to do it, so You can reveal Your love in a tangible way. Through Christ, amen.

Gone Forever

As far as the east is from the west, so far has he removed our transgressions from us (Psalm 103:12).

Scripture: **Psalm 103:1-12**
Song: **"Sinners, Rejoice: Your Peace Is Made"**

Science tells us that the universe is so vast and complex that even our most powerful telescopes can't measure its dimensions. No matter which direction we look, north, south, east, and west appear to go on forever, never meeting at any point in time or space.

What a great picture of God's forgiveness! When we humbly repent of our sin, He promises to forgive us for each one, every time we ask. The guilt of all our sin—past, present, and future—has been carried away into the wilderness by Jesus, the divine "scapegoat" (see Leviticus 16:7-26), never to return to us.

It boggles the mind to think of anyone offering forgiveness like that. God doesn't continue to bring up our sin once it's confessed. When He forgives, it's over, finished, gone forever. Therefore, let us forget too and move ahead with our lives. As someone once put it: "God buries our sins in the deepest sea and then places a floating sign above the spot. The sign says: No fishing!"

Dear Lord, when I think of Your forgiving me like this, I'm overwhelmed. I feel alive, loved, and humbled. My guilt and condemnation are gone because of Jesus, the one in whom I pray. Amen.

November 6–12. **Mabelle Reamer** is a recent graduate of Philadelphia Biblical University, having earned a master's degree in counseling.

One Turn at a Time

I will instruct you and teach you in the way you should go; I will counsel you and watch over you (Psalm 32:8).

Scripture: **Psalm 32**
Song: **"My Lord Knows the Way Through the Wilderness"**

It was almost 9:00 one Friday evening when my husband received a frantic call from our daughter. After visiting friends at a mall some distance from where we live, she had taken a few wrong turns as she drove home. Now she was lost. My husband, who was familiar with the area, talked her through the confusing exits and road signs until she found a street she knew led home.

Day-to-day problems and pains can be overwhelming, and they often leave us feeling as if we've lost our bearings. In our struggle to find our way through, it's easy to end up disoriented and worried, not knowing what to do next. It seems the more we try to figure things out, the more disoriented we can become.

Of course, God knows exactly where we are, and we don't have to go it alone. He's promised not to leave us floundering by ourselves. We have His promise that He'll go before us and talk us through each confusing, frightening turn, one at a time—until the day we go home to be with Him.

Father, quiet my heart and mind, and help me find peace in just being with You. Help me to trust You in the turmoil and to remember that You're already present in my tomorrow. So guide me through this day, one moment at a time. In Jesus' name, I pray. Amen.

Purifying Tears

Rend your heart and not your garments. Return to the Lord your God, for he is gracious and compassionate, slow to anger and abounding in love, and he relents from sending calamity (Joel 2:13).

Scripture: **Joel 2:12-17**
Song: **"Cleanse Me"**

When my children were small, part of their discipline for bad behavior would involve the occasional time-out. They'd have to go upstairs and sit quietly on a chair for a specified time. During one such occasion I sat down with my child to talk about *why* he'd been sent upstairs. He appeared to understand he'd done wrong, and he offered an apology. By all appearances everything went back to normal. I found out later that I'd only succeeded in making him change his outward behavior—not his heart.

Sometimes I secretly enjoy giving the *appearance* of walking closely with God, of saying sincere prayers, and deeply loving all of my fellow church members. It's easier that way, because seeing my heart—as it tends to be most of the time—is painful and humbling. But my gracious and merciful God knows I need to grieve over my heart, which so easily wanders into total self-interest. Is it perhaps only with tears that a heart can be purified?

Heavenly Lord, I know that my motives are often impure. Forgive me for my deceit and pride. May Your Spirit reveal those things in me that need to change. (I don't like asking this, Lord, because it's hard and it hurts. Give me the courage to do it anyway.) In Jesus' name, amen.

Eyes on the Prize

He did what was right in the eyes of the Lord and walked in all the ways of his father David, not turning aside to the right or to the left (2 Kings 22:2).

Scripture: **2 Kings 22:1-7**
Song: **"I Am Resolved"**

My favorite part of the Olympics is watching the sprinters as they scramble toward the finish line. They all strain mightily to receive a gold medal to hang around their necks. They must focus on their goal and not be distracted by the crowd or whomever is running next to them.

It's been said that what has our attention has *us*, and it doesn't take much to pull our eyes away. Loss, disappointment, fear of public opinion—these are only a few of the things that can distract us and keep us from finishing well.

In Old Testament times, King Josiah must have wanted to finish well, determining that nothing would keep him from being the person God wanted him to be. He didn't turn right or left, but headed straight to the finish line.

What would that mean for you or me today? For one thing, moving straight ahead for the Lord will affect our televised entertainment choices. How can we be "right in the eyes of the Lord" when our own eyes are filled with so much that *isn't* quite right?

Father, I want to run this race as the apostle Paul did—with my eyes always on the prize. Please help me to stay focused on you and finish well! In Jesus' name, amen.

A Treasure Found

Then Shaphan the secretary informed the king, "Hilkiah the priest has given me a book." And Shaphan read from it in the presence of the king (2 Kings 22:10).

Scripture: **2 Kings 22:8-13**
Song: **"Thy Word"**

There's something about a letter that keeps a person close to us even when they are physically far away. After my father died, I regretted not having any hand-written letters from him to tuck away and reread. So imagine my thrill a few months later when I discovered several letters he'd written to me years earlier. I'd forgotten about them!

Those precious missives were the next best thing to having him with me. They were a special gift that had been lost but found, something I would always treasure.

Somehow in the years before Josiah's reign, the Book of the Law (the first five books of our Bible today) had been lost and forgotten. Imagine the king's excitement at such a find after all the years of not having any writings from God himself.

Scripture overflows with messages from our God to us, with words that will encourage, inspire, and change us as we read them. Are they something we cherish and read over and over? Or are they more like a forgotten, lost treasure waiting to be discovered?

Great God of the Bible, without Your Word I can't know who You are—or become the person You want me to be. Make Your words so fresh and new in my heart that I'll want to reread them every day. In Jesus' name, amen.

Personal Influence

The king stood by the pillar and renewed the covenant in the presence of the Lord—to follow the Lord and keep his commands, regulations and decrees with all his heart and all his soul. . . . Then all the people pledged themselves to the covenant (2 Kings 23:3).

Scripture: **2 Kings 23:1-5**
Song: **"I Love You, Lord"**

By adopting the U.S. Constitution and Declaration of Independence, our nation's founders pledged themselves to keeping and protecting for the rest of their lives all that those documents asserted. The example of those men inspired others to take those writings as their own. Many of the early patriots, just ordinary citizens, would give their lives to insure the freedom proclaimed therein. And over 200 years later, we're still influenced by the men who penned the words of those great texts.

In fact, every human extends some form of influence, whether for good or bad. After God's Law had been found, King Josiah stood before the people and pledged to follow it with all his heart and soul, for the rest of his life. His example encouraged all the people to do the same.

You may be just one person, but one way or another you're having an impact on those around you. Be assured, someone is following your example.

Lord, thank You for those whose lives have encouraged me to reach for my dreams and to walk closer to You. Help me to provide the same encouragement to every person who looks up to me. Through Christ I pray. Amen.

Extraordinary Hall of Fame

Neither before nor after Josiah was there a king like him who turned to the Lord as he did—with all his heart and with all his soul and with all his strength, in accordance with all the Law of Moses (2 Kings 23:25).

Scripture: **2 Kings 23:21-25**
Song: **"The Greatest Thing in All My Life"**

Throughout the course of history, occasionally one individual stands out above the rest. The hall of fame list is long, of course, but here are some names that might immediately spring to mind: Moses, Alexander the Great, Augustine, Leonardo DaVinci, Abraham Lincoln, Albert Einstein. Each man's dedication to his life's purpose set them apart as the extraordinary, unique achievers they became. Although difficulties distracted them at times, they never lost sight of their dreams, pursuing them with everything they had.

Josiah won't be found in our secular history books, but God remembered him in His Book as one of the most extraordinary leaders who ever lived. This king hadn't led a great army or gathered tremendous wealth, but he did one thing that made him great: he kept sight of his determined purpose to be God's man.

Imagine having the king of the universe say, "There's never been one like you!" That's what separates the ordinary from the extraordinary in God's hall of fame.

Heavenly Father, *I want to follow You with all my heart. Give me the will and the strength to do it, one step at a time. In Jesus' name, amen.*

Wisdom Still Speaks

How much longer will you enjoy being stupid fools? Won't you ever stop sneering and laughing at knowledge? (Proverbs 1:22, *Contemporary English Version*).

Scripture: **Proverbs 1:20-33**
Song: **"O Boundless Wisdom, God Most High"**

It's becoming common in our modern society for true wisdom to be dismissed. Disguised, often thinly, as disdain for the traditional—or worse, "old-fashioned"—it's typically just the rejection of time-tested wisdom.

Today wisdom is often treated as a commodity that ebbs and flows according to the whims of culture and the popularity of trends, rather than standing on its own as something sacred. New studies, editorial opinions, scientific revelations, and strategically spun news reports—all can masquerade as authentic wisdom. So where shall we turn for genuine insight and good judgment?

In the book of Proverbs, wisdom is sometimes given a personality, as though it were actually a supernatural being alongside God at the time of creation. If we take the time to listen, wisdom's voice beckons, even today. In line at the grocery store, in traffic, at work . . . let us be alert to its matchless guidance.

Lord, I have access to true wisdom through Your Spirit who dwells within me. Help me listen closely to His guidance today. In Jesus' name, amen.

November 13–19. **Jeffrey Aran Leever** of Arvada, Colorado, is the author of *Even in Darkness* and *Daily Disciples*. He also contributes to Huskerpedia.com.

Why Won't They Listen?

Pay attention, my children! Follow my advice, and you will be happy (Proverbs 8:32, *Contemporary English Version*).

Scripture: **Proverbs 8:32-36**
Song: **"Listen to the Blessed Invitation"**

When it comes to listening, most of us have something in common. We've either made a parent wonder about the answer to the above title's question, or if we are a parent, we've asked it about our child.

As a youngster, far too often I disregarded the "pay attention" pleas issuing from my mother and teachers. Part of me knew the forthcoming information was important, that someone was trying to spare me from ignorance—or from getting into trouble. Still, the pleas usually failed to move me.

As an adult, I listen a little better, but sometimes God must still go to the extreme to grab my notice. This is strange, I suppose, because His Word clearly spells out the benefits of heeding Him: "You will be happy."

Seems like a pretty fair deal, doesn't it? Yet, as Benjamin Franklin once said: "He that won't be counseled can't be helped." Therefore, may we peel away the distractions of our eyes and the symphony of noise from our ears . . . and hear His caring voice. In the end, it is our lives that will benefit.

Dear Father, I pray for clarity in hearing Your voice and the courage to follow all You say to me. I do thank You for granting me Your Spirit as counselor and guide through all my days on earth. In Jesus' name, amen.

Today's Risky Business

Jeremiah, get ready! Go and tell the people what I command you to say. Don't be frightened by them (Jeremiah 1:17, *Contemporary English Version*).

Scripture: **Jeremiah 1:11-19**
Song: **"Be Bold"**

In our politically correct world, speaking out against wrongdoing takes more courage than ever. Christians today face a moral relativism that has turned traditional ethical formulations upside down. For example, only a few short decades ago, who could have imagined today's cultural outrage at the idea that sex be reserved only for marriage? Or the howls of protest at the suggestion that one religion might be more true than another?

When we feel that serious consequences loom, it's natural to want to avoid head-on collisions of worldview. Even Jeremiah must have had his fears about facing the evil of his day. But God told him to proceed with courage.

In this moment of quiet, I ask myself: How willing am I to point out wrongdoing, especially when I know I'll be called insensitive, offensive, or bigoted? We frequently long for guarantees that the risks will be worth it, that we'll succeed. But God has already given assurance in His Word: be faithful, and we will have our reward . . . here, or *there.*

Dear Lord, *make me a wise risk-taker for You, as Jeremiah was. Create in me a readiness and fearlessness to take on the challenges of a popular culture that abhors the idea of moral absolutes. In Christ's name I pray. Amen.*

Offer Refused!

But you refused to listen to my prophets . . . and you are the ones who were hurt by what you did (Jeremiah 25:7, *Contemporary English Version*).

Scripture: **Jeremiah 25:1-11**
Song: **"Not by Might"**

Hardened hearts keep more people out of Heaven than hardened arteries. The typical scenario goes like this: Something painful happens; a person feels wronged; bitterness follows but is pushed down and internalized. A heart becomes hardened to God. Admit it, we've all seen it. Or been there ourselves.

Later, God calls bitter people to repent and accept His love for them. Still, some people choose to reject His invitations, sometimes even blaming the voice that tried to help.

This is what happened to the prophet Jeremiah, a man who called the people of Judah (for 23 years!) to turn back to God from their idolatries. It certainly would have been much easier for Jeremiah just to blend in and ignore the evils around him. Yet he reminds us to speak out even amid a hostile and dangerous culture of unbelief.

We can debate whether or not Jeremiah actually made much difference; Judah's captivity ensued. But at least he presented the truth as God called him to do. Like him, we are simply to obey, leaving the results in God's hands.

Father, I desire to communicate the gospel to lost people, regardless of the reception. Through the power of Christ's sacrifice, I pray. Amen.

An Unfaithful Faith

All the leaders of the priests and the people became more and more unfaithful (2 Chronicles 36:14).

Scripture: **2 Chronicles 36:11-14**
Song: **"Believe Not Those Who Say"**

"Religion has not civilized man; man has civilized religion," said Robert Ingersoll, known as the King of American Orators in the mid-nineteenth century. He was also a committed agnostic.

Ingersoll was wrong about God's existence, but he was certainly right that human beings can attempt to "civilize" the true God, to make Him wishy-washy, tolerant of everything, and largely irrelevant. However, as our Scripture passage today demonstrates, worship of God requires exclusive faithfulness.

Sadly, many today wish to associate with Christ only superficially, as their so-called religious leaders continue moving away from reverence for God's teachings. It seems the more things change, the more they stay the same.

It's interesting to visit the Web site for secular humanism and find a great tribute to Robert Green Ingersoll (1833–1899). And, among the list of humanist affirmations there, we read: "We deplore efforts to explain the world in supernatural terms, and to look outside nature for salvation." What could be more unfaithful?

God, show me clearly what it means to live in faithfulness to You today. Guide me as I take each step. By the power of Jesus Christ, I pray. Amen.

Our God: *Not* Safe!

They ignored what the LORD God was trying to tell them, until he finally became so angry that nothing could stop him (2 Chronicles 36:16, *Contemporary English Version*).

Scripture: **2 Chronicles 36:15-21**
Song: **"People Need the Lord"**

In an age of truth rejection, how far do we go to ensure that people get every chance to accept God's love? The task is so difficult because we now live under a different "covenant" than what was in place in 2 Chronicles: the philosophy of postmodernism. But in many ways the challenge is similar. God went to extraordinary lengths (through Jeremiah) to keep Jerusalem from destruction. Yet, even with God, there comes an end to restraint.

In one of C. S. Lewis's fiction books for children, *The Lion, the Witch and the Wardrobe,* Aslan the lion represents the person of Christ. Little Lucy contemplates what it will be like to meet him, asking: "Is he quite safe?"

The answer comes: "Safe? . . . Who said anything about safe? 'Course he isn't safe. But he's *good*. He's the King, I tell you." In another part of the book we read: "At the name of Aslan each one of the children felt something jump in his insides. Edmund felt a sensation of mysterious horror."

The love of God is gentle but never offered with a ticket to easy living. We do well to be in awe of Him.

Lord, help me never take Your Word for granted. I love You—and I also reverence Your almighty name. Through Your beloved Son I pray. Amen.

Righteous Indignation

Remember, O Lord, what the Edomites did on the day Jerusalem fell. "Tear it down," they cried, "tear it down to its foundations!" (Psalm 137:7).

Scripture: **Psalm 137**
Song: **"Let God Arise, and by His Might"**

You can't read the Bible for long without noticing the distinctly human tone of voice. The peaks and valleys of God's Word demonstrate a variety of emotions—very humanlike. And the psalmist's personal attachment to Jerusalem reflects God's long-suffering nature as well as a righteous indignation that longs for justice.

Have you encountered your own version of the Edomites in your life? If so, you know what it feels like to be misunderstood, mocked, and mistreated. Your soul then cries out for justice and the restoration of your dignity. Psalm 137 shows us that God has heard this type of angry, forlorn lament before.

While we're free to bring such pleas to His throne, God reminds us: "It is mine to avenge; I will repay" (Romans 12:19). Scripture never calls on us to carry out our own version of holy justice on God's behalf. Rather, we are invited to lay our burdens down before Him, trusting that His peace—a peace that transcends all understanding—will guard our hearts and our minds until everything is put right.

Lord, *I weep for all that's wrong in the world, but I also thank You for promising to make all things new at the last day. Through Christ, amen.*

Driving Past Disaster

In you my soul takes refuge. I will take refuge in the shadow of your wings until the disaster has passed (Psalm 57:1).

Scripture: **Psalm 57**
Song: **"A Shelter in the Time of Storm"**

It was the last leg of our trip to Hot Springs, Arkansas, from Pennsylvania. On the outskirts of Little Falls, we saw the billboard advertising Carl's Motel. My boss's name was Carl, and since it was already late, I suggested, "Let's stay there and send Carl a postcard."

But we missed the exit, so we continued on to our destination though it was getting quite stormy before we settled into a motel in Hot Springs. The next morning we heard the news that a tornado had touched down in Little Falls. Curious to see the damages, we exited there on our return trip. Only the sign poles were left standing in the debris that had recently been . . . Carl's Motel.

According to the heading in my Bible, Psalm 57 was written to a tune called "Do Not Destroy." When the psalmist found refuge in the midst of disaster, his response was to sing and make music. As I drove through the storm-torn area, I prayed for those who experienced physical devastation. But I also offered a song of praise for the soul-keeping refuge of the Lord, my God.

Lord, *You spare me from so many dangers, most of which I never know. Praise to You, my shelter in the time of storm. Through Jesus I pray. Amen.*

November 20–26. **Penny Smith** of Harrisburg, Pennsylvania, has authored the books *Gateways to Growth* and *Keys to Christian Growth and Maturity.*

Personal Construction

It will be said: "Build up, build up, prepare the road! Remove the obstacles out of the way of my people" (Isaiah 57:14).

Scripture: **Isaiah 57:14-19**
Song: **"Builder of Ages"**

The construction for the new high school was a major undertaking, and radical changes to the whole area took place daily. Even the roadblocks and detours were constantly being changed—and our church sat right in the midst of it all.

The transformation that truly boggled my mind was the rerouting of a creek to create a new road. Each trip to church showed us the process, step by step. Workers removed trees and brush with earth-moving equipment, built up a solid foundation for the new road, and eventually tore out the old one. And the creek still flowed.

It's been said that we Christians are constantly under construction. Our creator-redeemer has given us the building materials. His Holy Spirit within us is our guide; the Bible is our blueprint. He may allow an interruption to slow us down, prevent us from financial crisis by blocking the approval of a loan, or clear the way for a new job. Divine diversions may be His pathway to our divine destiny. When crisis comes, praise Him for the comfort and restoration that is promised to follow.

Forgive me, Lord, for complaining about unwanted changes in my life. Thank You that I am being built together with other believers to become a dwelling in which You live by Your Spirit. In Christ's name, amen.

Productive Waiting

I wait for the Lord, my soul waits, and in his word I put my hope (Psalm 130:5).

Scripture: **Psalm 130**
Song: **"Be Still, My Soul"**

When it snows, my neighbor plows our shared driveway. But since he plows for many others, our driveway waits until the end of the day.

Once an unexpected snowstorm hit overnight, and I was to meet a friend at the airport in the morning. I prayed, "Lord, that plow needs to be here by 10:00 for me to get up the driveway." Of course, it wasn't my neighbor's custom to do such a thing. Besides, he knew nothing of my plight.

I was sorting laundry, wondering whom I could call upon to collect my friend on such a miserable day, when I heard a familiar engine roar. There was my neighbor, plowing the driveway. I checked the time. Exactly 10:00.

Waiting is one of the most strenuous spiritual challenges we face. The psalmist's posture seems to be one of inactivity. He says, "I wait . . . my soul waits." Then he reveals the key to his ability: he placed his hope in the Word of the Lord. But hoping, by faith, is hardly inactive; it is spiritual *exercise*. When we wait with an expectant posture, our belief is hard at work.

Teach me Your ways, Father, so I can stretch the limbs of my spirit to embrace Your Word. As I learn to place all my hope in You, I thank You for every productive time of waiting in Your presence. In Jesus' name, amen.

God Has a Plan

"I know the plans I have for you," declares the Lord, "plans to prosper you and not to harm you, plans to give you hope and a future" (Jeremiah 29:11).

Scripture: **Jeremiah 29:10-14**
Song: **"Hymn of Promise"**

She had filled our lives with chuckles and cheer, demonstrating what our senior years were meant to be. Whether speeding down the mountain on a snow slide, or dressing for a comedy act, she performed with superabundant joy and delight. Now she lay silenced by the brain tumor that had so quickly ravaged her life.

At first she would squeeze my hand to let me know she understood—and that she was still there. Now her hand lay limply in mine, death's dew formed on her brow.

It is one thing to trust the Lord for a bright future when you are in good health, but quite another when that health has failed. God doesn't tell us where our future lies or when our time on earth will end. Our confidence is in knowing that *all* of our times are in His capable hands.

While we remain here on earth, God's plans for us provide our hope for the future. If my friend could have responded in those last moments, I know that the squeeze of her hand would have indicated the strength of her confidence in our risen Lord.

Lord over all time, because of Your great love for me, my future is bright. While I draw breath, keep my faith in You vibrant and confident, through all the changing seasons of my days. In Jesus' name I pray. Amen.

The Upward Look

This is what Cyrus king of Persia says: "The Lord, the God of heaven . . . has appointed me to build a temple for him at Jerusalem in Judah. Anyone of his people among you—may the Lord his God be with him, and let him go up" (2 Chronicles 36:23).

Scripture: **2 Chronicles 36:22, 23**
Song: **"Let Zion's Watchmen All Awake"**

On my last visit to Israel, I learned that the house in which I stayed had been used as a blackout shelter during Operation Desert Storm in 1991. The occupants described how they had crowded into a dark inner hallway when the nightly curfew sounded. They would be there for hours, or even several days, hoping to avoid Saddam Hussein's Scud missile attacks.

When the all-clear signal sounded, they immediately left their hideout and climbed up the stairway to the roof above to assess any damage. What relief they felt upon going up, out of the darkened hiding place!

When I saw where they gathered, I could hardly believe they were able to exist there. But they passed the time by sharing stories, and also by turning their hearts' gaze upward—praying for one another and for the situation. Their prayers became proclamations of God's goodness, His protection, and His power. It made me think: is my heart propelled upward in the midst of trouble?

Heavenly Father, I thank You for being the lifter of our heads, and for helping us to lift our eyes to You in the worst of times. In Jesus' name, amen.

Packing to Move

Then rose up the chief of the fathers of Judah and Benjamin, and the priests, and the Levites, with all them whose spirit God had raised, to go up to build the house of the Lord which is in Jerusalem (Ezra 1:5, *King James Version*).

Scripture: **Ezra 1**
Song: **"Higher Ground"**

Some years ago I found myself in the embarrassing position of being homeless. Thankfully, it was for a short period of time, during which my hatchback car served as my official residence. I camped in style, moving about with a small mattress on the roof, my plasticware and a cook pot in the hatch with suitcases, my office in the back seat, and a dalmatian and dachshund in the passenger seat beside me. Don't ask me how we all fit.

The Lord had "raised my spirit," and I knew a time of preparation was at hand. I would sit on a park bench reading my Bible while the dogs exercised, and various passages would impress me: "Fear not." "Take no thought for your life." "Knock, and it shall be opened unto you." "Follow me." I had been stripped of most of my earthly possessions, dreams, and ambitions. Now it was time to rebuild.

Are you in transition? If so, there is no better time than this to prepare your heart and renew your mind for the next move. If you are following the Lord, He will provide.

Father, in times of uncertainty, lead me. Help me always to be willing to move if it serves Your kingdom purposes. Through Jesus I pray. Amen.

Do Not Enter!

We are the servants of the God of heaven and earth, and we are rebuilding the temple that was built many years ago, one that a great king of Israel built and finished (Ezra 5:11).

Scripture: **Ezra 5:6-14**
Song: **"I Will Go in the Strength of the Lord"**

Have you ever innocently entered a room, only to discover that you were in an Authorized Personnel Only area? With my poor sense of direction, this has taken many forms for me. For instance, I once not only entered a gent's rest room but actually started into a stall before I realized it. I've entered the exit ramp in parking garages, and then tried to exit the entrance ramp. I've tried to make my key work in someone else's locker, rushed into a private courtroom, and absentmindedly invaded the restricted area of an airport. Where will I end up next?

In a few of the above scenarios, I immediately heard the question posed to Ezra's temple builders: "Who has authorized you to be here?" I'd cringe, stutter, and back out with a red face.

On the other hand, when we're moving in the authority that has been given us, we enter the privileged places with confidence. As Christians, we are to walk in the authority that is ours through the sacrifice of Christ. We are indeed servants of the God of Heaven and earth, just as were the workers of Ezra's day.

Heavenly Father, *may the authority of the resurrection power of Christ empower me to do Your will today. In Jesus' name, amen.*

Precious Gift

They had no children, because Elizabeth was barren; and they were both well along in years (Luke 1:7).

Scripture: **Luke 1:5-20**
Song: **"Happy the Home When God Is There"**

Married for three years, both were in their late 30s. Although they were anxious to start a family, pregnancy eluded them. As a last resort, they tried in vitro fertilization. But when that failed, the doctor asked, "Would you consider adoption?" Instead, they traveled to another hospital in another state. And nine months later they became the parents of a beautiful, eight-pound baby girl.

The in vitro procedure was expensive, exhausting, and risky. Yet the happy couple says, "It was worth every cost, every obstacle. We are so thankful for God's goodness."

Zechariah and Elizabeth, dutiful servants of the Lord, had longed for, and prayed for, a child. But time had passed, and perhaps they had resigned themselves to being childless. Can you imagine Zechariah's astonishment and disbelief when the angel of the Lord appeared to announce their desire would be granted? And this child would be a key player in God's redemptive plan, preparing the people for Christ's coming. This couple too offered thanks for the goodness of God.

Gracious God, praise to You for the children among us. May every parent be reminded this day: how precious are these gifts! Through Christ, amen.

November 27–30. **Cos Barnes,** of Southern Pines, North Carolina, is a mother of three and grandmother of seven. She enjoys playing handbells for her church.

The Benefits of Silence

When he came out, he could not speak to them. They realized he had seen a vision in the temple, for he kept making signs to them but remained unable to speak (Luke 1:22).

Scripture: **Luke 1:21-25**
Song: **"Silently the Shades of Evening"**

My friend Sandra's parents were both deaf, her father from birth, her mother from the age of 6. She tells me they had no telephone until she was 8 years old. At that time, Sandra became her parents' communicator, the one who phoned for doctor's appointments, car inspections, or prescription deliveries. The three of them used sign language to communicate, so Sandra grew up in a silent household—which had its limitations and benefits.

Zechariah learned about silence the hard way. He was made unable to speak from the time the angel Gabriel appeared until the day the promised son entered the world. After the angelic encounter, Zechariah could only sign and gesture to the worshipers outside the temple.

I have a feeling that after he returned home and somehow conveyed his miraculous encounter to Elizabeth, Zechariah spent the next nine months in prayerful thanksgiving. He knew the limitations of silence, but surely over the years of observing his son John's ministry, he must have reveled in its awesome benefits.

Dear God, I pray today for people who are deaf or hard of hearing. I know sometimes they feel alone and isolated. Please help them know how special they are to You. In Christ's holy name I pray. Amen.

Fatherly Preparation

You, my child, will be called a prophet of the Most High; for you will go on before the Lord to prepare the way for him (Luke 1:76).

Scripture: **Luke 1:67-80**
Song: **"Prepare the Way, O Zion!"**

After the birth of their child, Zechariah praised God not only for sending a son but for providing salvation for the world. Directing his words to his son, Zechariah told John he would give knowledge and salvation to the people and prepare the way of the Lord. John the Baptist would be the forerunner of Jesus and would acquaint the people with God, for they really did not know what He was like.

I've noticed how fathers take pride in their sons. They are just as proud of their daughters, of course. But there seems to be a special father-son relationship in mentoring a boy into manhood—something a mom can't accomplish.

I witnessed it when my husband and son would discuss football strategy, school relationships, business tactics, and marital challenges. I remember their early games of catch and my husband demonstrating the butterfly stroke, removing the training wheels when it was time, and fixing the flats on both bike and car. Dad was always there with mature guidance when trouble loomed. He served as best man at his boy's wedding and soon babysat the grandchildren. The cycle starts once again.

Thank You for parents who faithfully guide sons and daughters in righteousness. Give them wisdom and strength this day. Through Christ, amen.

Shout the Good News

People went out to him from Jerusalem and all Judea and the whole region of the Jordan (Matthew 3:5).

Scripture: **Matthew 3:1-6**
Song: **"Gospel Echoes"**

John came proclaiming the Messiah. Living in the wilderness, John was dressed in coarse attire and spoke in no-nonsense words to the multitudes who came to hear him. Appealing to their intellects, as well as their hearts, he stressed repentance because the kingdom of Heaven was at hand. The penitents, after confessing their sins, received baptism from John, the water signifying God's gracious gift: cleansing from sin.

John was privileged to prepare the people for Christ's appearance, and he had great influence with them. We too have influence with people, even when we are unaware of its full extent. But we can go beyond this passive influence to have an active, positive witness.

By our words, and also by our actions, we can joyfully proclaim the goodness of God in our lives, clearly identifying ourselves as servants of King Jesus. We may feel as if we're in the wilderness when we do so. And the crowds may not go out to us. But look for that person—here . . . there—who seems to have an open heart. He or she is ready for your life-giving testimony. Let it bubble forth loud and clear.

God, keep me alert to people around me today. May I catch the eye of one whose heart You have prepared for good news. In Jesus' name, amen.

My Prayer Notes

DEVOTIONS®

*N*othing
is impossible
with God.
　　　—Luke 1:37

DECEMBER

Photo © Digital Stock

Gary Allen, Editor　　　　Volume 50, Number 1

© 2005 STANDARD PUBLISHING, 8121 Hamilton Avenue, Cincinnati, Ohio, 45231, a division of STANDEX INTERNATIONAL Corporation. Topics based on the Home Daily Bible Readings, International Sunday School Lessons. © 2003 by the Committee on the Uniform Series. Printed in the U.S.A. All Scripture quotations, unless otherwise indicated, are taken from the HOLY BIBLE, NEW INTERNATIONAL VERSION®. NIV®. Copyright © 1973, 1978, 1984 by International Bible Society. Used by permission of Zondervan. All rights reserved. Where noted, Scripture quotations are from the following, used with permission of the copyright holders, all rights reserved: *New American Standard Bible (NASB),* © 1960, 1962, 1963, 1971, 1972 by The Lockman Foundation, La Habra CA.

Such Potential!

To us a child is born, to us a son is given, and the government will be on his shoulders. And he will be called Wonderful Counselor, Mighty God, Everlasting Father, Prince of Peace (Isaiah 9:6).

Scripture: **Isaiah 9:2-7**
Song: **"Jesus, Name Above All Names"**

When we stand at Christmas and sing those glorious words, "Wonderful, Counselor, the Mighty God, the Everlasting Father, the Prince of Peace" from Handel's *Messiah*, we rejoice once again at the birth of Jesus. According to the prophet Isaiah, the coming of this new Davidic king was the advent of a new day for God's people—a reign of righteousness and peace.

Today we rarely witness the ascension of someone to a kingly throne, but we often rejoice at a baby's birth. I remember the breathless tone in my daughter's voice when she, as a nurse trainee, called to tell me, "Mom, today I helped a baby into the world! It was a beautiful baby boy, and the parents were so happy."

"You assisted in a beginning with great potential," I said. For at no time are we more aware of our responsibility to nurture our young ones in the faith. Each birth is the start of a life that can be lived for the Everlasting Father.

Father, Your Son's birth was like no other in its world-saving effects. Help me as I seek to bring children into His presence. Through Christ, amen.

December 1–3. **Cos Barnes**, of Southern Pines, North Carolina, is a mother of three and grandmother of seven. She enjoys playing handbells for her church.

What Would You Give?

We pray this in order that you may live a life worthy of the Lord and may please him in every way: bearing fruit in every good work, growing in the knowledge of God (Colossians 1:10).

Scripture: **Colossians 1:9-14**
Song: **"Victory in Jesus"**

I was asked to judge the essays of first- and second-graders for a national contest. The theme was: "If I could give the world a gift, what would I give?" I was to rate the essays on originality, literary content, and theme interpretation. But I found it difficult to reject any of the papers because of their creativity and compassion. These children yearned to give peace to the world, save the endangered environment, rescue abused and orphaned children, and care for the poor and for mistreated animals.

As I pondered the thoughtfulness of such responses, I considered my own gift to the world: I would like to impart to others a growing knowledge of God. This is what Paul strove to do among the early Christians at Colosse. He filled them with an understanding of the true God, strengthening them for service and assuring them they would not fail in the face of enduring opposition. His prayer for them was that they would attain the full knowledge of God's will. What a gift!

O God, I know that sometimes little children lead us. Bless all the first- and second-graders in our schools. Let their hearts be ever open to knowing and serving You as they grow into world-changers. In Jesus' name, amen.

December 3

Touched by the Master

He is the head of the body, the church; he is the beginning and the firstborn from among the dead, so that in everything he might have the supremacy (Colossians 1:18).

Scripture: **Colossians 1:15-23**
Song: "Majesty"

I asked my adult son to repair a lamp before he departed from his visit. He went to his deceased father's tool box, secured the tool he needed, and fixed the lamp in no time. "Aren't you glad you're so handy?" I asked.

"I was taught by the master," he winked and smilingly replied, referring to his father, who was adept at home repair. Earlier in our visit, I had discussed with my son the increase in a yearly bill. He told me all prices had gone up and to go ahead and pay it. Dissatisfied, I persisted with customer service until I received a lower rate. Later I e-mailed him: "I too was trained by the master" (referring to his dad, who would have shown the same dogged determination in getting the matter corrected).

In our Scripture today, Paul reminds the Colossians that Jesus is supreme and by His death has redeemed them from sin. Knowing these early Christians had been threatened by false teachers who advocated angel worship, Paul points them back to the master, the one who reigns supreme in everything. Unlike any human master, He is worthy not only of emulation but of worship.

Father God, I bow my heart and my knee to Your Son, the one You sent to rule my life today and tomorrow. In His holy name I pray. Amen.

Skip the Fanfare

Here is my servant whom I have chosen, the one I love, in whom I delight; I will put my Spirit on him, and he will proclaim justice to the nations (Matthew 12:18).

Scripture: **Matthew 12:15-21**
Song: **"My Wonderful Lord"**

What fanfare and pomp came with our past presidential elections! Elaborate dinners to introduce candidates, televised debates, and the constant media coverage made it all seem so important. Yet this picture thoroughly contrasts with something much more significant—the greatest event in history: the coming of Jesus, His preaching of the kingdom, and His willing sacrifice to redeem us. Unlike any celebrity candidate, He changed the world . . . but quietly, as a meek and loving servant of all.

The Pharisees had rejected Jesus, but the people were excited about being healed and wanted to proclaim His works with much ado. Jesus remained true to form, however, warning them not to tell who He was. It was important to Jesus that He walk in the ways of His Father, respecting the words of Isaiah that Matthew quotes for us.

I'd like to be able to witness to the kingdom that way too, in quietness and confidence and in the power of the Spirit. A sincere willingness to serve requires no fanfare.

Loving Father, show me each new day what I can do to further Your work here on earth. Through Christ I pray. Amen.

December 4–10. **Dorothy Minea** is a Christian writer and speaker living in Camarillo, California. She has four children and four grandsons.

He's Good

Having come in, the angel said to her, "Rejoice, highly favored one, the Lord is with you; blessed are you among women!" (Luke 1:28, *New King James Version*).

Scripture: **Luke 1:26-33**
Song: **"God Is Good All the Time"**

My friend Debbie always ends our phone conversations with, "God is good." Her faith amazes me because life isn't easy for her these days. She has four little children and is expecting baby number five. Her husband is a gifted minister but presently out of work. As he patiently and prayerfully awaits a new calling, Debbie says she knows God has good plans for her entire family.

Mary, betrothed to Joseph, a descendant of David, waited patiently for her role to unfold after Gabriel appeared. She'd been raised in a family steeped in Hebrew law and God's love. She had heard the beautiful stories of Abraham, Isaac, Jacob, and Joseph. She knew of the courage and loyalty of Moses and David. Yet she was troubled at the angel's announcement of favor.

None of us are expected to cruise through life without some intensely troubling times. And deep faith can flourish even amidst serious questioning. Yet Mary surely believed that God was good. In His way and time, He would bring forth good things in the life of His servant.

Dear Lord, thank You for loving me just as I am—but also calling me to become more like Your precious Son. Keep me growing and rejoicing in Your goodness! In the name of Jesus, my Savior, I pray. Amen.

Omnipotence Does It!

Nothing is impossible with God (Luke 1:37).

Scripture: **Luke 1:34-38**
Song: **"What a Mighty God We Serve"**

Esther in the Old Testament; Mary, mother of Jesus; and Esther, my friend—they all have at least one thing in common. They all said, "Yes, Lord," to His calling. My friend opened her small mobile home to four family members who had no place to live. It was a big yes for Esther and her husband, who willingly put their retirement plans on hold, gave what they had, and endured cramped quarters for several months.

And because the mother of Esther's 2-year-old great-grandson couldn't properly care for him, Esther and her husband adopted the little guy. The new parents' ages? Both were in their 70s.

Esther lived her life helping others. And she must have completed all that God had for her to do because He took her home to be with Him recently.

Mary, like Esther, realized she was God's servant and accepted His calling. Yet her initial response was, "How will this be?" Isn't that often how it is for us as we seek to discern God's will? He calls us to a task, a mission, that from all human perspectives appears undoable. Then we remember: omnipotence solves a multitude of problems.

Dearest Lord, even when I'm overwhelmed by the problems and obstacles of Your calling, let me trust Your wonder-working power. In the name of Jesus my faithful Savior I pray. Amen.

Grateful for New Life

My spirit rejoices in God my Savior, for he has been mindful of the humble state of his servant (Luke 1:47, 48).

Scripture: **Luke 1:46-55**
Song: **"Every Day with Jesus"**

A Christian man had been fighting depression for years. "It's as though my body is tied down," he said. "I have no desire to accomplish anything. My spirit just feels dead."

One morning, while reading a devotional piece titled "A New Beginning," the man's heart was touched as never before. The writer spoke of each new day being a gift from God, a new beginning coming with each sunrise. Though the writer lived 3,000 miles away across the Pacific, her message spoke powerfully to him. Like Mary, he experienced a rejoicing of spirit, and with this seemingly small change in perspective, he gradually developed a new eagerness to serve his Savior.

Years have marched by, but he still glorifies the Lord by working during the week to keep the church facilities in order and singing in the choir each Sunday. He also wrote a song—using words from the devotional that renewed his heart so many years ago. "I will always praise God for sending me, through a simply piece of writing, His wonderful words of life," says this grateful servant.

Father, I give all of myself into Your hands with the dawn of this new day. Thank You for Your loving care—for my body, my soul, my spirit. All honor and praise to Your name, through the Lord Jesus Christ. Amen.

Heavenly Reassurance

While he was still speaking, a bright cloud enveloped them, and a voice from the cloud said, "This is my Son, whom I love; with him I am well pleased. Listen to him!" (Matthew 17:5).

Scripture: **Matthew 17:1-5**
Song: **"Blessed Assurance"**

You needed some reassurance, a few encouraging words, or a pat on the back to help you keep going amidst tough obstacles. We've all been there.

As I watched the U.S. figure skating championships on television, I noticed that most of the skaters received a few brief words from their coaches before launching onto the ice to present their programs. The words seemed to fuel their enthusiasm and usually sent them to the ice with a confident smile. A little reassurance can do wonders.

Peter, James, and John were at a low point. A few days earlier, their beloved Jesus had spoken to them of His coming death. Jesus knew their discouragement. Is that why He asked them to accompany Him to the mountain-top to witness a spectacular, miraculous light show?

One thing is certain. Seeing Jesus' heavenly splendor, glimpsing the great Moses and Elijah, and hearing the voice from Heaven must have launched Peter, James, and John into their future ministries with all the confidence in the world.

O God, speak words of comfort and encouragement into my life today. I do not ask for miraculous demonstrations, but should I hear Your still, small voice today, I will be thankful. Through Christ, amen.

What Status!

The Son is the radiance of God's glory and the exact representation of his being, sustaining all things by his powerful word (Hebrews 1:3).

Scripture: **Hebrews 1:1-9**
Song: **"All Glory, Laud and Honor"**

My father was a harsh disciplinarian. Whenever I got a bit out of line, he reminded me of his status in the family—which automatically reminded me of mine! I realize now that he was simply acting according to his own experience with his father. He stayed with the old ways and seemed closed to new methods in parenting.

Many years ago, around AD 60, Jewish converts to Christianity found it difficult to accept the new covenant and the status of Jesus in relationship to angels. Their ancestors had been guided by great men like Moses, Joshua, and David. But they had also experienced the guidance and miraculous interventions of angels. As wonderful as these creatures were, they couldn't hold a candle to the superiority of God's Son.

We humans often struggle to see things in a new light, even when the change comes from God himself. Some of those early converts turned back to the old covenant. In those days, as in our day, it took faith to see the radiance of God's glory in Jesus.

Dear God, what a beautiful image—to see Your Son sitting at the right hand of Your throne. And I am blessed to know His sustaining power in my life even now. All praise to Jesus, the one in whom I pray. Amen.

Care, As He Did

To which of the angels did God ever say, "Sit at my right hand until I make your enemies a footstool for your feet"? (Hebrews 1:13).

Scripture: **Hebrews 1:10-14**
Song: **"O Jesus, I Have Promised"**

Our Scripture tells us that God clearly spoke to Jesus when He said, "I will make your enemies a footstool for your feet." But this caused me to wonder: Who are Christ's enemies? Are they not those who reject Him, who motivate unbelief and persecute the church?

No doubt. But perhaps another way to reject Christ is to ignore the kinds of works He did and refuse to emulate them. Works don't save us, but they can reveal the state of our heart. Jesus went about doing good, caring for human needs. So I'm convicted in my own heart: Let me not be found fighting against the Lord and His ways! Let me be ready to care for others through acts of kindness.

One small example springs to my mind at the moment. A sweet shop near my home is giving away free ice-cream cones, for which the Christian owner asks for a $5 donation. The money goes to our local chapter of the American Red Cross to aid victims of mud slides in our county.

Workers like this are working upon the earth as Jesus once did. He sits at the right hand of God; we are His hands and feet down here.

Father, I long for the second coming of Your Son. But when He arrives, may I be found working for His cause. In His name, amen.

Beyond the Appearance

An angel of the Lord appeared to him in a dream and said, "Joseph son of David, do not be afraid to take Mary home as your wife, because what is conceived in her is from the Holy Spirit" (Matthew 1:20).

Scripture: **Matthew 1:18-25**
Song: **"Remember Christ, Our Savior"**

Why do automobile manufacturers make door mirrors that require the warning "Caution: Objects in mirror may be closer than they appear"? If the objects in our mirrors are closer than they appear, how can we ever know for sure when it is safe to change lanes? We have to turn our heads and check our blind spots, right?

After Joseph learned his wife-to-be was pregnant, he took time to consider the situation. He knew he wasn't the baby's biological father, so he paused to check his blind spots. What was he failing to see? Unwilling to disgrace Mary in public, he thought about various ways he could end their relationship quietly. But things weren't as they appeared, and it took an angelic visit to open his eyes.

It's a good thing Joseph had integrity, because it stopped him from acting on pure emotion. It's a great reminder for us too: consider others' feelings—even when it seems they've horribly offended.

God, when I feel hurt by another, help me to relax and look to You. Remind me of Your ability to work in all circumstances. In Jesus' name, amen.

December 11–17. **Lee Warren,** of Omaha, Nebraska, has written devotions for numerous publications and authored a singles book called *Single Servings*.

Majestic Observations

We did not follow cleverly invented stories when we told you about the power and coming of our Lord Jesus Christ, but we were eyewitnesses of his majesty (2 Peter 1:16).

Scripture: **2 Peter 1:16-21**
Song: **"Book of Books"**

Ever heard people say that they believe the Bible is great literature but that it can't be fully trusted because fallible humans wrote it? I've noticed that such folks rarely think twice about accepting the facts of history books—especially those written by human eyewitnesses.

Not only does apostle Peter claim to be an eyewitness of what Jesus did and said, he goes one better. He says that "no prophecy of Scripture came about by the prophet's own interpretation. For prophecy never had its origin in the will of man, but men spoke from God as they were carried along by the Holy Spirit" (vv. 20, 21).

As an eyewitness—and as one inspired by the Holy Spirit—Peter, like all the persons who wrote books in the Bible, recorded the words that God desired. We may not witness all the majesties that Peter did. However, I know I've observed the powerful effects of God's proclaimed Word upon individuals and congregations. These transformations happened right before my eyes.

__Heavenly Father,__ I know Your Word conveys timeless truth, but when people question the authority of the Bible, or when I'm struggling with difficulties, I am tempted to doubt. Strengthen my faith in Your eternal Word today. Through my Savior, Jesus Christ, I pray. Amen.

In God's Hands

We have renounced secret and shameful ways; we do not use deception, nor do we distort the word of God. On the contrary, by setting forth the truth plainly we commend ourselves to every man's conscience in the sight of God (2 Corinthians 4:2).

Scripture: **2 Corinthians 4:1-6**
Song: **"Seek Ye First"**

I've been witnessing to my friend Tom for over a decade. He listens patiently to me but makes no affirmative decision about Christ. One evening, he was even willing to sit next to me in my living room as I opened the Scriptures and had him read aloud several passages regarding the gracious salvation we can find in Jesus. Tom showed no reaction, though, as he handed the Bible back to me. When I asked him whether he understood what he read, he said, "I guess I'm just not interested."

I believe that I "set forth the truth plainly" before Tom's conscience, yet he didn't respond. As much as this has grieved me over the years, I have taken comfort in knowing that I've done what God asked me to do. And I'll continue to share with Tom for as long as he will listen.

Thankfully, we aren't responsible for the responses of others to God's Word. Conversion is God's business. Sharing its availability is our business.

Dear God, I long to see my friends and relatives taste Your forgiveness. I am grieved by their seeming lack of response, but I will continue to share plainly of Your goodness and grace. Thank You for breathing Your life into every open heart. In Christ's name I pray. Amen.

Children of Light

You were once darkness, but now you are light in the Lord. Live as children of light (Ephesians 5:8).

Scripture: **Ephesians 5:8-14**
Song: **"Holiness unto the Lord"**

I hit the interstate early one morning a couple of years ago. I needed to be in Kansas City by 9:00 AM for a conference. I live two hundred miles away from downtown. It was still dark as I crossed the border into Missouri and soon thereafter saw a deer running straight toward my car. I swerved, the deer jumped, and a deadly collision was avoided! My headlights may well have saved my life that morning.

In the passage above the apostle Paul calls believers to "live as children of light" because God has placed His light within them. In verse 13 Paul tells us that "everything exposed by the light becomes visible." Just as my headlights saved me from disaster, exposing our sin to the light of God's Word keeps us free from the various devastations that sin always brings into our lives.

Before we placed our faith in Christ, we drove through life without headlights—a dangerous situation. But thanks be to God! Aren't you glad you can now depend on the light of His wisdom and guidance as you journey through each day ahead?

Father, too often I seek comfort by hiding in some form of darkness. Yet in Your light is the peace that satisfies—eternally. Give me the courage to live as a child of the light today. Through Christ I pray. Amen.

Jesus, Eternal

The life appeared; we have seen it and testify to it, and we proclaim to you the eternal life, which was with the Father and has appeared to us (1 John 1:2).

Scripture: **1 John 1:1-4**
Song: **"At the Name of Jesus"**

Recently I watched a documentary about the Cold War. At one point the producers aired footage from 1964 showing American leaders discussing the possibility of war with Russia. I was born in 1966—two years after these events occurred. I found myself losing track of what the leaders were saying because I was thinking about life before I existed, but I just couldn't grasp the reality.

It can be hard to imagine what life was like before we had life. Then we read a passage like the one above.

We tend to think of Jesus only in His human form, either as a baby in a manger or as the Messiah dying for our sins. While He certainly did take on flesh, dwelt among humans, and ultimately died for them, He has existed with the Father from eternity.

Will you meditate on that thought today with me? The Jesus whom the apostle John proclaimed, who saved you from your sins, is the God of the universe who has always existed and will never cease. Thus, He can guarantee your own eternal life.

Father, I am moved by Your majesty and the thought that You have always existed with Your Son and Spirit. And I am undone by the love that caused You to enter space and time for me. Thank You, in Jesus' name. Amen.

Walk in the Light

If we walk in the light, as he is in the light, we have fellowship with one another, and the blood of Jesus, his Son, purifies us from all sin (1 John 1:7).

Scripture: **1 John 1:5-10**
Song: **"Walk in the Light"**

As I was growing up, my dad always told me that if I did something wrong, I should tell him about it rather than trying to cover it up. He said he would listen and help in any way he could. And, if necessary, he would do what he thought best regarding any punishment I deserved.

His calm, loving approach made it a bit easier to tell him when I had done something wrong. Once I understood how he would deal with me, I didn't feel compelled to cover my sins around him. I didn't know it at the time, but I was walking in the light. I was in a good relationship with my dad. His love covered my wrong actions as I confessed them. It was a purifying process for me.

God's love for us is far greater than the love that flowed between my dad and me. And when we are willing to confess our sins to God, our fellowship with Him grows deep. The problem comes when we think we've done something that's just too sinful. While we may say something like that about our actions, what are we saying about the power of Christ's purifying blood?

Heavenly Father, today let my sins drive me to Your mercy and grace. I want to maintain our relationship! Thank You, in Jesus' name. Amen.

Setting the Standard

Whoever claims to live in him must walk as Jesus did (1 John 2:6).

Scripture: **1 John 2:1-6**
Song: **"My Jesus, I Love Thee"**

Quite a few years ago, I worked in the customer service department of an insurance company. Our boss was always under enormous pressure to make sure that policy changes requested by our customers were handled in a timely fashion. But we had a relatively small staff—probably too small—to process the requested changes.

However, no matter the circumstances, my boss always remained calm. She was always available to help her employees. When overtime was necessary, she was there. When we went home for the day, she was often still working. She modeled what a customer service employee ought to be. She set the standard for all of us.

None of her employees could claim that we outworked her. But if we were to be good representatives of the department, we knew the standard for which to strive.

In similar fashion, if we claim to represent Jesus Christ, we're privileged to follow His lead and live out His commands to love and serve both God and humankind as He did. What a blessed way to live!

Father, when I think about trying to live up to the standard Jesus set for us, sometimes I'm overwhelmed. I know I can't do it on my own, and I'm thankful that You empower me by Your indwelling Spirit to become more and more like Your holy Son. In His name I pray. Amen.

Census Records

In those days Caesar Augustus issued a decree that a census should be taken of the entire Roman world (Luke 2:1).

Scripture: **Luke 2:1-7**
Song: **"O Little Town of Bethlehem"**

When my dad and I began doing genealogical research we discovered that my great-great-grandfather was a Confederate cavalryman during the U.S. Civil War. We also found a fascinating, handwritten letter he had addressed to the pension board. The letter describes an injury he sustained and tells about how his unit learned of the war's end. Reading about the Civil War through the words of my very own kin made the event much more real and personal to me.

In today's text Luke, the historian, mentions a Roman census taking place at the time of Jesus' birth. The event shows Jesus far from the realm of myths and fairy tales. Unlike Zeus or Hercules, our Jesus is a documentable person of human history. And like my great-great-grandfather, Jesus has left us a letter. In it we discover the eternal God, who chose to enter history at a time we now celebrate as Christmas. At this time of year, we not only connect with the past in a personal way but look forward to being part of a glorious future.

God, thank You for the Gospel writers who, under inspiration of the Holy Spirit, carefully documented the life of Jesus. I pray in His name. Amen.

December 18–24. **Brian Waldrop** is a writer and professional copy editor living in Cincinnati, Ohio, with his 25-pound cat named White Sox.

December 19

Birth Announcement

I bring you good news of great joy that will be for all the people (Luke 2:10).

Scripture: **Luke 2:8-20**
Song: **"How Great Our Joy"**

Often a man can tell you in exquisite detail all the intricacies of a make and model of car. But when it comes to remembering the vital statistics of a newborn baby, some men do well to recall even the gender of the child!

Interestingly, it was men who first received news of the Savior's birth. The birth announcement came to these shepherds via what some might call a singing telegram. The shepherds were thrilled to hear the news and rushed to the "maternity ward" to see the infant child. Mary, the baby's mother, "treasured up all these things and pondered them in her heart" (v. 19). Even a musty stable couldn't dampen the joy of birthing this promised child.

Sometimes the human side of Jesus' birth gets overlooked when we reflect upon the Christmas story. Just as glorious as a divine Savior coming to earth is the fact that He came as a bouncing baby boy. Like us (and *with* us) Jesus experienced all the ups and downs and twists of life. At Christmas, the supernatural and the natural became one in the person of Christ. What good news!

Dear God, my joy is great when I, like Mary, ponder all the events that unfolded on that very first Christmas. I stand in awe of Your love that orchestrated the events leading to my salvation. Thank You, Father, in the name of Your worthy Son. Amen.

The Wait Is Over

The gospel he promised beforehand through his prophets in the Holy Scriptures regarding his Son (Romans 1:2, 3).

Scripture: **Romans 1:1-6**
Song: **"While Shepherds Watched Their Flocks"**

Like most children, I could hardly wait for Christmas to come each year. Brightly wrapped presents needed unwrapping! Likewise for the Jewish people longing for their promised Messiah, the centuries from the days of Abraham must have seemed like an awfully long wait. But when He finally came, most did not recognize Him by His "wrappings."

Yet the prophets had foretold a much needed gospel, which means "good news." It was a way of being right with God apart from the Old Testament law. Jesus' coming to earth was the fulfillment of this plan of salvation. How God must have longed for the day when the contents of that glorious gift would be revealed to the world.

For us in the twenty-first century, the wait is long over. Now we see clearly the great gift of God. Because Jesus was fully man, He perfectly represented us in fulfilling the law's demands. And because He is fully God, His sacrifice on the cross is eternally effective for us. Could there be any better good news than that?

Dear God in Heaven, thank You for the gift of salvation through Jesus. And thank You for the thought and care that went into this gift. It's much more than I could ever have imagined. In the name of the Father, the Son, and the Holy Spirit, I pray. Amen.

Adopted and Adored

In love he predestined us to be adopted as his sons through Jesus Christ, in accordance with his pleasure (Ephesians 1:4, 5).

Scripture: **Ephesians 1:3-10**
Song: **"A Child of the King"**

Zoe and Scooter are the two adult cats my sister adopted from our local humane society. As a result of their adoption, they've received many blessings, including quality food, superior shelter, and nearly every known cat gizmo and toy. Their adoptions elevated them from unwanted animals awaiting euthanasia to priceless pets who are loved and adored.

Jesus left His home in Heaven, in a sense, to be adopted into the earthly home of Mary and Joseph. His adoption ultimately made way for our unlikely adoptions as God's children. Now we have "every spiritual blessing in Christ" (v. 3). We enjoy "the riches of God's grace" and have "redemption through his blood, the forgiveness of sins" (v. 7). We have been rescued from eternal condemnation, elevated to full family membership.

It is a marvelous thing to be adopted by royalty, to have legally become part of the king's own bloodline with its full inheritance. And Jesus is currently building a home for us beyond our wildest dreams (see John 14:2, 3). Truly, we are both adopted and adored.

Heavenly Father, *You loved me when I was anything but lovable. You paid an immeasurable price to redeem me and to adopt me into Your family. I am eternally grateful. All praise to You, in Christ's name. Amen.*

Guiding Lights

The true light that gives light to every man was coming into the world (John 1:9).

Scripture: **John 1:1-9**
Song: **"Lead, Kindly Light"**

Several years ago I rode through the air in a small commuter plane at night. Since the curtain separating the passenger cabin from the cockpit remained open throughout the flight, I could see the control panels with all their glowing monitors. When the plane landed, I watched through the front windows. As we descended and finally touched down, I saw the runway lights guiding our path.

Guiding lights played an important role in that first Christmas. A supernatural star led the wise men to Jesus. An angelic host of heavenly light appeared to shepherds announcing the Messiah's birth in Bethlehem. And, of course, the greatest guiding light in the Christmas story was Jesus himself, who said, "I am the light of the world. Whoever follows me will never walk in darkness, but will have the light of life" (John 8:12).

I have sometimes needlessly stumbled through days in darkness. It helps me to remember that Christ can illuminate even the darkest pathways of the human heart with His forgiveness, wisdom, and guidance. He leads to Heaven all who look to Him for light and life.

O God, may the twinkling lights of my Christmas tree remind me to follow more closely the one to whom the star led. And help me become a source of guiding light to those still living in darkness. Through Christ, amen.

A Better Way

The law was given through Moses; grace and truth came through Jesus Christ (John 1:17).

Scripture: **John 1:10-18**
Song: **"Grace Greater than Our Sin"**

The law that came through Moses was like a piece of fine art. This masterpiece perfectly defined right and wrong, and through it the Jews learned that God is holy and just. In this way the law was good. As a way of becoming right with God, however, it fell short. It demanded a perfect obedience that even the great Moses couldn't attain.

Jesus Christ offered the better way to God. Through Him we experience not only God's justice but also His grace and truth. Justice was fulfilled when Jesus took the punishment for our sins. Grace was bestowed when God freely credited this sin-payment to our account. Truth was upheld when Jesus fulfilled every demand of the law on our behalf.

Truly Jesus is the better way—the *only* way—to enter a right relationship with God. Looking at the law we see a picture of our sin and a waiting condemnation. But by looking at Jesus, we see forgiveness, grace, and an eternity with God that is picture perfect.

Heavenly Father, in my baptism I accepted the grace and truth so freely offered to me in Christ. Help me rely only upon this great salvation today that I might avoid any misplaced loyalties to man-made legalisms. I pray this prayer in the name of Jesus, my merciful Savior and Lord. Amen.

Messiah's Mission Statement

To open eyes that are blind, to free captives from prison and to release from the dungeon those who sit in darkness (Isaiah 42:7).

Scripture: **Isaiah 42:5-9**
Song: **"Joy to the World"**

Nearly everyone has a mission statement these days: businesses, churches, and even many individuals. In today's text we read about the mission of the Messiah.

The original hearers of Isaiah's message were Jewish captives languishing in Babylon for having rebelled against God. But God forgave their sin and, through the prophet Isaiah, promised them an anointed deliverer, or messiah, who would conqueror their Babylonian captors and allow them to return home to Jerusalem. The immediate, historical fulfillment of this promise came in the form of Cyrus, the Persian king.

Prophecies like Isaiah's normally have a "close" and a "far" application. That is, when viewing twin mountain peaks in the distance, we may think both peaks stand side by side. Moving closer, though, we see them separated by long distances. Thus Isaiah also referred to another King-Messiah who would come at a later time and free those captive to Satan and sin. What a mission—and how wonderful to remember it on the day before Christmas!

O God, You have set me free by Your grace. Please open my eyes today to others seeking Your freedom. Help me invite them into the light. In the name of my Lord and Savior, Jesus, I pray. Amen.

Motives and Methods

Go and make careful search for the Child; and when you have found Him, report to me, that I too may come and worship Him (Matthew 2:8, *New American Standard Bible*).

Scripture: **Matthew 2:1-11**
Song: **"Angels, from the Realms of Glory"**

My friend Heather had never shown much interest in God. I hesitated to mention my own faith, since I thought it might somehow alienate her. So I wrote to a minister who lived close to her, asking him to visit her. My plan was that he would appear to drop in as he canvassed the neighborhood, asking people to come to church. "Remember not to mention my name," I added. (I didn't want Heather to be mad at me for interfering in her life!)

The minister refused to act on my terms, however. He pointed out in a reply letter that, while he appreciated my interest in Heather's welfare, he wondered why I wanted to remain anonymous. "Why don't you contact Heather and tell her of your belief in God? Then ask if I can visit her and talk about her beliefs." After reading his reply, I realized I'd been planning a bit of a deception. Motive, good; method, bad.

Herod was deceptive in his concern for the Christ child. But in his case, the problem was more than method.

Father, today I rejoice in Your Son's incarnation. Help me witness to Him with loving motives and winsome methods. In His precious name, amen.

December 25–31. **Kayleen Reusser,** of Indiana, has written hundreds of articles, including pieces for the entertainment section of a major daily newspaper.

Senior Saints

She came up and began giving thanks to God, and continued to speak of Him to all those who were looking for the redemption of Jerusalem (Luke 2:38, *New American Standard Bible*).

Scripture: **Luke 2:22-38**
Song: **"The First Noel"**

Being in mid-life and good health, I marvel at the gracious attitudes and cheerful faces of elderly people I know who suffer with health problems. Lou, age 78, is a widower dealing with pancreatic cancer. Yet he attends church with a smile on his face. Loren, 80, has a hand that refuses to straighten. Yet he prepares and serves communion. My parents, in their late 70s, struggle with a multitude of health problems—and yet they thank God for each day of their lives.

The prophetess Anna was a widow, had no children, and could have spent her days in lonely bitterness. Instead, for years she helped care for the temple. Furthermore, after she'd seen the infant Jesus, she turned to bystanders and declared that the child was Messiah, the hope of Israel, the redeemer of the world.

Why was this gentle, elderly woman the first to make this grand announcement? Though she was an old woman, Anna was young in hope. She, like my friends, never ceased to believe in the great wonders of God.

Heavenly Father, *thank You for the wonderful examples around me—of loyal servants who remain faithful all their days. Day by day, make me one of them! I pray through my Redeemer, Jesus Christ the Lord. Amen.*

Easily Made, Easily Broken

"I will put my trust in him." And again he says, "Here am I, and the children God has given me" (Hebrews 2:13).

Scripture: **Hebrews 2:5-13**
Song: **"'Tis So Sweet to Trust in Jesus"**

In the movie *Mary Poppins,* two lonely children become enthralled with their new nanny. One night, after a particularly exciting day, they implore her, "Promise you'll never leave us!" For all of her zany actions, Mary Poppins replies wisely, "That's a pie crust promise—easily made, easily broken."

People do crave stability, but most of us have had to deal with vows that crumbled. Not only friends, family, and neighbors disappoint us, but even the government frequently reneges on its promises. So whom can we trust?

Our Scripture passage today tells us that Jesus calls us brothers. This is one relationship that we can trust with the full weight of our lives. His promises provide a solid foundation—a much better place to stand than the crumbling crusts of good intentions. As Abraham Lincoln once said: "We must not promise what we ought not, lest we be called on to perform what we cannot."

My trustworthy Lord, You've made us as frail beings who need to depend on each other; yet sometimes that backfires. Then we come running to You for help. Teach me to trust You with my hurts and disappointments—and then to learn to trust others again. In the holy name of Jesus, my Lord and Savior, I pray. Amen.

Taming Temptation

Because he himself suffered when he was tempted, he is able to help those who are being tempted (Hebrews 2:18).

Scripture: **Hebrews 2:14-18**
Song: **"Holy, Holy, Holy"**

The wind whistled past my ears as tears gathered in my eyes, blinding me. Desperately, I tried to grasp the reins that flopped against Lady's neck, but they were too far away. I clung to the saddle horn, praying her racing feet wouldn't find a hole in the field.

A tractor had entered the field we were walking in, but I'd been too busy conversing with a fellow rider to notice. Startled by the machine's loud noise, Lady had bolted, jerking the reins out of my hands. Now she ran faster than ever toward a fence looming at the end of the field. Lunging forward, I snatched the reins from Lady's neck and pulled back hard. Lady fought against the pressure of the bit in her mouth but finally stopped.

The Bible's words about temptation remind me of that scary ride. It didn't take much for Lady to lose control. Temptation is like that. When it comes, we must call on Jesus to help us pull back. Thankfully, He has experienced every temptation and is willing to come to our aid with understanding and incomparable strength.

O God, each of us faces temptation as we strive to serve You daily. When tempted, help me relax and consider: "What do I really want?" Then restore to me the joy of my salvation. Through Christ Jesus, my Lord, I pray. Amen.

Kindhearted Words?

To sum up, let all be harmonious, sympathetic, brotherly, kindhearted, and humble in spirit (1 Peter 3:8, *New American Standard Bible*).

Scripture: **1 Peter 3:8-12**
Song: **"O God, Our Help in Ages Past"**

Our Bible study had concluded for the day, and we began to gather our purses and Bibles. As Helen, a newcomer, moved into the hallway, Alexa said to us, "Has anyone seen Tom Smith's house recently?" Several of us shook our heads with curiosity, so Alexa continued: "He's parked more old cars in his yard. That man has more trash at his place than a junk yard!"

We chuckled and turned to leave. Helen stood a few feet away. Her face was white, eyes wide with disbelief. Without a word she picked up her Bible and hurried out of the church. I liked Helen and hurried after her. Her keys were in the ignition by the time I caught up with her. "What's wrong, Helen?"

"You might think Tom is trash," she said tearfully. "But he's my father, and it hurt to hear all of you talking about him like that!" In one brief moment we'd offended a new Christian and violated Peter's commands. Thankfully, the wisdom of Peter's words sunk in like no sermon could. Over the weeks that followed, we learned about forgiveness and reconciliation too.

God, it seems I often utter words before thinking them through. Keep working in me a kind and humble spirit. In the name of Jesus I pray. Amen.

Just Reach Out

Do not merely look out for your own personal interests, but also for the interests of others (Philippians 2:4, *New American Standard Bible*).

Scripture: **Philippians 2:1-5**
Song: **"Channels Only"**

Todd gripped the jail cell's window bars and looked outside in despair. He hadn't meant to get caught selling cocaine. Now he was locked up for a long time.

He'd been learning about the occult and figured he'd use his jail time to learn more about psychic phenomena. As he pondered these things, Todd looked up and saw two inmates looking at him. One held out his hand. "We wanted to introduce ourselves," the man said.

When they discovered his interest in psychic matters, the other man said he'd pursued the same thing, but "then I met Jesus Christ and was baptized." Todd listened closely and then began meeting with the men for a Bible study led by a jail volunteer. Todd was baptized in jail. After his release, Todd married, became a business owner, and eventually served as a deacon in his church.

Todd's two jail mates could have chosen to read their Bibles or pray that day. Instead, they reached out to help someone else. And so I'm seriously considering: Who in my world of associations needs a helping hand today?

Lord, I don't know exactly who I'll encounter today, but give me the eyes to see needs and a willingness to help. Thank You, in Jesus' name. Amen.

Sink or Swim?

Being found in appearance as a man, he humbled himself and became obedient to death—even death on a cross! (Philippians 2:8).

Scripture: **Philippians 2:6-11**
Song: **"Love Lifted Me"**

When my kids were small, I took them to swimming lessons. Trained instructors demonstrated how to perform each stroke. But there was something my kids didn't know about their instructors. They were also certified lifeguards. Before my kids entered the water, I wanted to know their instructors could save them from drowning.

We're all swimmers in the sea of life. In the beginning we dip our toes in the water. Then we get braver and venture out further. We may even try to swim to the other side of the pool. But suddenly we reach the middle and feel scared. Temptation, worry, and doubt drag us down, and we cry out for help. Jesus, our lifeguard, quickly swims to our side. He secures us next to his body and delivers us safely to the edge of the pool.

It wasn't enough for Jesus to instruct us on how to live. He had to become our Savior by dying on the cross. By His humility and obedience, we shall be brought to the far shore. Until then, out of gratitude, let us follow His instructions and example as best we can.

Father, thank You for allowing your Son to die on the cross to give me eternal life. His obedience to You and His love for me is overwhelming. Now help me live as He lived. Through His precious name, amen.